ECONOMIC DEVELOPMENT AND URBAN MIGRATION

Tanzania
1900–1971

BY
R. H. SABOT

CLARENDON PRESS · OXFORD
1979

Oxford University Press, Walton Street, Oxford OX2 6DP

OXFORD LONDON GLASGOW
NEW YORK TORONTO MELBOURNE WELLINGTON
NAIROBI DAR ES SALAAM CAPE TOWN
KUALA LUMPUR SINGAPORE JAKARTA HONG KONG TOKYO
DELHI BOMBAY CALCUTTA MADRAS KARACHI

© *Oxford University Press 1979*

British Library Cataloging in Publication Data

Sabot, R H
  Economic development and urban migration
  1. Labor supply—Tanzania
  2. Rural-urban migration—Tanzania
  I. Title
  331.1'379678   HD5841.3   78–40254

ISBN 0–19–828403–9

Typeset by CCC and printed and bound at William Clowes & Sons
Limited, Beccles and London

ECONOMIC DEVELOPMENT
AND
URBAN MIGRATION

For my father
and in memory
of my mother

PREFACE

THERE is a generally recognized need for microeconomic analyses of
labour markets in developing countries to improve our understanding
of the marked sectoral, occupational, and geographic shifts in labour
supply and demand observed in the course of economic development
and structural change, and to improve the formation of employment
and incomes policies in those countries. This study is an attempt to
comprehend and analyse the experience with urban migration
gained by Tanzania in the course of its development between 1900
and 1971. Tanzania was selected because it is one of the world's least
urbanized countries. It is one of the few places where contemporary
observations can be made of the early stages of a migration process
that has already contributed to the transformation of work and
settlement patterns in middle and high income countries. Also, the
Tanzanian government's willingness to innovate in its development
policies holds out greater hope than in many other developing
countries for reducing some of the social and economic costs
associated with urbanization.

The project was conceived in Oxford in 1969. Fieldwork was
conducted in 1970–71, while I was associated with the Economic
Research Bureau of the University of Dar es Salaam. The National
Urban Mobility Employment and Income Survey of Tanzania
(NUMEIST, 1971) was specially designed to generate the data
necessary for the study. Preliminary data processing and analysis
were conducted in Paris while I was a consultant to the Development
Centre of the O.E.C.D. The analysis was refined and a draft of the
current volume was prepared in Oxford during 1972–74 when I was
on the staff of the Institute of Economics and Statistics and a senior
member of St. Antony's College. The volume was subsequently
rewritten in Washington, D.C., in 1975–76.

In the course of its long gestation period a large number of people
have taken an interest in and helped with this study. They are not
responsible for remaining errors, nor do they agree with all the views
expressed, but without their help the project would not have reached
term. I must thank, in the first place, Jere Behrman of the University
of Pennsylvania who introduced me to the economics of developing
countries, Arthur Hazlewood, my first tutor in the subject at Oxford,
who had a great influence on my decision to do research in East

viii PREFACE

Africa, and Paul Streeten who supervised the early stages of my work on this project and was a source of inspiration and encouragement throughout. Also, Keith Griffin, Teddy Jackson, and Ian Little provided extensive and valuable comments on an earlier draft of this volume. Other Oxford colleagues whose suggestions I gratefully acknowledge include: Paul Collier, Heather Joshi, Vijay Joshi, John Knight, and Robert Mabro. The study also benefited from the comments of participants in conferences and seminars at Bellagio, sponsored by the Rockefeller Foundation, at Geneva, sponsored by the I.L.O., at Toronto, sponsored by the Econometric Society and at Harvard and Oxford Universities, where various chapters were presented.

I collaborated with Manfred Bienefeld, currently at the Institute of Development Studies, University of Sussex, on the design and administration of NUMEIST and with Howard Barnum, currently at the University of Michigan, on the specification, estimation and analysis of Tanzania's migration function. Their attention to detail and technical expertise markedly increased the confidence with which I can state the findings of the research. Many other people assisted with the field work, with data processing and with the preparation of the manuscript for publication. Without the support of Ian Livingstone, Gerry Saylor and Simon Mbilinyi, successive directors of the Economic Research Bureau, and of Officials of the Ministry of Economic Affairs and Development Planning, the survey on which this study is based could not have been undertaken. Nor would it have been successful had it not been for the extraordinary efforts of the twenty-four economics students at the University of Dar es Salaam who served as enumerators, half of whom accompanied my wife and me on the 4,000 mile research safari to Tanzania's major urban areas. Joseph Rugumyamheto of the Manpower Planning Unit of Devplan and Judith Sabot, who supervised the interviews, deserve special mention, as do Susan Joekes, my research assistant in Oxford, Katherine Tait who edited the manuscript and Judy Chance and Kamal Tengra who typed the various drafts. To all, I extend my thanks.

As the project grew beyond the bounds of the original plans, so did its costs; now I must gratefully acknowledge the foundations and international organizations that provided financial support: the Canadian International Development Agency, the Danforth Foundation, the O.E.C.D. Development Centre, the Rockefeller Foundation, the Thouron Fund of the University of Pennsylvania, and the World Bank. They have been most generous and patient patrons and the following members of their staffs were often constructive critics as well: Kirby Davidson, Friedrich Kahnert, Mark Leiserson, Michael Todaro, David Turnham, and Montague Yudelman.

Thanks are also due to the O.E.C.D. for permission to reprint here parts of *Migration, Education and Urban Surplus Labour* (1975) and *The Social Costs of Urban Surplus Labour* (1977) volumes I wrote (the former with Howard Barnum) as contributions to the Employment Series of the Development Centre. I am also grateful to the editors of the *Oxford Bulletin of Economics and Statistics* and *Oxford Economic Papers* for permission to include in various chapters material first published in those journals.

The World Bank   RICHARD SABOT
Washington, D.C.
January, 1979

CONTENTS

INTRODUCTION

ALTHOUGH it appears to be essential for sustaining economic growth and to have important connections with labour market problems, migration has been neglected in the analytic study of economic development. The present work attempts to remedy the situation by means of an intensive analysis of the nature, micro- and macro-determinants, and consequences of migration in one country. The decreasing share of total product from agriculture and the increasing share from manufacturing and services, a principal feature of structural change,[1] is accompanied by a decrease in the proportion of the labour force engaged in agriculture and living in rural areas, implying a net flow of urban migration. In his seminal study of economic growth Kuznets emphasizes migration's significance:

> The disparities between demographic and economic trends in the increase of population and labour, and between internal capital accumulation and differentials in investment opportunities, are numerous and widespread; and the required transfers and migrations were far-reaching processes whose role in the rapid structural shifts and high rates of modern economic growth can hardly be exaggerated. (Kuznets 1966.)

The assumption that the transfer of labour from low to high productivity sectors is a fundamental mechanism by which increase in per capita output takes place is the central feature of the dual economy genre of growth models (Lewis 1954, Fei and Ranis 1964), though their abstraction from a consideration of the actual determinants of migrant behaviour assumes a simple, direct, and instantaneous relationship between migration and spatial income differentials.[2]

Despite substantial investment and high rates of growth of industrial output in many less developed countries (LDCs), rates of increase in urban wage employment (Baer and Herve 1966, Morawetz 1974) have remained relatively low and have often been outstripped by the rapid growth of the urban labour force. Assessment of the global magnitude of the problem is hampered by

---

[1] See Bean 1946, Chenery and Syrquin 1975, Clark 1957, Kuznets 1966, Little, Scitovsky, and Scott, 1970.

[2] Lewis. A somewhat more explicit treatment of the spatial dimension of the growth process in a dual economy model is found in Kelley, Williamson, and Cheetham 1972.

the scarcity of statistical surveys of urban labour markets and, more fundamentally, by confusion as to the conceptual issues underlying the measurement of urban surplus labour. Available evidence does, however, indicate that urban unemployment is significant in developing countries and that in many instances its rate has been increasing (Turnham 1971). Rapid urbanization implies that even where the rate is constant the volume of urban unemployment will grow rapidly; it is frequently asserted that open unemployment is only the tip of the iceberg. The reports of the I.L.O. employment missions to Colombia, Kenya, and Sri Lanka assert that for every unemployed worker there are three or four underemployed (I.L.O. 1971, 1970, 1972a).

The chronic nature of the problem, the fact that surplus labour is not generally accompanied by equivalent underutilization of complementary urban resources, and the frequent coincidence of urban surplus labour with scarcity in rural wage labour markets, suggest that Keynesian demand deficiency cannot explain urban labour market imbalance in LDCs. The availability of employment opportunities in the agricultural or urban non-wage sectors also casts doubt on the relevance of structural explanations which attribute unemployment to inadequate savings or inappropriate technology and hence to a low total demand for labour (Eckaus 1955, Krishna in I.L.O. 1972b).

Evidence that rural–urban migration provides a significant part of the urban labour supply suggests a link between migration and urban labour market imbalance. Recently a class of models has been developed to explain the coexistence of high levels of urban unemployment with rural–urban migration. The principal hypothesis is that the wages of some urban workers are above the level that would equilibrate labour supply and demand and that as a consequence there are queues for urban jobs. With the wages in question rigid, the conventional market clearing mechanism—a decline in wages—is replaced by a quantity adjustment mechanism. The excess supply of urban labour increases until there is equality between the expected income of migrants, the product of the urban wage and the probability of obtaining a job, and the rural wage.[3] In

[3] The basic ideas regarding the relationship between migration and urban unemployment were first formalized in Todaro 1969. See also Frank 1968, Green in Sheffield 1967, Wellisz 1968. The model has been extended to allow for the analysis of welfare implications (Harris and Todaro 1970). For dynamic considerations see Lal 1973 and Stiglitz 1974. For intersectoral capital flows see Corden and Findlay 1975.

contrast to the Keynesian and structural models, which are economy-wide and focus on the demand side of the labour market, the new models focus on intersectoral relations and on the supply side of the labour market; they can apply to long periods.

Migration has also figured in the explanation of the difference in labour productivity between developed and developing countries, a difference which is pervasive even when comparisons are drawn at the sector level (de Briey 1955). Narrowing the income gap between nations requires not only a shift of labour from one sector to another but an increase in the level of productivity of all sectors. Although the lower level of labour productivity in developing countries is partly due to scarcity of capital, the post-war belief that incomes could be raised simply by injecting massive doses of capital has rapidly given way to the recognition that development is multidimensional (Robinson 1971, Sabot 1972). Recognition of the importance for economic growth of investment in human capital is part of this new understanding. In studies of the sources of growth the 'residual' is large: conventional measures of increase in inputs of labour and capital, which do not adjust for improvements in quality, account for little of the increase in output. Increase in investment in schooling, on the job training, health, and migration which enhance the productivity of labour have been suggested as an explanation. The recognition that the stock of human capital has increased has also contributed to the reconsideration of the apparent decline in the capital–output ratio in the rich countries (Schultz 1962, Denison 1962).

In Africa, the form of migration in the colonial period seriously restricted the formation of human capital. The primary economic and social commitments of migrants to their areas of origin precluded strong commitments to residence and employment in the receiving urban areas and agricultural estates. As a consequence migration was frequently short term only, leading to the negative linkage of:

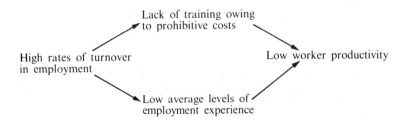

As long as the instability of the wage-earners reduced the rate of return on employers' investment in human capital, attempts to raise the level of productivity in the wage sector and to develop a modern industrial sector, which requires a disciplined and moderately trained labour force, were seriously hampered (Great Britain 1955, Kamarck 1971).

In this study we are concerned with a fairly narrow range of consequences of migrant behaviour. The focus of the analysis is on the problems rather than the benefits of migration, because it is the problems that require remedial action and because sound economic analysis is essential to sound economic policy. The focus is on urban problems only; we do not analyse the consequences of urban migration for the rural source area because our data base is urban. A study of the source areas would require information on villages and households which is not available in Tanzania;[4] the aggregate data available on rural areas do not adequately reflect the effects of out-migration.

The focus is further narrowed to a particular sub-set of urban migration-related problems, namely those associated with labour utilization. We concentrate the analysis on urban surplus labour and low labour productivity and turnover. These two problems are linked not only by their association with migration but also by their association with the difference between rural and urban incomes. To substantiate and clarify the linkages between urban surplus labour, migration and the rural–urban differential, and those between labour productivity, migration, and the rural–urban income differential requires evidence regarding the micro-determinants of migrant behaviour.

Human capital theory, the theory of investment in man, is the foundation on which our analysis of the determinants of migration is based. When he included all the acquired and useful abilities of the inhabitants of a country as part of its wealth, Adam Smith was applying the concept of capital to human beings. The essence of the modern theory was articulated by Irving Fisher (1966), who regarded 'capital' as anything that yields a stream of income over time, and

---

[4] One aim of a project currently under way in West Africa is to integrate collection of data on off-farm management and migration into the more traditional format of farm management surveys. The results should provide the foundation for a rural-oriented analysis of the consequences of urban migration. See Eicher *et al.* 1970.

'income' as the product of capital. From this perspective all categories of income describe yields on various forms of capital and can be expressed as rates of return on the corresponding items of capital. Conversely, all forms of assets that yield income can be given an equivalent capital value by capitalizing the income they yield at an appropriate rate of interest. However, it is only in the last twenty years that human capital theory has been elaborated in detail.

We noted the application of the theory to the analysis of economic growth. It has also been applied to the analysis of the distribution of income (Mincer 1970). Particularly in the industrialized countries it is clear that the functional or factor-share approach and related social-class analysis that dates back to Ricardo is of diminished relevance, because variance in labour incomes is the dominant component of total income inequality. Since returns to investments in human capital are measured in the first instance by income differentials, it follows that the distribution of earnings can be analysed as at least a partial function of differences in investment in individuals. As wage employment opportunities and the stock of human capital increase in developing countries, the relevance of this approach to income distribution will become of greater importance. Even now, one 'non-institutional' explanation suggested for the persistence of rural–urban income differentials, despite 'excessive' migration and chronic problems of urban surplus labour, that we consider has been that high urban wages minimize costs per efficiency unit of labour. Better health and nutrition or greater stability among better-paid workers may increase worker productivity and thus provide higher rates of return to firms from investment in on-the-job training.

Our primary interest is in the third line of development of human capital theory as a way of analysing behaviour in situations where activities undertaken affect primarily future rather than present well-being. The analogy between human and physical capital has been extended to cover the individual's decisions to invest. If migration is only a means to an end, the process by which a barrier between the individual and his goal is overcome, then it can be viewed as one of the costs of achieving the migrant's goal. Since migrants must move to achieve their aim, there is a necessary delay between their outlay on costs and their achievement of the goal, what we call the returns to migration. Thus the decision to migrate can be analysed as an investment in human capital and the only underlying assumptions are that migration represents purposive behaviour, the costs of which are borne in the present as a means of enjoying returns anticipated in the future. A somewhat more rigorous formulation of this proposition is:

Migration may be viewed in a costs and returns framework such that for an individual to migrate his expectations must be that the costs, money and non-money, of migration are equal or less than the difference in the present discounted values of the streams of benefits in the source and receiving areas. (Schultz 1961, Sjaastad 1962.)

Human capital theory provides guidelines for the selection of those dimensions of the socio-economic environment which are relevant to the rural residents' decision to migrate. The direct cost of moving is the cost of transport and the increase in expenditure on food and lodging; the opportunity cost of migration is the source area income forgone while *en route* and in the receiving area; the income the rural resident expects to receive in the urban area constitutes the returns to migration when measured *ex ante*. Where jobs are rationed by a non-price mechanism as a consequence of high and rigid urban wages the framework is easily extended to take account of the probability of employment.[5]

The economic costs and returns can be related to the rate of migration in a general functional form. Using subscripts r and u to designate rural region of origin and urban destination area, respectively, we express the migration relationship as the following function, continuously increasing with W_u and P_u and decreasing with W_r and *DIST* between the boundaries of zero and one;

$$M_{ru} = F(W_u, W_r, P_u, DIST_{ru}, E_{ru})$$

where M is the rate of migration; W_u and W_r are the average values of urban and rural incomes; *DIST* is the geographic distance between source and receiving areas and serves as a proxy for direct costs; P_u is the urban employment probability; E is an error term included to capture effects on the migration rate arising from imprecision in specification and measurement and is assumed to be orthogonal to the independent variables and to have zero mean and uniform variance. Once the costs and returns to migration are quantified, hypotheses associated with the individual components of the framework can be tested and the contribution of the specified

[5] See Appendix B for discussion of problems of measuring the income and probability variables.

variables, both individually and collectively, to the explanation of variance in migration rates among sub-groups of the rural population assessed. Of particular interest is the contribution of employment probability as an explanatory variable. Econometric estimates of the relation between consumption and income have been interpreted as 'tests' of the Keynesian model of unemployment. Similarly, the significance of employment probability in a migration function can be interpreted as a 'test' of the intersectoral misallocation model of urban unemployment.

The human capital framework has several advantages over the two alternative approaches frequently used in studies of the determinants of migration, one of which cannot be used as the basis for hypothesis testing, while the conceptual inadequacies of the other make it clearly inferior to human capital theory in establishing empirical models of migration. The first alternative approach is to avoid the explicit use of theory in the design of applied research; this is the aim of numerous studies of migration in which the motivation of rural residents who have moved to town is ascertained by asking them directly. However, if interviewers present migrants with a predetermined set of categories, some conceptual framework must have influenced the writing of the questionnaire. Only where migrants are asked a completely open-ended question as to why they came to town can the claim be made that there is no theoretical foundation. This non-behavioural approach may yield valuable insights into migrant decision-making and may provide the basis for useful extensions of existing theory. However, even with in-depth interviews there is no way to attach accurate weights for aggregation to the reasons given, with the consequence that the significance of individual factors cannot be tested, nor can the degree of responsiveness of migration flows to changes in potential policy variables be assessed.

The second approach, which divides factors influencing the decision to migrate into those that 'push' individuals out of the rural areas and those that 'pull' them into the urban areas, is frequently only a crude version of human capital theory. To say that push factors, such as low rural wages or lack of availability of land, are strong is roughly equivalent to stating that the opportunity costs of migration are low; to say that pull factors such as high urban wages and the availability of work are strong is roughly equivalent to stating that expected gross returns to migration are high. The 'push–

pull' approach abstracts from the direct costs of migration and tends to emphasize absolute values of either costs or returns rather than the difference between them. In some extreme cases differences in the strength of push factors among source regions are viewed as determining rates of migration while differences in the strength of pull factors among urban areas are viewed as determining the direction of migration. In these cases the underlying model of decision-making, in which the rural resident acts on the basis of the opportunity costs of migration without regard to expected returns, is unrealistic. To paraphrase Marshall, focusing exclusively on costs or returns is the equivalent to claiming that the top or the bottom blade of the scissors is cutting the paper. The view that rural conditions alone influence the migration rate is also inconsistent with the historical evidence that countries with relatively rich agricultural sectors have had relatively high rates of out-migration and that within developing countries the poorest rural regions frequently have relatively low rates of movement to the towns.

It is well to be aware of the weaknesses as well as the strengths of human capital theory as conventionally elaborated. Where only economic costs and returns are included, this model of decision-making is consistent with the most narrow 'classical' concept of economic man. The individual is viewed as a bundle of productive services which he can offer for sale or employ himself to produce goods and services for self-consumption or for the market. His choice of residence from among the alternatives open to him is determined exclusively by the spatial structure of employment opportunities and of prices for his services (directly, in the form of wages or indirectly in the form of prices or imputed prices for output). It is assumed that just as the entrepreneur will select the investment he expects to maximize profits, so a migrant will choose the situation he expects to maximize income. This approach predicts that migration will occur whenever expected net economic returns are positive.

The assumption of strict economic rationality has been criticized by some economists on the ground that people are not observed making the rather complex calculations necessary for the estimation of rates of returns to human capital investments.[6] However, the fact

[6] J. Vaizey's comment (in O.E.C.D. 1965) on economists' estimates of the rate of return to human capital investments is but one example: ' "Let us take Junior out of school—it's yielding 8 percent, and we can get 9 percent on mending Grandma's broken thigh-bone." Do they think this computing is a possible human activity among normal people, let alone a desirable one? This is to say, I do not believe this

that decisions about migration or schooling are not made on the basis of intricate mathematical calculations does not distinguish them from decisions about physical capital investment nor does it necessarily undermine confidence in the realism of the assumption of the economic rationality of investors. Empirical studies reveal that businessmen do not literally solve the equations in terms of which economists specify profit maximizing situations (Simon 1966); they are frequently guided by apparently conventional rules of thumb. For the analysis of decisions to invest in both human and physical capital, the assumption is that investors behave 'as if' they are seeking rationally to maximize expected returns, have all the data needed for this attempt, and perform all the required calculations. Whether this assumption is acceptable depends on the strength of the justification on which economists rely; whether the analogy between physical and human capital decisions breaks down with regard to the goals of investors depends on whether the justification for the 'as if' assumption is markedly stronger in one case than the other.

Johnson claims that to argue against the concept of investment in human capital by referring to how individuals actually make decisions 'is equivalent to disputing the law of gravity on the basis of the commonsense observation that if a feather and a bullet are dropped from the top of Notre Dame the bullet will hit the ground first' (Johnson in OECD 1965). Confidence in the ability of the market to reject participants who engage in 'deviant' behaviour leads economists to equate the income maximization assumption with a law of nature.

Let the apparent immediate determinant of business behavior be anything at all—habitual reaction, random chance, or what not. Whenever this determinant happens to lead to behavior consistent with rational and informed maximization of returns, the business will prosper and acquire resources with which to expand; whenever it does not, the business will tend to use resources and can be kept in existence only by the addition of resources from outside. The process of 'natural selection' thus helps to validate the hypothesis—or, rather, given natural selection, acceptance of the hypothesis can be based largely on the judgement that it summarizes appropriately the conditions for survival. (Friedman 1953.)

procedure is either an "is" or an "ought" statement. I believe it to rest on an elementary fallacy likening these expenditures to outlays on physical capital as a result of mistakenly pressing an analogy too far'.

If the law of natural selection is not completely effective, if, in other words, the market does not impose the ultimate sanction of banishment on all participants whose behaviour does not conform to the model of income maximization, then the non-economic goals and decision-making rules of the individual must be taken into consideration when framing hypotheses regarding the determinants of migrant behaviour. The concept of economic rationality refers to maximization of control over goods and services, the consumption of which entails opportunity costs because scarce resources are employed in their production. Yet numerous dimensions of the environment to which individuals attach value do not have opportunity costs as conventionally defined. Thus the maximization of income is not synonymous with the maximization of welfare. If the market is not selective of income maximizers and if we continue to assume that individuals assess their goals rationally, then we would expect them to attempt to maximize total welfare.

There is considerable debate on the extent to which the market, in fact rather than in theory, is selective of firms whose decisions on physical capital investment are in accord with economic rationality. The prevalence of imperfections and consequently of monopoly power is thought by some to allow entrepreneurs and managers with motives other than profit maximization to survive (Simon 1966). There appears to be less ground for controversy over the proposition that natural selection ensures income maximization as the goal for investors in human capital. Johnson's comment notwithstanding, it is difficult to see how the market can perform this function effectively. Though an individual who decides not to invest may have to accept a less appealing job at a lower income than an investor, his survival as a participant in the labour market is rarely, if ever, at risk. At any given time there is likely to be an abundance of individuals in employment, who in their human capital investment decisions have balanced a lower level of expected income against a higher level of non-economic benefits.

The apparent difference in the strength of sanctions imposed by the market on human and on physical capital investment for not maximizing returns qualifies the analogy between the two. The relative weakness of market sanctions in the case of human capital makes the consideration of non-economic factors of particular importance when analysing migration investment decisions. The differences between the economic and welfare costs and the

economic and welfare returns to investment in migration are called
the psychic costs and returns. While they do not represent resource
costs and returns, they do affect resource allocation. Some early
analyses of the determinants of migration in Africa by social
scientists relied almost exclusively on this category of explanatory
factors.[7] Subsequent studies have shown this emphasis to be
misplaced. Nevertheless differences in psychic costs and returns are
likely to be a significant part of the explanation of different rates of
internal migration and to be more important in LDCs than in
industrialized countries. The explanatory power of non-economic
factors is a positive function of the magnitude of the gap between
economic and total private net returns and of its variance. Rural-
urban differences in the socio-cultural environment are likely to be
more pronounced in poor countries, as are the differences in socio-
cultural characteristics among source area populations.

Conceptually, there is no difficulty in incorporating this class of
costs and returns into the analysis of human capital investment
decisions. As Becker (1964) states, 'since many persons appear to
believe that the term "investment in human capital" must be
restricted to monetary costs and returns, let me emphasize that
essentially the whole analysis applies independently of the division
of real earnings into monetary and psychic components'. However,
in his theoretical analysis, by stating that 'real earnings are the sum
of monetary earnings and the monetary equivalent of psychic
earnings' he evades the measurement problem that economists must
confront when applying the conceptual framework to the empirical
analysis of migration or other human capital investment decisions.

Unfortunately, since there are no direct quantitative estimates of
psychic costs and returns, it is difficult to determine with precision
how much of the difference in migration rates among sub-groups can
be explained in terms of movement along a migration function and
how much by shifts of the function. For example, rates of urban
migration are higher among relatively young rural residents,
probably because a young man has a longer remaining working life
in which to reap the benefits of the rural–urban income differential
and thus gain higher net economic returns to migration. But it is also
conceivable that a systematic increase in aversion to risk occurs over

[7] Discussions of the importance of psychic and sociological factors in Africa, and
also the less easily qualified economic factors, can be found in Kuper, Caldwell,
Gugler 1968.

the course of a person's life. No less plausible is the hypothesis that 'place attachments' grow stronger with age (David 1973). The age-related nature of such factors makes it difficult to separate the non-economic from the economic determinants of migration. A similar problem, on which we concentrate greater attention, arises in the analysis of the influence of education on the propensity of rural residents to migrate. Education selectivity is a frequently observed characteristic of urban migrant streams, and in Africa, where the annual number of school leavers has only recently exceeded the increase in urban employment opportunities, education has been linked with the emergence of chronic urban unemployment (Caldwell 1969, Byerlee 1974). However, whether education's influence on the decisions of rural residents to migrate is due to better economic opportunities for the educated or to their greater willingness to change remains an open question.

Psychic costs and returns cannot be precisely specified, yet it is possible to list some non-economic dimensions of the environment which may influence the rural resident's perception of spatial welfare differentials, even though we cannot say with assurance whether these factors should be entered as costs or as benefits. For example, the 'bright lights' of the towns are frequently referred to as influencing the rural residents to undertake a move. The meaning of 'bright lights' is unfortunately vague. The anonymity, variety, fast pace, liberality, modernity, and complexity of urban surroundings, together with the pervasiveness of the monetary nexus in the urban environment, all appear relevant. But there is no reason why rural residents should not see the difference in environments as a net psychic cost rather than a benefit. This will depend on their preferences. For some rural residents the traditional family structure prevailing in rural areas may be oppressive, while for others it may be a source of support which is left only with reluctance. This is true also for other differences between the rural and urban environments, such as the level of political activity and the proportion of jobs in which one is subject to the authority of others.

Non-economic factors can also have a bearing on investment behaviour indirectly, through their influence on the economic costs and returns. There is frequently an explicit break between the generation that bears the costs of human capital investment and the generation that reaps the benefits, while in the case of physical capital a continuum of investors and beneficiaries is more usual.

With regard to migration in Africa, parents frequently bear the direct costs and a significant portion of the opportunity costs (value of labour time on the family farm) of investment in education and migration. One extreme view is that they do this with the welfare of their children in mind. If the motive is altruistic, as it may well be, then investment in migration can be expected to continue as long as net returns to the child beneficiaries are positive, with migration rates higher than in situations where the beneficiaries bear the costs. At the other extreme, parents may invest in migration because they expect a positive return in the form of remittances from urban areas. In this case, the migration rate will be a positive function of the proportion of the child's income the parents expect to receive. In part, this expectation will be a function of the strength of the prevailing social *mores* that reinforce the practice of remittances. This suggests that the analysis of migrant behaviour would be improved by analysis of these *mores* and of the determinants of the intra-family distribution of income.

Let us consider briefly three other distinctions between investment in physical and in human capital. The latter does not yield returns in the form of tradable assets, but in the form of a higher price for labour services. This not only suggests that investment in human capital is for a relatively long period, but implies that an individual's decision to invest in human capital raises the price of his leisure. The present value of the difference in earnings between investors and non-investors may overstate the value of economic returns because some of the higher earnings are compensation for additional hours worked (Lindsay 1971). Like physical capital, human capital is subject to economic obsolescence before the end of its physical working life through technological change or other changes in the occupational and spatial composition of labour demand. However, human beings are more adaptable than machines, and a decline in demand for their skills may prompt them to learn new ones, posing the problem of separating the returns on a given human capital investment from the returns on subsequent investments. Unlike physical capital investment, investment in human capital may yield consumption benefits. While this is likely to be the case for education, separating consumption from investment expenditures is unlikely to pose a problem in the analysis of migration decisions.

These qualifications to the analogy between physical and human capital investment do not negate the usefulness of the concept of human capital as applied to the micro-analysis of migration. They show, however, that our model of investment behaviour is still only crudely specified, and that some improvements in specification are likely to require collaboration between economists and other social scientists.

The analysis of why people move and why the migrant stream has the demographic and economic characteristics and consequences it has, is not complete without an examination of the processes by which the signals (variables) to which rural residents respond are themselves determined. The analyses of the macro- and micro-determinants of migrant behaviour are complementary. Of course, given its interdependent nature, all dimensions of the economic system and its change are more or less relevant to the migration process. Selecting particular dimensions for consideration is made somewhat easier by the changes in the structure of the Tanzanian economy that have occurred during the period on which we concentrate our analysis, since there is a presumption that these changes have had a relatively strong impact on the spatial distribution of incomes and employment opportunities. The extent of structural change, defined as the change in the relative importance of different industries in terms of output or in terms of resources employed, has been small when measured in relation to the economy as a whole. Within the wage sector, however, which has dispropor-tionate significance for migrant returns, the changes have been far-reaching.

Structural change can in certain respects be seen as an endogenous variable in the growth equation. As incomes increase, differences in income elasticities of demand among consumer goods, and sectoral differences in capital intensities and the ease of factor substitution, will generate different sectoral growth rates. In Tanzania, however, the highly open economy together with the government's powerful influence on the wage sector of the economy, directly through ownership and control and indirectly through wage, price, tariff, and tax policies, mean that internal market forces are not the only forces, and indeed, may be only minor forces, effecting structural change. The important role of exogenous factors has led us to broaden our definition of the phenomenon somewhat to include changes in other wage labour market parameters that are exogenously induced or controlled. Thus, for example, the dramatic increase in educational opportunities is viewed as another dimension of structural change, as, in certain sub-sectors, are the rapid increases in wages. The role of exogenous factors also emphasizes the link between government policy and changes in the patterns and consequences of migration, though policy-makers have only occasionally been aware of the implications of their decisions for migration and for such of its negative consequences as the growth of an urban labour surplus.

Since so little of a quantitative nature is known about urban migration, a subsidiary aim of this study is to document the economic background of migrants and the demographic and educational composition of the migrant stream, the level of stability of migrants in employment and in urban residence, and how migrants fare in the urban labour market compared to the urban-born. Neither this nor the work on the determinants and consequences could be accomplished with existing sources of data. Labour force surveys in LDCs which generate data on employment, and in some instances on incomes, do not collect information on mobility; nor do household budget surveys, which collect data on incomes, and in some instances on employment; and population censuses, which frequently generate at least some data on migration, do not collect adequate information on incomes and employment. Even where all three sources of data are available, as in Tanzania, the lack of foresight of government statistical bureaux and survey designers has meant that they cannot be dovetailed. For this study it was necessary to design a survey to integrate the collection of demographic, mobility, employment, and income data. Though still not ideal, since rural areas are not covered and there are data for only one period, the *National Urban Mobility, Employment and Income Survey of Tanzania (NUMEIST)*, a random sample of 5500 households in seven Tanzanian towns, permits a more comprehensive and disaggregated view of urban migration than has previously been possible. It is the empirical foundation on which this study is built.

In the production of material goods a highly sophisticated capital-intensive technology may be less efficient in economic terms than a less sophisticated labour-intensive technology, depending on the class of goods to be produced and the availabilities of factor inputs. Similarly, given the different availability of relevant data and the degree of refinement of the conceptual framework for different sub-topics, there is considerable variation in the sophistication of the economic tools we consider appropriate. The sketchiness of the data on colonial period migration for instance, permits only a statistically non-rigorous analysis, although it has been an important influence on the evolution of the labour market in the post-Independence period. Also, even though the conceptual and empirical bases are weak, it is important in some contexts to assess the influence of psychic costs and returns.

Our discussion will be adequate if it has as much clearness as the subject-matter admits of, for precision is not sought for alike in all discussions. . . . We must be content, then . . . to indicate the truth roughly and in outline, and in speaking about things which are only for the most part true and with premises of the same kind to reach conclusions that are no better. . . . It is the mark of an educated man to look for precision in each class of things just so far as the nature of the subject admits. (Aristotle, *Ethics*, I. iii; trans. Ross 1915.)

I

MIGRATION AND THE COLONIAL WAGE LABOUR MARKET

ALTHOUGH the locus of wage labour demand during the colonial period was predominantly rural, most of the labour was supplied by migrants from other rural localities. The colonial wage labour market and its attendant rural–rural migration provide a background of comparison for the changes of the post-war era in wage labour supply and demand. Though less detailed and lacking in empirical rigour, in broad outline the analysis parallels our consideration of the present-day phenomenon of urban migration.

1. RURAL–RURAL AND RURAL–URBAN MIGRATION, 1900–1948

Although population figures for Tanzania before 1948 are piecemeal and often inaccurate, they are sufficient to demonstrate that only a small proportion of the population lived in towns and the urban population was increasing at a low rate. Table 1.1 shows that in nearly half a century from 1900 to 1948 Dar es Salaam's population grew by only some 50 000 people from a base of approximately 20 000. If the natural growth rate of Dar es Salaam was at the upper end of the 1–2 per cent range estimated for the population as a whole, then net migration contributed little more than 1 per cent a year to the population of the country's largest urban area (U.N.

TABLE 1.1
Population estimates, Dar es Salaam 1900–1948

Year	Total population
1900	20 000
1913	22 500
1921	24 600
1931	34 300
1943	45 100
1948	69 277

Source: Sutton 1970.

TABLE 1.2
*Numbers of migrant wage labourers using government rest
centres 1927–1947*

Year	Estimated number
1927	72 000
1929	98 000
1930	80 000
1940	110 000
1947	135 000

Source: Tanganyika, Labour Department 1928–48.

1949). The rate of growth of other urban areas does not appear to
have been any higher. In 1948, the degree of urbanization was
still extremely low; though the mainland population was nearly
7 500 000, only 197 000 people, 2·6 per cent of the total, lived in areas
classified as urban.[1]

The magnitude of rural–rural migration during this period stands
in sharp contrast to the insignificance of the movement of people
from rural to urban areas. Though data on the number of migrants
into rural employment areas are non-existent before 1927 and, in
general, rather crude, the bias in Table 1.2, derived from records of
the number of people using government rest centres, appears to be
definitely downward.[2] In 1927 approximately 72 000 people left their
homes for other rural areas and travelled up to 700 miles, often on
foot and in the face of considerable health hazards. The number of
migrants increased to 98 000 in 1929, then declined sharply in 1930
as the depression in North America and Europe reached the colonies
through the primary commodity markets. By 1940 rural–rural
migration had surpassed pre-depression levels, and it continued to
expand during the war, when sisal was considered an essential
commodity, and during the immediate post-war commodity boom.
In 1947, 135 000 people, nearly 8 per cent of the entire adult male

[1] In most countries for an area to be classified as urban the minimum population
must be 5000–10 000 people. As the urban population in 1948 included a number of
townships with population of less than 5000, these figures overestimate the degree of
Tanzania's urbanization. In the 1967 census the 5000 minimum population was
adopted as the definition of an urban area. Tanzania, Central Statistical Bureau 1968.
[2] While some migrants stopping at rest centres were likely to have an urban
destination, it is estimated that an even greater number of rural–rural migrants did
not use the centres at all. Tanganyika. Labour Department 1930.

population of the territory, moved from one rural area to another in pursuit of employment.

The important point is that during the first half of the century, rural–rural migration was far more significant than rural–urban migration. However, one further qualification is in order. The figures for rural–urban movements are for net migration, while the rural–rural movements are in gross terms. Since there was a high level of turnover in urban employment, with migrants returning to their home areas after only a short period in town, the gross rate of urban migration would be considerably higher than indicated. But even a doubling or tripling of the net annual increase would leave urban migration as a small proportion, 25 per cent at most, of the rural–rural movement.

2. DETERMINANTS OF MIGRATION DURING THE COLONIAL PERIOD

P. H. Gulliver's study of migration (1955) among the Ngoni of southern Tanzania concluded: 'Without question the overwhelming reason why Ngoni leave their homes and their country to seek work abroad is economic. Men cannot, or feel they cannot, earn sufficient money at home to satisfy their basic cash needs and their minimum standard of living; alternatively men feel that it is easier to earn sufficient income abroad than at home.' Rural residents were responding to a spatial differential in income per unit of effort. The empirical evidence, even in Gulliver's own study (1955), is inadequate to test this hypothesis rigorously. Nevertheless, such evidence as exists on the relationship between the structure of migration rates and differentials among rural groups in costs and returns, does provide a basis, albeit a crude one, for assessing responsiveness to economic incentives.

2.1 *Migration rates and wage employment opportunities*

The structure of investment, production, and trade that emerged during the German period, was reinforced by the British, and was characteristic of the colonial pattern of development throughout Africa, had a corollary in the spatial distribution of wage-earning opportunities. Investment was outwardly focused and heavily concentrated in two sectors, export agriculture and infrastructure, with some additional investment in mining. Port facilities were developed at Dar es Salaam and Tanga, and one railway line followed the old caravan route through the centre of the country to Dodoma, Tabora, and Mwanza, while another was laid in the north from Tanga to Moshi. A crude road network was established, and administrative and trading centres with modern buildings and water supply, electricity, and sewers were constructed in fourteen geographically dispersed areas (I.B.R.D. 1961).

There was a rapid expansion of major primary product exports during the period 1913–50. Sisal, introduced in 1892, increased from an output of 2000 tons in 1913 to 120 000 in 1950, an average annual rate of expansion of nearly 5 per cent. Coffee output and exports grew even more rapidly and stood at 15 000 tons in 1950, while cotton and cashew nuts, Tanzania's other major export crops, followed suit (I.B.R.D. 1961).

This rapid expansion of exports took place although the level and growth of foreign investment were constrained by the absence of major mineral resources to be exploited, the small size of the settler population, and the international economic and political situation. Tanzania was a battleground during the First World War; this put a halt to most modern sector production and interrupted the flow of new investment. Though pre-war levels of performance were achieved again in 1924, the depression and Hitler's increasingly vociferous territorial demands, often including former German East Africa, created an environment of uncertainty clearly unfavourable to foreign investment (Listowel 1968).

Throughout this period imports consisted predominantly of consumer goods, manufactured in Germany until the First World War, in England after it. In addition, a sizeable amount of capital equipment such as railway engines, construction machinery, and tractors was imported for infrastructure and export sector investment. Capital imports for the establishment of a manufacturing sector constituted only a small proportion of total imports. Of the 569 manufacturing establishments in Tanzania employing ten or more persons in 1965, only 18 per cent had been established before 1946, and half of those were involved in the export-oriented activities of sisal decortication and cotton ginning, the small remaining number producing beer, leather goods, soap, and other items for domestic consumption (Rweyemamu 1971).

Our concern is with the implications of this evolving structure of investment, production, and trade for the wage labour market. There are no accurate employment estimates prior to 1944, the year of the first employment census. What evidence there is, however, suggests that, before the arrival of the Germans in 1880, there was little wage employment beyond a few porters in the caravan trade and some wage labourers on the Zanzibari estates. Though there was co-operative pooling of labour in peasant agriculture, one man offering his labour to others for harvesting or house-building in exchange for the use of theirs in return, this did not involve payment of wages. The increasing level of economic activity generated an increasing demand for wage labour, however, and by 1944 some 320 500 people were engaged in part- or full-time wage employment (Tanganyika, Labour Department 1945), increasing to 443 600 by 1951. The introduction of wage employment was a significant change in the structure of the economy, though even in 1952 wage labour was still less than 10 per cent of the economically active population.

Table 1.3 gives the breakdown of employment by industry and region for 1952, the earliest date for which accurate figures are available. Over 50 per cent of all wage employees were engaged in agriculture, somewhat more than 20 per cent in non-agricultural private industry, another 20 per cent were employed by the government, with the remaining 5 per cent serving as domestic servants in private households. The further breakdown of the agricultural and non-agricultural sectors in Tables 1.4 and 1.5 is of particular interest. Reflecting the pattern of production, only 22 per cent of those employed in non-agricultural private enterprises, less than 5 per cent of the total, were in manufacturing; while over 50 per cent were to be found in the three sub-sectors of mining and quarrying, construction, and commerce. In agriculture, 70 per cent of all wage labourers were employed by the foreign-owned sisal industry on large estates, which frequently ran to 1000 and more acres and employed over 500 workers. Production on these estates was labour intensive, in part because of relative factor costs and in part because the technology for the mechanization of sisal had not yet been developed.

The concentration of wage jobs in agriculture naturally entailed a rural skew in the distribution of employment opportunities. In addition, the construction, transport, and mining industries, the largest non-agricultural private employers of wage labour, were not concentrated in urban areas. Though no precise measure of the distribution is available, the greater part of wage-earning opportunities appears to have been in rural areas throughout the colonial

TABLE 1.3
Regional distribution of wage employees classified by main employer groups 1952

Region	Private households	Agriculture	Non-agricultural private industry	Government	Total	Regional groupings as % of Total
Dodoma Singida	1417	2248	4835	9881	18381	4·1
Coast Morogoro	5985	49039	28919	22520	106195	23·9
Mara Shinyanga Mwanza West Lake	2144	3948	15423	12843	34358	7·7
Arusha Kilimanjaro	2341	29608	8813	11217	51979	11·7
Mtwara Ruwuma	2137	19206	11470	8237	41050	9·2
Iringa Mbeya	1865	18037	8036	5987	33925	7·6
Tanga	2739	105710	11830	7211	127490	28·7
Kigoma Tabora	1802	5231	11295	11891	30219	6·8
Total	20430	233027	100621	89787	443597	100·0
Main employer group as % of Total	4·6	52·5	22·7	20·2	100·0	

Source: East African Statistical Department 1953.

TABLE 1.4
Non-agricultural wage employees classified by industrial group 1952

Major non-agricultural industrial group	Number of employees	Industrial group as % of Total
Mining and quarrying	16529	16·4
Manufacturing (including electricity)	22539	22·4
Construction	21253	21·1
Commerce	14627	14·5
Transport and communications	6951	6·9
Services (non-government) (excluding domestic service)	16874	16·8
Not adequately described	1848	1·8
Total	100621	100·0

Source: East African Statistical Department 1953.

TABLE 1.5
Agricultural wage employees classified by type of farming 1952

Type of farming	Number of employees[a]	Type of farming sub-group as % of Total
Sisal	160788	69
Tea	6990	3
Coffee	13981	6
Tobacco	2330	1
Mixed	48935	21
Total	233027	100

[a] Assumes that distribution of casuals among types of farming is same as for regular employees.
Source: East African Statistical Department 1953.

period. This is what we would predict, given the difference in the rate of rural–rural and rural–urban migration. That rural residents went where the jobs were is consistent with the hypothesis that migration represented economically rational behaviour.

2.2 *Migration rates and regional economic opportunities*

The sale of labour was not the only activity from which rural dwellers could derive a cash income; there were also opportunities to sell cash crops. Cotton and coffee, whose production expanded at roughly the same rate as that of sisal, have been predominantly peasant crops. Although coffee was the second largest export crop, only 5 per cent of the agricultural labour force was employed in its production in 1952.[3] Is there any connection between the location of these cash crop opportunities and the regional structure of rates of emigration?

Let us first consider the regional distribution of wage employment opportunities. Most colonial agricultural investment and settlement was in a belt running north from Dar es Salaam and Morogoro to Tanga, and from there inland to the Usambara Mountains and the slopes of Mount Kilimanjaro and Meru. The north-eastern section of the country was favoured by its climate: rainfall and soil fertility were more favourable to high levels of agricultural productivity than in the semi-arid plains of the central territory. The Southern Highlands, with equally favourable climatic conditions, received only sporadic investment and settlement because the north-east had been developed first and had rapidly established an advantage in transport, communications, marketing, and other facilities. Table 1.3 indicates that in 1952 over 64 per cent of all wage employment opportunities were located in Coast, Morogoro, Arusha, Kilimanjaro, and Tanga, the five regions of the north-eastern belt; the remaining 36 per cent were divided in roughly equal proportions among the other twelve regions. This regional difference in wage employment opportunities was reinforced by a difference in wage rates. Most of the few wage jobs available in the southern and western segments of the country were with the public works department, which in 1952 paid sh 23 per *kipande*[4] as compared to sh 28 for heavy cultivation on the sisal estates and sh 39 for a sisal cutter (Gulliver 1955). The demand throughout the colonial period was predominantly for unskilled labour. As Table 1.6 indicates, less than 5 per cent of the jobs open to Africans in 1952 were non-manual, a reflection of the structure of the economy, the scarcity of educational opportunities for Africans, and the high proportion of white-collar jobs reserved for Europeans. Skilled and semi-skilled jobs constituted 15 per cent of the total, and unskilled jobs made up the remaining 80 per cent. In agriculture the proportion of unskilled

[3] Table 1.5 above.
[4] *kipande:* a card on which the daily work of a labourer is recorded; the number of days per card did not vary among tasks.

labour was considerably higher: nearly 90 per cent of agricultural
wage employees required muscle-power only, as compared to 60 per
cent in other sectors. One consequence of this occupational
distribution was a highly compressed distribution of wage incomes,
the vast majority of workers receiving wages within a narrow range.

Peasant cash crop agriculture was also concentrated in the north-
east and near Lake Victoria. Even in 1965, after considerable
government attention to the agricultural development of the south
and west, Tanga, Kilimanjaro, and Morogoro, the regions with the
greater concentration of wage employment, still generated, together
with Mwanza, 60 per cent of peasant cash crop production (Jensen
1968). The other thirteen regions produced the remaining 40 per
cent. The good climate and transport facilities of the north-east were
as important to the peasant cultivators as to the estate owners. While
cotton and coffee were grown under different conditions from sisal,
the natural environments favourable for their production tended to
be in the same areas, with coffee growing on the mountain slopes
and sisal below.

Potential cash crop producers in the fertile portions of the southern
and western regions were at an extreme cost disadvantage because
of their remoteness from modern transport facilities and markets.
Songea, in the Southern Highlands, for example was nearly 400
miles from a coast port, with no railway to service the area, and a
road open only in the dry season (Gulliver 1955). Production costs

TABLE 1.6

*Occupational distribution of adult males in non-government wage
employment 1952[a]*

	Non-agricultural private industry %	Agricultural private industry %	Total %
Non-manual	10·0	1·6	4·1
Skilled and semi-skilled	29·9	8·9	15·3
Unskilled	60·1	89·4	80·5
Total	100·0	100·0	100·0

[a] Occupational data are for a sub-sample of wage employees.
Source: East African Statistical Department 1953.

for coffee in Ngara, in the far west, were the same as in Mwanza, but the extra transport costs the farmer had to bear made cultivation competitive with migrant wage employment only when international coffee prices were high. When coffee prices declined, Ngara was the first area to revert to a non-cash crop economy (Iliffe 1971).

The production of food crops for the labour force on the estates in the north also provided high cash crop earnings from which more remote regions were excluded. Government policy contributed to economic divergence by concentrating rail and road investments in better endowed regions and by its tendency to favour the 'progressive farmers', the peasants most likely to succeed, in the provision of seed and credit. Both policies favoured the African population living in areas of European settlement. Geographic variations in entrepreneurial ability should also be considered, though their importance is difficult to assess.

Although there were pockets of extremely high population density, land alienation was not a serious impediment to cash crop development, because colonial settlement was limited by government policy even in the most fertile areas of Tanzania. European settlement never became official policy in Tanzania, which was one of the few places in Africa where neither the European farmer, as in Rhodesia and Kenya, nor the African farmer, as in Ghana and Uganda, established dominant control over agricultural cash crop production (Iliffe 1971).

Whether to increase foreign exchange earnings and tax revenues by encouraging European settlers to establish large farms using modern technology and African labour or by encouraging Africans to expand and transform their own agriculture within the traditional land tenure system had been debated since the first decade of the current century. Rechenberg, colonial governor during that period, opposed a settlement approach for three reasons. First, the opening of the Uganda railway, which gave inland areas access to foreign markets and resulted in a rapid expansion of cotton and coffee production by Africans within its reach, convinced the governor that the African peasant was an 'economic man', who would respond to market opportunities on the basis of an intelligent understanding of his own self-interest. Second, the economic marginality of the early estates raised questions about their profitability. Third, he feared that the forced takeover of African land would incite another uprising like the Maji Maji rebellion, which swept the southern half of the territory in 1904–5 and was associated with the use of forced labour on a cotton development scheme (Iliffe 1969).

Similar decisions were made by Cameron, British governor in the latter part of the 1920s, and by the British Labour government in 1929. The considerable pressure to establish a 'Great European Dominion' in East Africa was resisted on the ground that large-scale settlement would violate the terms of the League of Nations mandate by which Britain ruled the territory (Listowel 1968). Only 1 per cent of the country's land area was alienated for Europeans[5] in contrast to Kenya, where fully 20 per cent of arable land was alienated (Wolff 1969, Brett 1973). The smaller-scale alienation in Tanzania helped to raise local African incomes rather than lower them.

The concentration of employment and cash cropping opportunities in the same area was an essential reason for the growth of the colonial migrant labour system in Tanzania—not that there was inadequate local population to man the estates, for the north-eastern regions were among the most populated in the country. Rather, the evidence suggests that the opportunity cost of taking up wage employment, measured in terms of agricultural income forgone, was high enough to make working on the estate an unattractive alternative for the local peasant. The limited cash earning opportunities and low incomes of the south and west made opportunity costs low enough for employment on the estates to be an attractive alternative, despite the higher costs involved in migrating long distances. Nearly 70 per cent of all agricultural wage employees were long-distance migrants.

Though the data on rates of migration and differentials in wage income, employment opportunity, and cash crop earnings lack the desired precision, the available evidence, which reveals considerably higher migration from the poorer south than from the richer north-east, supports the hypothesis that rural residents migrated in response to differences in the level of cash earning opportunities.

2.3 *Migration rates and intra-regional income differentials*

Culturally homogeneous regions of Tanzania are not economically homogeneous. Even within the relatively underdeveloped south and west, some areas are more prosperous than others. All the Ngoni, for instance, can expect similar direct costs and returns from migration,

[5] See Iliffe 1971.

but for those in the eastern areas of the tribe's territory, where cash crop cultivation is possible, the opportunity costs of migration are higher. Comparing Ngoni rates of migration from a cash crop area, Gulliver (1955) found, as we would expect, considerably heavier migration from the western, non-cash crop areas than from the eastern, better-off areas (Tanganyika, Central Statistical Bureau 1963).

Environmental factors such as differences in soil fertility and rainfall contributed to the emergence of intra-regional cash crop income differentials, as did the availability of land. Despite the low level of alienation of land and the over-all low population density (22 persons per square mile in 1957), isolated areas of land scarcity emerged as early as 1912 (Iliffe 1969). On the slopes of Kilimanjaro, in Sukumaland amongst the Nyakyusa, in the Usambara mountains, and on the islands in Lake Victoria, land shortage became a serious problem. The rapid population growth produced by in-migration and a rate of natural increase accelerated by better medical care was only one cause of this shortage. The spread of modern medical knowledge also led to decreases in cattle disease and thus to increases in the cattle population, whose demands on grazing land exacerbated the problems of population density. Much peasant farming was still based on traditional methods of shifting cultivation which presuppose such abundance of land that a family can exhaust one patch and move on to clear and cultivate another while the first regenerates itself over a long period. The demands of increasing human and livestock population on the limited available land shortened the fallow period and led to land deterioration, which decreased the amount of fertile land in the areas affected (Dumont 1966, Yudelman 1964). Land scarcity also resulted from attempts by peasant farmers to increase their incomes. A study of Nyakyusa land tenure found that pressure on fertile land resulted primarily from the introduction of cash as a supplement to food crops for family consumption (Gulliver 1958). The result was that the age at which young men were entitled to land went up and the average size of plot passed on from father to son decreased, leading to differences in income for young men between areas in which land was scarce and those in which it was plentiful.

In many Nyakyusa villages more than half the young men were landless, which naturally cut them off from a cash crop income. For them the opportunity cost of migration was minimal. The Gulliver study (1958) revealed that where the proportion of young men without land was two to three times as great as in other areas, the proportion of young men away at work for wages was twice as great. Differentials in the net returns to migration resulting from differentials in the opportunity costs of migration are again shown to be associated with differentials in the rate of migration in a way consistent with our economic interpretation of migrant behaviour.

2.4 Migration rates and income changes

A secular increase in opportunity costs or an increase in the return to cash cropping can result from technological innovation, from an upward trend in prices for the crop, or from a decrease in transport costs. Assuming a crop with a short gestation period, cyclical or short-term upturns in opportunity costs can result from brief expansions of demand and prices, or from good weather generating bumper crops with high marketable surpluses. In Ngara, where cash crop production was hampered by high transport costs, a decrease in the world market price of coffee turned the peasants from cash production to wage labour migration. As the opportunity cost of migration decreased, Ngara's economy moved from exporting coffee to exporting labour (Iliffe 1971). Among the Nyakyusa, as the proportion of young men without land increased during the immediate post-war era, the level of local cash-earning opportunities and the opportunity cost of migration were lowered and the rate of migration increased (Gulliver 1958).

Another example of the relationship between change in the structure of opportunity costs and change in the rate of migration is found among the Sukuma. Higher cotton prices in the late 1940s and 1950s, greater availability of credit, and more widespread knowledge of cotton production technology enabled local economic opportunities to rival migration as a source of money income. Land being in ample supply, the result was a rapid expansion of Sukumaland cotton production, an increase in the proportion of men raising cash crops, and a dramatic reduction in the rate of migration to the agricultural wage employment areas. The bureau established in the 1920s to engage Sukuma labourers for work on the sisal estates was closed in 1952 because of the decline in the number of volunteers (Heijnen 1968). A similar decline in rates of out-migration in response to increased returns to local economic opportunities was noted among the Ngoni (Gulliver 1955).

2.5 *Migration rates and changes in the cost of travel*

During the 1920s there was a significant drop in the cost of travel as road or rail transport was introduced into areas from which people had had to walk to the estates. Instead of investing three or four weeks and much energy in walking, the migrant could for a small charge (or 'free' in the case of those who signed a labour contract) ride on a truck or train. However, a decline in the cost of travel for migrants also meant a decline in transport cost for cash crops. The relative importance of direct costs in the potential migrant's decision is indicated by the apparent increase in migration from the newly opened areas, despite the increase in opportunity costs. In discussing the effect of the opening of the railway on labour supply, the colonial labour commissioner noted:

The development of recruiting in Mwanza is of special interest in connection with the effect of the construction of the railroad and the production of native grown economic crops. Before the building of the line, fears were sometimes expressed that the great encouragement this offered to native production would have an adverse effect upon the labour supply from the areas tapped, the enormous advantage of improved transport facilities being overlooked. In practice, the effect has been to increase the exodus of labourers substantially; in 1927 contract labourers from Mwanza numbered 71; in 1928 this number increased to 1107 while for 1929 it rose to 2513. Since the output of native-grown crops has also risen considerably, it is clear that the time formerly lost in the long journey on foot to work or to a market, is now saved and utilised to earn more wages or grow larger crops.[6]

The importance of travel cost in the structure of costs and returns to migration during the colonial period is clear. We should also consider the implication in the example noted that rural residents took advantage of the improvements in transport to increase their total cash income. It is, of course, possible that paralleling of the increase in out-migration by the increase in cash crop production could have derived from increased participation of the population in the money economy rather than from increased income per producer. Whether rural residents sought to raise their income above a relatively low minimum level bears on the issue of the responsiveness of potential migrants to increases in the wage rate.

2.6 *Migration rates and conditions of work in receiving areas*

Within a rural receiving area, we would expect migrants to prefer

[6] Tanganyika. Labour Department 1930. See also 1928 for documentation of a similar phenomenon among the Ngoni.

employers offering a high return to migration in the form of higher
wages or better working conditions. This response is manifest in the
migrants' attitude to signing a contract with a recruiter: only about
one-quarter of all migrants came as contract labourers, despite the
fact that recruiters frequently offered free transport in exchange for
a commitment to work for a minimum of five months for a specified
employer (Tanganyika, Labour Department 1930). Most migrants
came as volunteers in order to maintain flexibility in choice of
employer and length of stay. Conditions on estates varied widely in
quality of housing and food, nature of supervision, and size of the
daily task, but not, for the most part, in wages. Given the labour
scarcity existing during much of the colonial period, migrants not on
contract could choose to work on the estates offering the best
conditions, thus minimizing the effort price of income and
maximizing the returns to migration. As one commentator noted:
'The constant shortage of labour puts the employer at a disadvantage;
a property with a bad reputation is speedily boycotted and this acts
as a steady incentive towards improved conditions.' (Orde-Browne
1946.)

3. SUPPLY AND DEMAND IN THE COLONIAL WAGE LABOUR MARKET AND BEHAVIOUR OF MIGRANTS AND EMPLOYERS

One particularly important dimension of the relationship between
the structure of migration rates and that of costs and returns we have
not yet analysed is that between migration rates and wage rates over
time. It is important because of the particular view of the wage
elasticity of the individual's supply of labour adopted by private and
government employers to justify their approach to one of the most
significant labour problems of the colonial era.

3.1 *Wage labour scarcity*

Whereas many African governments today face the problem of
overabundant urban labour, during the colonial period employers in
Africa were troubled by a scarcity of wage labour (Berg 1965, Mason
1958). The current stress on unemployment and underemployment
is, for reasons which will emerge later in this study, a post-Second
World War phenomenon. In the earlier literature on employment problems in Tanzania, the paramount concern was the per-
sistent shortage of labour encountered by government and private

employers. The chronic inadequacy in the numbers of Africans volunteering for the new wage employment opportunities was so serious that German government reports of 1906 talk of a 'labour calamity' threatening the further development of plantation agriculture (Iliffe 1969, Tanganyika, Labour Department 1928). Although there were some years of adequate supply, usually those in which there was a short-fall in peasant food or cash crop production, or the opening of a new transport facility, shortage of labour[7] was common during British colonial rule. One response of employers was the practice of 'crimping' labour, enticing workers to break their contracts and move from one estate to another. The lure generally consisted of the offer of less work or better conditions (Tanganyika, Labour Department 1930). Another response was to import labour. The railways, for example, were built with a significant proportion of Indian industrial labourers,[8] and the sisal estates recruited as many as 45 000 workers in a single year from outside the territory (Lawrence in R.D.R.C. 1976). A third set of responses will be discussed in section 3.4.

3.2 *Low wages and backward-bending supply curves*

A significant aspect of the employers' response, however, was what they did not do. The evidence suggests that, if an adequate supply of labour was not forthcoming at the going wage, raising the level of wages would increase the supply by increasing the return to migration. The employers held, however, that increasing the level of wages would actually lead to a decline in the supply of labour. The labour supply function of the individual labourer was held to be backward sloping.

There is nothing unique or economically irrational about a wage employee who offers less of his services at a higher wage. The effect of a wage change on any person's offer of services can be broken down into an income effect and a substitution effect. The income effect of a rise in a person's rate of earnings means that with increased income he can afford more leisure, more time for non-cash-earning economically productive activities and less time for wage employment. If leisure and goods produced for self-consumption are not inferior, an individual with increased income will tend

[7] Orde-Browne 1946 and Tanganyika. Provincial Commissioner, Western Province 1936.
[8] See Orde-Browne 1946.

to consume more of them. The substitution effect works in the opposite direction. A rise in wages means that the opportunity cost of leisure and non-market goods, in terms of the goods and services that an additional hour's work can buy, has increased. They have become more expensive and an individual will tend to substitute other goods and services for them. Thus, the income and substitution effects pull in opposite directions; where there has been a rise in wages and the level of the individual's total offer of services is not institutionally constrained, either effect may prevail. In other words, a rise in wages in Africa or in an industrial country may lead people to work less or to work more.[9]

In Tanzania, as elsewhere in Africa during this period, it was held that wage labourers had strictly defined target cash incomes. Beyond a certain level, the income elasticity of demand for all wage goods would approach zero, which implied that the substitution effect of a wage increase would be nil or very weak. An increase in the rate of pay would simply result in the wage earner achieving his target after a shorter period in employment.[10] Major G. Orde-Browne, formerly labour commissioner in Tanzania and in 1946 Labour Adviser to the Secretary of State for the Colonies, believed this to be so:

Conversations with travelling labourers will usually elicit the fact that they have a definite sum in view, and that they hope to earn that amount and then go home again. The sooner that this can be done, therefore, the quicker the worker's return to his village. Consequently, the offer of more money seldom has much attraction for him; increased wages enable him to leave earlier but do not persuade him to remain longer. This accounts for the statement frequently made that the offer of a higher wage means less work and not more. (Orde-Browne 1946.)

An explanation was suggested for the low income elasticity of demand for wage goods. On the one hand, because of the widespread availability of land, the African did not have to depend on the money economy for provision of food. Also the 'traditional' or non-money economy produced housing and utensils that decreased

[9] We argue below that during the period under consideration there was a shift in preference towards manufactured goods. If this was the case then handicrafts produced for self-consumption may well have been inferior goods and an increase in wages would have decreased the amount of time allocated to their production. In this case if an increase of wages is to lead an individual to decrease the amount of labour services offered, then the income–leisure effect must outweigh not only the substitution effect but the income–traditional goods effect as well.

[10] If, in fact, the target income was completely rigid, this would imply a negative unit elasticity of the individual's offer curve of labour.

dependence on cash. On the other hand, Africans had been rooted for so long in stagnant tradition-bound societies where per capita income remained constant that they were not open to consumer innovation. Even when the effort prices of the goods were the same and the manufactured goods more varied, they preferred traditional hand-made goods. Apart from the need for tax money or bride-price, the African was said to have very limited cash wants. Increased income would thus have little appeal, for the Africans were satisfied with what little they had: 'What European population is nearly as fortunate? The African has a low standard of living, according to that standard he is very well off.' (Tanganyika, Labour Department 1929.)

In addition to the weak substitution effect of higher income on the offer of labour, Africans were reputed to have an unusually high preference for leisure as opposed to any income, cash or non-cash.

The Tanganyika African as a worker is inherently indolent, and in this respect he is not dissimilar from the great mass of mankind. The real difference arises from the low apparent cost to himself at which he can indulge his indolence. His direct wants are few; the climate is warm and he needs little clothing; as has been said already, leisure ranks high in his scale of preference. (Guillebaud 1966.)

Recently the hypotheses of economic stagnation and lack of consumer innovation, and that of high preference for leisure, have had considerable doubt cast upon them. Our view of African history was for a long time determined by what could be gleaned from colonial government documents, which constituted almost the only written record of the continent in the nineteenth and early twentieth centuries. Advances in historical research have opened a mine of oral and archaeological evidence, and the economic history of the continent has been revised as a result.

Compared with the complex exchange economy of nineteenth-century West Africa, there was little economic specialization in Tanzania before the arrival of foreign capital with the Germans. There was, however, a clove-producing plantation economy on Zanzibar, and coastal trade under the control of Omani Arabs, Portuguese, and local Swahili-speaking peoples. The coast and the interior were linked by trade routes, emanating from Kilwa in the south, from Dar es Salaam and Bagamoyo in the centre, and from Pangani in the north. These routes, reaching Lake Victoria and beyond, were traversed by caravans of 1000 men or more, and their activity sent impulses of economic change throughout the territory. Ivory, skins, beeswax, salt, and—much to the detriment of local development—slaves were exported; cloth, cooking pots, guns, gunpowder, knives, hoes, and other manufactured goods were imported (Alpers in Kimambo and Temu 1969). Capital markets grew up on Zanzibar to finance the trade, and local agriculture responded by selling surplus production to the Zanzibar plantations and the caravans. Partly in response to the influx of migrants from the south and the consequent pressure on traditional agricultural systems in certain localities, new crops such as mangoes, peas, cashew-nuts, ground-nuts, and rice were introduced (Greenway 1944–5). Internal trade was also developing in such commodities as cattle, salt, and locally manufactured iron hoes (Roberts 1968). The colonial economic structure was not superimposed on stagnant, entirely tradition-bound, subsistence tribal economies. There is evidence to suggest that, far from being rejected as untraditional, the new imported goods were valued highly and earned their owners considerable status within the tribal community (Powesland 1957). Thus the explanation of a rigidly defined target income resulting from a limited appreciation of manufactured imported goods must be qualified.[11] Moreover most analysis using the target-income concept is short term, with the implication that the income goal is fixed independently of income-earning possibilities (Berg 1961). Rising incomes in some sectors, combined with the demonstration effect, would be expected to raise income goals; yet the limited-want hypothesis was still being used to explain African behaviour in the 1950s as in the first decade of the century.

Recent research into the economies of peasant production has revealed that labour inputs, measured in number of hours per week, are frequently quite high, though unevenly distributed through the year (Kao et al. in Eicher and Witt 1964). It also has been recognized that activities away from the fields, in what was thought to be leisure time, frequently meet essential social and political needs of the community, suggesting that work time was underestimated. The view of the leisure-income preference function of the African has had to be revised in the direction of the more conventional form found in richer societies, thus raising additional doubts about the validity of the backward-bending individual labour offer curve.

[11] An argument for the revision of the limited-want hypothesis in Central Africa is found in Miracle and Fetter 1970.

There are strong arguments against the hypothesis that the Africans had a target income so rigid that any increase in wages would lead to a cut-back in the amount of labour offered in the same proportion. Indeed, the evidence casts doubt on the notion that the individual labour-offer curve sloped back at all. Leaving the analytic arguments aside, what evidence was presented that Africans in Tanzania actually responded to a wage increase with a shorter length of stay?

There was substantial evidence of such behaviour only during the Second World War, when the rapid expansion of military manpower needs led to a sharp increase in over-all labour demand and to wage increases by some employers (Orde-Browne 1946). The response of wage employees was to shorten their length of stay in employment. This, however, was not because of limited wants, but because the flow of consumer imports into the country had been interrupted by the war. The first response of employees was to save the money with which there was nothing to buy, and the purchase of cattle, the traditional form of savings, increased markedly in labour source areas. However, as the shortage of consumer goods persisted and the proportion of income saved increased, early termination of employment by wage earners began to occur. Apart from this case, which of course does not provide support for the backward-bending labour offer curve under normal circumstances, no positive evidence of such behaviour was noted in thirty years of Labour Department Annual Reports, in the two special reports on labour conditions commissioned by the colonial government, or in the few academic studies carried out.

The analytical arguments and empirical evidence qualifying the assumption of the individual's backward-bending labour offer curve, strong though they may be, constitute only half the case against the aggregate backward-bending supply curve of labour during the colonial period. The effect of a change in wages on the supply of labour was a function of its effect on the participation rate in the wage labour force as well as on the average length of stay of migrants in employment.

The evidence presented in the last section indicates that the supply of labour, measured in numbers of people volunteering for wage labour, is positively sloped. For the aggregate number of hours to decrease when wages increased, it would not be enough for the number of hours worked by each individual to decrease. Rather, that decrease would have to outweigh the increase in the number of people entering wage employment. Given our doubts about the shape of the individual offer curve of labour, we find it highly unlikely that the aggregate supply curve was backward-bending. When wages finally began to rise rapidly in the 1950s and 1960s after nearly half a century of virtual stagnation,[12] the supply of labour increased dramatically, making labour scarcity a historical phenomenon. This increase resulted not only from an increase in the participation rate but also, contrary to the notion of an individual backward-bending labour offer curve, from an equally dramatic increase in the length of stay of migrants in employment.[13]

3.3 Oligopsonistic power and wage determination

We have outlined a situation of chronic labour scarcity in the colonial wage labour market, and have shown that the most common contemporary justification for stagnant wages, a backward-bending labour supply function at an extremely low level of income, does not appear to have general validity for the whole period. If there was a free market for labour, why did not the employers bid up wages in their attempts to attract adequate numbers of workers for the estates? An answer consistent with the evidence is that the market for labour was not free and that the small number of large estate owners and the government took advantage of their oligopsonistic position to administer wages at a level below that which would equilibrate the market. This interpretation, emphasizing non-market demand side factors in the determination of the wage level, is consistent with the fact that there was considerable competition among employers to provide better living conditions and food or smaller tasks. Constrained from using the wage mechanism, employers turned to other forms of competition for labour, including the 'crimping' or stealing of labour.

That estate employers followed what was recognized as a 'cheap labour' policy of keeping wages below the market-determined level is also consistent with the economics of the sisal industry. While they were price makers in the labour market, the estates were price takers in the commodity market for sisal (Guillebaud 1966), and any

[12] There are no accurate wage and price series for the colonial era. However, one estimate has placed average real wages for agricultural labour in 1951 at the same level that held in 1927. See Iliffe 1971.
[13] See Chapter VII below.

increase in wages not offset by an increase in labour productivity cut into profits. On the one hand, it could not have been clear at the time how big an increase in wages would be necessary to secure an adequate supply of labour. While it is probable that the aggregate supply curve was positively sloped, it is also likely that it was inelastic owing to the prevailing poor communications and transport, strong aversion to leaving the village community, and still undeveloped preference for manufactured as opposed to hand-made goods. It would have taken a considerable wage increase to elicit the necessary increase in supply.

On the other hand, if the increase in labour supply resulted from an increase in the participation rate and not from the stabilization of the labour force, then it was unlikely that the higher wages would yield a more productive labour force. The new labour force participants would have been completely inexperienced workers, raw recruits to the world of estate labour. Since 90 per cent of the estate jobs were unskilled, it is unlikely that productivity would have declined, but in these circumstances a rise in wages would not have led to an increase. At the time, to increase the capital intensity of production as a means of economizing on labour and raising its productivity did not appear a viable alternative, both because the appropriate technology had not been developed and because increases in capital intensity require complementary increases in the skill and stability of the labour force.[14] To have increased wages would have cut into profits; or at least the prospect of raising wages would have led to the expectation of lower profits because of the apparent low wage elasticity of supply and the increased risk in the relationship between wages and level of productivity.

3.4 *Coercion*

The fact that wages were not determined by the free interaction of supply and demand but were kept at an artificially low level by a handful of non-African employers, raised the issue of exploitation of labour among nationalists and trade unionists and contributed to the newly independent government's strong support for rapid increases in the level of wages. The issue of the unfair use of economic power by the minority colonial population, in whose hands it was

---

[14] See Chapters VII and VIII for a fuller discussion of wages, stability, and productivity.

concentrated, was exacerbated by the policy of coercing the rural population to take up wage employment in support of the low wage policy.

While a coercive action by definition is one that entails compulsion or restraint by force, there is considerable room for disagreement about what is legitimate inducement and what is illegitimate coercive behaviour. Labour extracted at gunpoint under the threat of physical harm or imprisonment is clearly coercive. Such action is more coercive than the imposition of a head tax that can only be paid in cash, and which thus forces the African into the monetary sector, without dictating how he earns his money. Between these two examples would be a money-only head tax combined with a prohibition on African cash crop production, which would leave wage employment as the only source of cash but would not dictate where or for whom the individual worked.

The issue of compensation enters here. It could be said that the higher the wages paid for the labour extracted, the less coercive the action, especially where the wage offered is below the supply price of labour. The greater the gap between the compensation and labour's supply price, the greater the coercion. In addition, there is the issue of the agent. The same action might be considered a legitimate form of inducement, if legislated and carried out by the government rather than private employers. Furthermore, an action taken with the aim of increasing labour force participation, or raising the level of involvement with the money economy, might not be considered coercive when executed by a government claiming to represent the welfare of the African majority rather than the white minority. The issue of the degree and legitimacy of coercion is important not only in assessing its role in the colonial wage labour market in Tanzania. As the government has taken increased initiative in directing the national development effort, the issue of what forms of policy implementation constitute illegitimate coercive behaviour has once again become central. This is certainly true of policies related to current labour market problems, namely the control of rural–urban migration and urban unemployment.

The use of forced labour, the most clear-cut form of coercion, was widespread in Tanzania during the German era. The Gotzen cotton scheme employed large numbers of men against their will at extremely low levels of compensation; its existence has been put forward as an explanation of the Maji Maji rebellion. Forced labour for short periods in payment of taxes, without any compensation, was often the means by which roads and other public works were built, though instances of estate owners using such methods during periods of extreme labour scarcity were not infrequent (Iliffe 1969). It was only in 1922, four years after the beginning of British rule, that the colonial governor issued the Involuntary Servitude Abolition Ordinance banning the use of forced labour (Listowel 1968). However, in 1928 over 21 000 Africans were conscripted for a total of 150 000 man-days to serve as porters in areas not yet reached by motorized transport. Labour was conscripted during the Second World War when an acute scarcity resulted from buoyant conditions in the commodity markets for sisal, pyrethrum, and rubber, the increasing size of the local contingent in the army, and increased opportunity costs in the form of rising cash crop prices. In 1943 nearly 23 000 people, or 8·5 per cent of the total wage labour force, were conscripted at the going wage of sh 12 a month for minimum periods of 9–11 months for work on non-military projects, predominantly agricultural estates (Orde-Browne 1946).

The war was an exceptional period; for the most part, forced labour, the crudest sort of coercion, was on the decline and virtually passed out of existence during the period of British colonial rule. Nor did the British in Tanzania resort to the form of direct force common elsewhere in British colonial eastern and southern Africa. Very few attempts were made to limit the level of African non-wage cash earning opportunities and incomes. There was little direct prohibition of Africans raising cash crops and Africans were not forcibly removed from the most fertile agricultural areas to 'native reserves'.

There were some restrictions on the type of crops Africans could grow in the first areas of German settlement. Government discouragement of small-holder production in sisal continued in areas contiguous with the sisal estates as a way of inducing local people to work on the estates (Lawrence in R.D.R.C. 1976). Peasant cash crop agriculture was generally encouraged as a means of increasing exports and revenues from export taxes and duties on the low-priced manufactured imports that constituted a large proportion of African cash expenditure (Iliffe 1969). In areas near the sisal estates, marketable food crops were encouraged in order to provide the large wage labour force with food.

There were other less crude forms of coercion, the most common being the imposition of taxes that could only be paid in cash. This of course raised the general level of participation in the cash economy and, in regional backwaters where cash crop production was uneconomic, put men under pressure to migrate and seek wage employment. The first taxation ordinance was imposed in 1897 in the areas under full German political control. The main object was 'educational', in that it was intended to oblige Africans to accept paid labour and accustom themselves to European administrative discipline (Iliffe 1969). Taxation as a labour-force-generating device soon lost effectiveness as other components of the demand for cash income increased in importance and the opportunities for local cash earnings increased. In much of Tanzania it had little effect after the First World War, and revenue became the aim of taxation. It remained, however, an important device in the process of widening the labour market in Tanzania in the 1920s and 1930s. The fact that labour demand was increasing, while wages were constant and non-wage cash earning opportunities and income were rising in labour source areas, meant that previously untapped labour reserves had to be found. Raw recruits remained a significant part of the labour market. For example, in 1928–9, as the administrative grip (and hence the grip of taxation) tightened in Kigoma region in the extreme western portion of the country, the Ha began to travel to the north-east in large numbers.

Coercion also entered into the method of recruiting labour, whereby private European contractors were paid on a commission basis to enlist labour in distant regions and bring it to the north-east. Before 1909, no contract was required and force and deception were widely employed (Tanganyika, Labour Department 1929). In 1929 the Labour Commissioner wrote that 'there remains a tendency to resort to bribery to headmen for assistance in recruiting; this highly objectionable method is, of course, liable to heavy punishment, but it is not easy to detect offences.' (Orde-Browne 1946.)

The government attempted to ameliorate the coercive conditions in the labour market, fearing that such abusive measures would lead to political instability. In addition to eliminating forced labour, it introduced licensing and regulation of recruiters. However, because of the politically influential position of the estate employers, the government was under considerable pressure not to put an end to the need for coercive measures by doing the one thing that would have solved the problem of the scarcity of labour. Though not subject to the same constraints as private employers, the government, which employed 20–30 per cent of the entire wage labour force, did not use its substantial weight in the labour market to push up wage rates. Though there tended to be a positive differential between government and private employment for the same type of work, and though the government argued that the 'cheap labour' concept was illusory and that wage increases would be more than offset by productivity increases, it chose not to force the private employers' hand by acting as an aggressive wage leader.

Rather, the government attempted to ameliorate the labour shortage by indirect measures, most of which were aimed at lowering the costs of moving for the potential migrant. Transport facilities were improved and nearly a dozen rest centres were opened along major migrant paths, reducing the discomforts of travel and the exploitation of travellers. The rest centres also functioned as dispensaries, reducing the considerable risks of disease and increasing the productivity of the labourers on arrival (Tanganyika, Labour Department 1928, 1929, 1930). As we have seen, these measures were inadequate and labour shortage on the estates continued until the 1950s.

4. SUMMARY

The colonial period in Tanzania witnessed the introduction and rapid expansion of a market for wage labour. As a consequence of the distribution of foreign investment, the locus of labour demand was rural. Wage employment and agricultural money-earning self-employment were concentrated in the same regions. The unequal regional distribution of opportunities for engagement in the rapidly growing money economy, in conjunction with lower returns to labour in wage employment than in cash cropping, gave rise to a migrant labour system. The supply of wage labour, mainly long-distance migrants responding to regional differences in economic opportunities, fell chronically short of meeting the demand of the estates and other employers for labour. The employers, who were in an oligopsonistic position in the labour market, paid wages below the supply price of labour because of the inelasticity of the labour supply; an apparent lack of opportunity for profitable factor substitution and the nature of their position in world commodity markets; and because they could use coercion to increase the supply of labour.

II

STRUCTURAL CHANGE AND URBAN MIGRATION

THE analysis of the relationship between the shift in destinations and changes in costs and returns in the last three decades offers the first of a number of perspectives on the micro-determinants of contemporary migrant behaviour. Here we go beyond documenting the changes in costs and returns to a consideration of the macro-economic determinants of those changes. The measurement of the magnitude of population flows is also essential to our subsequent assessment of the consequences of migration for the urban labour market.

1. RURAL–RURAL AND RURAL–URBAN MIGRATION, 1948–1971

The vast majority of rural residents who left their homes during the pre-war colonial period moved to other rural areas; in peak years more than 150 000 people moved from the southern and western regions into the rural north-eastern employment areas. In sharp contrast, less than one-third this number of migrants chose to go to one of Tanzania's fourteen registered townships in any given year. The net annual rural–urban population shift during the half-century prior to 1948 was very small, with urban population increasing not much faster than the natural growth rate.

Although inadequate for precise quantification of the north-eastern stream of migration since 1948, the data are sufficient to indicate the relative level and slope of the trend line. Throughout the late 1940s and 1950s large numbers of people continued to use the government rest centres along the routes to the established receiving areas. About 178 000 rural–rural migrants used the facilities in 1959, but in the following two years the annual number declined to 76 000. By 1965 the number had fallen below 10 000 and the centres were closed (Tanganyika, Labour Department 1966). For over half a century rural residents in large numbers had been making the journey to the north-east. Now they no longer chose to do so.

The data on rural–urban migrants available from the censuses of

1948, 1957, and 1967 and *NUMEIST* allow two alternative methods of measurement for the post-war rural–urban shift. The first method entails calculating the total urban population increase over a given period and, given the natural rate of growth of the urban population, determining the proportion of the total increase due to net urban migration.[1] Table 2.1 shows that in 1948 the total population of the six regional centres was 62 500. During the 23-year period to 1971 the population of these urban centres nearly quadrupled, implying an average annual growth rate of 6 per cent. This is more than twice the rate of growth of the rural population over the same period, and more than twice the rate of growth of the same towns over the preceding half-century. There were over 175 000 more people living in the six towns in 1971 than in 1940. If we assume that the natural population growth rate (births minus deaths per 1000 people) of the urban areas is no higher than the natural growth rate of the rural areas,[2] then the population increase of the six towns due to natural growth was only some 48 000, or a little more than one-fourth of the total increase. The other three-quarters, nearly 130 000, was made up of people who left their birthplace to come to the six towns. The post-war growth rates of the six towns have varied considerably. Arusha's population has multiplied sevenfold, 86 per cent of the increase being due to migration, while in Tabora natural population growth has contributed as much as migration to the growth of the town.

In Dar es Salaam, after a period of virtual stagnation, the population grew rapidly, quadrupling over the period 1948–71. The annual growth rate of nearly 7 per cent was almost three times that

[1] This approach establishes a lower limit to migration's contribution to urban population growth rate; to the extent that the urban-born migrate to the countryside, migration's contribution will be greater. The outflow of those born in the city is not insignificant: in 1971, 11 per cent of non-migrant urban population indicated that they intended to leave the city and take up permanent rural residence. Nearly 28 per cent of those planning to leave intended to retire or take over a relative's *shamba* (cultivated field; farm), and another 36 per cent expected to find better economic conditions in the countryside. Bienefeld and Sabot (*NUMEIST*) 1971.
[2] No detailed data on rural–urban natural growth rates exist for Tanzania. Studies in the Central African Republic, Dahomey, Guinea, Cameroon, Togo, and the Congo have found that the lower death-rates in urban areas resulting from superior economic conditions and health and sanitary facilities are outweighed by lower birth-rates caused by later marriage and changing attitudes. The end result is lower urban natural growth rates. The relatively high male/female ratios found in all towns during most of the period under consideration (see Chap. IV) make it probable that the situation in Tanzania is similar. See Conde 1971.

of the rural population and more than double what it had been during the first half of the century. Fully 78 per cent of the total population increase of 242 000 was due to migration. Dar es Salaam's population base in 1948 was greater than the combined total for the six towns. This implies that, with the same rate of natural increase in the capital and the regional centres and the same average length of stay of migrants, the absolute magnitude of net migration to Dar es Salaam would be greater than to the six secondary centres combined. Since Dar es Salaam has in fact been growing faster, this means that, as administrative capital, chief industrial centre, and primary port, it has reinforced its position at the top of Tanzania's urban hierarchy. The choice of Dar es Salaam by most urban migrants in the post-war period perpetuated the high primacy characteristic of the urban hierarchy in Tanzania since urbanization began in the late nineteenth century.[3] In 1948 the capital was 3·3 times the size of the next largest city; in 1971 the ratio was 4·2:1. The index of rank-size balance, with quotients greater than one indicating deviation from a normal distribution, increased over this period from 1·95 to 2·20.[4]

Aggregation of urban migration over the entire post-war period may hide important deviations from the trend and thus give a wrong impression of what is currently happening. The annual flow of migrants to the towns need not be a regular one. On the contrary, the small size of the urban sector in production terms and the fact that investments are lumpy and largely centrally controlled mean that the rate of employment growth may vary considerably for each town from year to year, in response to government decisions on the location of new infrastructure and industrial projects. If migration rates are sensitive to changes in employment opportunities, the stream to a given town will probably be uneven, at times well

[3] High primacy is defined as a deviation from a lognormal distribution of cities such that a stratum of small towns and cities is dominated by one very large city and there are a deficient number of cities of intermediate size. See Jefferson 1939 and Berry 1961. By itself this urban ordering is not a sign of underdevelopment. Rich countries such as Denmark and Japan as well as poor countries have primate cities. Nor is it associated with the relative population size, degree of urbanization, or geographic size of countries.

[4] $\text{Quotient} = \dfrac{\text{population of largest city}}{(\text{population of second- and third-largest cities} + 1/6 \text{ population of fourth-largest city})}$

See Herrick 1965.

TABLE 2.1
The contribution of migration to urban population growth

	Total population			Rates of growth (%)				Population increase	Population increase due to natural growth	Increase due to net migration
	1948	1967	1971	1948–67	1967–71	1948–71		1948–71	1948–71	1948–71
Mainland Total	7 480 400	11 877 000		2·5						
Dar es Salam	69 200	272 821[a] / 280 603[b]	311 185[a] / 327 333[b]	7·5	3·3 / 4·0	6·8		241 983	52 900	189 083
Tanga	20 600	60 900	73 900	5·9	5·0	5·7		53 300	15 750	37 550
Arusha	5 300	32 300	34 700	10·0	1·6	8·5		29 400	4 052	25 348
Mwanza	11 300	34 800	60 800	6·1	15·0	7·6		49 500	8 650	40 850
Tabora	12 800	21 000	25 600	2·7	5·1	3·1		12 800	9 780	3 020
Dodoma	9 400	23 600	24 700	4·9	1·1	4·1		15 300	7 190	8 110
Mbeya	3 100	12 400	19 100	7·5	11·4	8·2		16 000	2 371	13 629
Six towns	62 500	185 000	238 800	5·9	6·6	6·0		176 300	47 800	128 500

[a] Within administrative boundaries.
[b] Including contiguous enumeration areas in Mzizima district but excluding short-term non-citizen residents.
[c] Based on an assumption of a 2·5 per cent rate of natural increase in urban areas. Last 2 columns represent rough estimates only.
Source: NUMEIST 1971.

beneath the long-run trend line and at others well above it. Short-run variations in rural incomes might result in similar fluctuations in the rate of migration. Unfortunately, it is not possible to document year-to-year changes without a series of annual migration surveys, and no such series exists. It is possible, however, to separate the most recent four-year period from the entire post-war era, and it is important to do so because the Arusha Declaration of February 1967 made significant changes in government economic policy. Among the changes was a move towards more control of rural, urban, and regional distributions of investment.

The rate of growth of the seven towns appears to have declined somewhat during the period 1967–71, to 5·5 per cent a year, compared to 6·7 per cent for the previous nineteen years. This is due to the decrease in the rate of growth of Dar es Salaam, as the six-town growth rate increased. The increase in the rate of in-migration to the six towns was, however, by no means uniform: population growth rates were less than 2 per cent in Arusha and Dodoma, a marked decline from Arusha's earlier pattern of very rapid growth, while Mwanza grew at the very high rate of 15 per cent per year, nearly 2·5 times its rate for the previous nineteen years.

For Dar es Salaam two measures of the population for 1967 and 1971 are presented. The first considers only the population within the administrative boundaries of the city. On this definition the rate of growth is 3·3 per cent, less than half what it was for the early period. The second measure, recognizing that urban growth often results as much from geographic spread as increasing density, includes all the census enumeration areas in neighbouring Mzizima district contiguous with the administrative boundaries of Dar es Salaam proper.[5] The higher growth rate arrived at by the inclusion of the outlying areas is evidence of a high proportion of the increase in the city's population now living in Swahili *makuti*[6] housing settlements on the outskirts of town.

Even with its expanded boundaries, Dar es Salaam increased only 4 per cent a year, a significant decline from the period 1948–67. There is good reason to believe, however, that despite the extremely high growth rate recorded for Mwanza, the *NUMEIST* figures

---

[5] All discussion of the Dar es Salaam population in subsequent chapters refers to the functionally as opposed to the administratively defined population.

[6] *makuti:* leaves of the coconut plant, used as material for roofs and walls.

underestimate the 1971 population for each of the seven towns.[7] Compensating for the bias, we may conclude that the growth of the seven towns has continued at much the same high rate as in the pre-1967 period, implying an ever-increasing magnitude of migration. In 1948 the net movement to the seven towns was approximately 6500 people, increasing to approximately 18 000 in 1967 and 28 000 in 1971. The adjustment brings the Dar es Salaam growth rate more in line with past experience and raises the six-town rate well above the rate for the earlier period. There was no significant diminution in the pace of urban migration in Tanzania in the period 1967–71, though there was a slight shift in the direction of migration from Dar es Salaam to the six towns.

For a given population base, the higher the net rate of in-migration relative to the natural rate of population growth, the higher will be the proportion of migrants in the total urban population at the end of the period. The cross-section of Tanzania's 1971 urban population in Table 2.2 shows the significance of migration for population growth. Fully 83 per cent of the total adult population of both Dar es Salaam and the six towns was born elsewhere. An urban resident is classified as a migrant in this study only if he came to town after the age of 13.[8] Even with this narrower definition, approximately two-thirds of the seven-town adult population qualify as migrants. Although our main concern is with rural–urban migration, our definition of migrant covers people from both urban and rural areas. Nearly 90 per cent of Dar es Salaam and six-town migrants come from rural areas, and over 70 per cent of the urban population was born in a rural area. Rural–urban migration is clearly the predominant factor in the growth of Tanzania's towns.

---

[7] There are five sources of downward bias in the 1971 estimates. First, in Tanga, Arusha, Tabora, Dodoma, and Mbeya aerial photographs were used as the sampling frame. Some of the photos were six months to a year old. New structures built during the time between the photographs and the survey, and the people living in them, were omitted from the sample. In Dar es Salaam and Mwanza, aerial photographs were not used. Census enumeration areas were selected for the first sampling stage, and each area mapped just before second-stage sample selection (see Appendix B for a more detailed discussion of sample selection). Second, the survey focused on the adult urban population. Additional information on children was gathered for the sake of making population estimates, but there was greater likelihood of missing children in a house than adults to whom questions were addressed. An underestimate of children means an underestimate of urban population. Third, the survey excluded the institutional population in military and police barracks, hospitals, and prisons. Fourth, non-citizens on relatively short-term contracts were excluded, though this

TABLE 2.2
Proportion of migrants in the total urban population
(%)

	Born in town	13 or younger on arrival	14 or older on arrival	Total
Dar es Salaam	18	16	66	100
Tanga	21	18	61	100
Arusha	8	15	77	100
Mwanza	16	13	71	100
Tabora	28	18	54	100
Dodoma	19	19	62	100
Mbeya	14	13	73	100
Six towns	17	16	67	100
Total	17	16	67	100

Source: NUMEIST 1971.

The urban perspective on migration made necessary by the data leads to two important qualifications. Both the rate of urban population growth and the proportion of migrants in the total significantly underestimate the volume of migration, as they are measures of net rather than gross in-migration. There is no precise way to calculate the number of people who came to town and returned to rural areas, though there is evidence that the numbers are considerable. While the rate of migration has been very high when viewed from the perspective of the towns, the impact of out-migration on rural population levels has been minimal. Over the last quarter-century, rural–urban migration has led to urban population

factor is taken into consideration in the estimates for Dar es Salaam, where non-citizen personnel are concentrated. Fifth, in Dar es Salaam there appears to have been an under-representation of high growth enumeration areas. The enumeration areas outside the administrative boundaries included in the first stage of sampling were those immediately contiguous with the city's boundaries. There is evidence that the population of Dar es Salaam has moved beyond even this larger area. If the boundaries were expanded to include these additional growth areas, the rate of growth for 1967–71 would be still higher.
[8] People who came to town as children are not considered migrants because the aim of this study is to describe and analyse the behaviour of rural residents who came to town of their own volition. It is such people government policy will have to reach if it is to influence the rate of urban migration. (The position of women in this regard is discussed in Chaper IV.) In terms of access to education and degree of familiarity with the urban setting and with the labour market, people who come as young children may be just as urbanized as those born in town.

growth rates two and three times the rural rates, doubling the proportion of Tanzania's population in urban areas; but this shift of population from the countryside to the towns has not equalled the natural increase of the rural population. Far from it: despite net out-migration, the population of rural mainland Tanzania increased by nearly 4 000 000 during the period 1948–67. After nearly a quarter of a century of rapid growth, the urban population in 1967 still constituted only 6 per cent of the total population. The pace of urbanization is considerably slower than the rate of urban growth and Tanzania remains one of the least urban countries in the world.

2. INCOME FROM AGRICULTURAL SELF-EMPLOYMENT

What has happened to the income of the rural agricultural self-employed in the post-war era? Aggregate trends in rural income data cannot provide an explanation for both the decrease in rural–rural migration and the increase in rural–urban migration. While the explanation for these divergent trends in the rate of migration must be sought in the differential returns to migration that we examine in succeeding sections, information on rural incomes is necessary to specify the trends in the differences in income of the rural self-employed and wage earners, whether in rural or urban areas. The data problems in constructing a rural income series are daunting. The only relevant data available prior to 1960 are price and quantity figures for agricultural exports. There is very little information on non-export cash crop production and virtually nothing on production for family consumption. Time series consumption data for the rural areas are non-existent. National income data, including estimates of non-market and cash incomes in the agricultural sector, are available for the period after 1955, though subject to serious qualification. Much of what is said about the post-war trend in per capita income has to be inferred from trade data, national income data, and isolated studies of yields per acre per man.

2.1 *Trends in non-labour inputs and agricultural exports*

A number of available indicators reveal rapid changes in Tanzanian agriculture during the post-1945 period. Trends in such capital inputs as tractors, storage dams, irrigation works, and wells have been sharply upward. Purchased inputs of seeds, insecticides, and fertilizers have also been growing rapidly. From 1945 to 1960 the tonnage of fertilizer consumed increased twenty-five-fold (Fuggles-Couchman 1964). Infrastructural investment in the rural sectors, in main roads and feeder roads, storage and marketing facilities, has been expanding at a high rate. The figures on exports are evidence of significant change in the agricultural sector. Table 2.3 documents the rate of expansion of Tanzania's five most important current export crops. The value of exports of cotton, coffee, cashew-nuts, and tea grew at an extremely high rate.

TABLE 2.3
Value index of exports from Tanzania for the five leading crops, 1945–1970
Value index (1945 = 100)

	1945	1950	1955	1960	1965	1970
Sisal	100	385	324	503	465	291
Cotton, lint	100	191	735	1173	1623	1643
Coffee	100	387	770	817	958	1742
Cashew-nuts		100	425	1042	2021	2822
Tea	100	100	1049	2256	2960	4135

Sources: Fuggles-Couchman 1964, East African Customs and Excise Department, various years.

Since we are concerned with economic opportunities open to potential migrants, it is important to know whether the expansion was achieved by African peasant farmers, European settlers on large plantations, large-scale African landlords, or state farmers. The amount of land alienated did not increase after 1960. Nearly 70 per cent of the 1945–60 increase from 1 844 000 to 2 409 000 acres was held by the Overseas Food Corporation and its successor the Tanganyika Agricultural Corporation, organizers of the ill-starred ground-nut scheme. Less than 30 per cent of their holdings were in production in 1960. With the exception of sisal and, in part, tea, the expansion in output of export crops did not come from the estates.

There are few wage employees in non-estate agriculture outside the high-output regions of Arusha, Kilimanjaro, West Lake, Mwanza, and Iringa, where African farmers control plots in excess of 50 acres and employ considerable numbers of wage labourers. In 1967 the approximately 13 000 employers of wage labour constituted less than 0·3 per cent of the people economically active in agriculture (Tanzania. Bureau of Statistics 1969–71), though a downward bias in the enumeration of employers is likely. However, the census recorded only 16 000 wage employees in African agriculture. The low ratio of employees to total agricultural labour force and to employers indicates that most non-estate agricultural production and most of the recent increase in non-estate exports were produced by family agriculture.

2.2 *Trends in agricultural incomes*

This picture of dynamic small-holder agriculture must be severely qualified. The growth of average income in agricultural self-employment was slower than that of income from peasant export crops. Export cash crops accounted for less than a third of total agricultural income in 1970 (Tanzania, Bureau of Statistics 1972). Changes in cash crop production for the domestic market and the production of subsistence crops thus had important consequences for the over-all structure of economic opportunities in agricultural self-employment that potential urban migrants faced. Although the data are, unfortunately, extremely weak, it is clear that the rate of growth of production for domestic use was considerably lower than that for export.[9] A smaller share of total peasant agricultural income was derived from exports in 1945 than in 1970. In fact, peasant agricultural exports were extremely small in absolute terms at that time. In 1951 only £51 000 worth of tea, £752 000 worth of cotton, and £896 000 worth of coffee was exported by an agricultural peasantry numbering over 2 000 000 people. The small base accounts in part for the high growth rates. Immediately after the war the number of producers engaged in exporting was a small proportion of the agricultural self-employed. This meant that a relatively small increase in the participation rate of peasants in this market would result in large jumps in production, even if the output per head of the new export producers was low. The post-war boom in prices for coffee and cotton provided the incentive necessary for farmers to cultivate an additional half-acre or acre for the export market. Table

---

[9] There are, of course, numerous problems in estimating output that does not reach the market. The Ministry of Agriculture estimates of the production for self-consumption of maize, rice, sorghum, beans, cassava, sweet potatoes, coconuts, and fruits and vegetables, upon which the National Accounts figures for non-cash crop income were based, were considered to be gross underestimates of actual output. While some adjustment was made in later years, using Household Budget Survey data, the underestimate for earlier years contributed to an upward bias in the over-all growth rate of the agricultural sector. See Tanzania, Bureau of Statistics 1971b.

2.4 illustrates the expansion of the co-operative movement, which has emerged as the marketing agent of the small-holder export producers; this is one indication of the extent to which participation in this market has increased.[10]

TABLE 2.4
Growth of the co-operative movement in Tanzania 1949–1960

	Registered societies	Total membership
1949	79	60 445
1952	474	125 483
1957	546	304 786
1960	691	326 211

Source: Fuggles-Couchman 1964.

There does not appear to have been a similar incentive to expand output for family consumption or for the domestic market. Total wage employment was virtually stagnant over this period, limiting the growth of market demand for food, while demand for subsistence output grew only as fast as the rural population. The World Bank Mission in 1960 estimated the growth of agricultural output for the period 1949–58 at somewhat more than 4 per cent a year or approximately 1·5–2 per cent per capita (I.B.R.D. 1961). Fuggles-Couchman (1964), in his more comprehensive study of agriculture over the period 1945–60, did not hazard an estimate of over-all growth. Noting that the high growth rates for capital and purchased inputs entailed no change in the technology employed by the vast majority of African farmers—once again, because of the small base existing in 1945—he appeared less sanguine about the trend in total output. Our estimate of the trend in agricultural income per capita in the rural sector, 1955–70, derived from national income data and presented in Table 2.5, confirms the scepticism of Fuggles-Couchman (1964). The index shows that incomes in the rural sector have virtually stagnated throughout this period.

A more detailed examination of the trend in small-holder income for the period 1960–5 yields some insight into the reasons for poor

---

[10] The fact that co-operatives have increased their share of the marketing of peasant export crops means that the expansion of membership somewhat overestimates the growth in numbers of export producers.

TABLE 2.5
*Index of agricultural per capita real incomes in the
rural sector 1955–1970*
1955 = 100

Year	Index
1955	100
1960	101
1962	94
1964	102
1966	110
1968	109
1970	105

Sources: Jensen and Mkama, 1968; Tanganyika. Central Statistical Bureau, 1964;
Tanzania, *National Accounts of Tanzania*, various years; Tanzania. Central
Statistics Bureau, 1968; and Tanzania. Bureau of Statistics, 1971a, 1972.

performance in the rural areas. Table 2.6 summarizes the information. The 28 per cent increases in cash crop production is consistent
with the data in Table 2.3, the lower rate of growth here being due
to the aggregation of exports with slower-growing domestic cash
crop production, the calculation of growth rates by averaging non-
cash crop with cash crop producers, and the deflation of output
figures by the growth of the agricultural labour force and the rise in
consumer prices. As expected, cash crop output per worker grew

TABLE 2.6
Indices of small-holder incomes 1960–1965

Index	1960–2	1963	1964	1965
Real subsistence output per worker	100	102	105	95
Real cash output per worker (small holder)	100	112	132	128
Real cash output per worker (small holder) after tax	100	107	120.	110
Real total income per worker (small holder)	100	105	114	108
Real total income per worker (small holder) after tax	100	104	110	110

Source: Helleiner 1968.

faster than output for family consumption. Aggregating market and non-market output reveals that on small holdings total real income per worker increased by some 8 per cent from 1960–2 to 1965, at approximately the same annual rate as estimated for the period 1945-60. This, however, is before taxes on agricultural incomes.

Taxes can be expected to decrease the growth rate of agricultural income if the rate of taxation increases over time. In a country where cash income is very low, administrative personnel scarce, modern accounting practices rarely used, and much of the population engaged in unrecorded subsistence economic activity, it is tempting for the government to maximize revenue collections in the few sectors where such collections are feasible (Taylor 1970, Helleiner 1964). Income from cash crop agricultural production and from export crops in particular, which together comprise approximately 50 per cent of national income, is institutionally centralized in marketing boards. In Tanzania since Independence, taxes in the form of export duties, produce cesses, and Marketing Board surpluses have grown as a proportion of total agricultural output, imposing increasingly large reductions on the prices that the farmer received for his output. Export taxes have risen as a proportion of the total value of exports (Tanzania, Bureau of Statistics 1971b, 1972). Data on other taxes are less readily available, but in the *Ross Report* it was noted that:

The transfer of marketing to the co-operatives has led, initially, to a higher cost of handling produce; co-operatives and local authorities are increasingly imposing levies and cesses on agricultural commodities; Marketing Boards are setting their buying prices for certain commodities at levels which enable them to accumulate cash surpluses. All these factors are widening the margin between the market price of the product and the price received by the grower.

Table 2.6 indicates that taxation reduced the growth of cash output per worker over the period 1960–5 from 28 per cent to 10 per cent, while completely negating the real total income growth per worker of 8 per cent.

(Taxes on agricultural production reduce the level of income that small holders receive directly from the sale of output and may have negative consequences for expansion. They need not, however, reduce over-all rural per capita income unless government expenditure for the benefit of the rural areas is less than government revenue generated there. It is extremely difficult to calculate such figures.[11] However, one estimate for 1969–70 indicates that while only 35 per cent of monetary G.D.P. was produced in urban areas and a still smaller proportion of government revenues derived from urban production (Tanzania 1972), those areas received 24 per cent of the development budget directly. An additional 20 per cent of the total had its primary impact in the towns.

The result is a rural to urban income transfer or capital flow, which not only lowers rural incomes in a given period but constrains rural investment and, in the longer run, the growth of agricultural output. The government's urban bias, which was considerably stronger before 1967, is one reason why the rural self-employed did not share directly in the benefits of the economic growth of the Tanzanian economy in the late 1950s and 1960s.

TABLE 2.7
External trade indices[a]
(1960 = 100)

Index	1962	1963	1964	1965	1966	1967
Volume:						
Exports:	96	103	113	111	143	145
Imports	117	108	108	107	142	140
Value:						
Exports:	93	116	128	114	144	142
Imports	105	107	116	132	170	172
Price:						
Exports	98	112	113	103	99	95
Imports	91	100	109	114	113	117
Terms of trade[b]	108	112	104	90	88	82

[a] Mainland only.
[b] Ratio of export price to import price.
Source: Van Arkadie, in Faber and Seers 1972.

[11] On the expenditure side, there is no precise way to separate urban and rural benefit when both sectors make use of a facility such as a road or a hospital. On the revenue side, any calculation of the rural contribution to revenue from import duties, which would depend directly on the rural–urban distribution of consumption of imports and indirectly on the effects of tariffs on the rural–urban terms of trade, is likely to be imprecise.

The deterioration of the terms of trade facing the rural self-employed in the 1960s appears to have been as important as the government's urban bias in constraining rural income growth. Though it is difficult to calculate because of the unreliability of the import price index, the decrease of the real import purchasing power of Tanzania's exports, of which Table 2.7 presents estimates, has had a definite negative effect on rural income growth. Equally important is the change in rural–urban terms of trade. Internal terms will reflect external ones because the middlemen who distribute the imports are in the towns, but the real purchasing power of domestic cash crop production for locally produced manufacturers should also be considered. From 1960 to 1965 the producer of cash crops for the domestic market apparently got no more than before for the products he sold to the towns, but had to pay more for the products and services he bought from them. Evidence for this deterioration in the internal terms of trade is the sharp rise in urban wages not accompanied by a decline in pre-tax profits. From 1960 to 1963 the profits of enterprises employing wage labour seem to have increased by nearly sh 4 million. Higher wage costs per man were compensated for by reducing the labour force, reorganizing production to increase productivity, or replacing labour with machinery. The first two responses were common among firms facing a highly elastic demand curve in export markets. Domestic producers operating behind high tariff walls, on the other hand, were in a virtually monopolistic position and appear to have taken advantage of their situation by passing on wage increases to consumers through higher prices.[12] The result was a further weakening of the farmer's terms of trade with the town. The effect on a rural resident of increasing taxation and worsening terms of trade is a lower opportunity cost of migration and an increased incentive to move and take up wage employment, either on an estate or in town.

Taxation, tariffs, and the allocation of investment funds are not the only ways in which government policy influences rural incomes. The rate of return on government agricultural investments must also be considered. There has been considerable misallocation of the resources the government was willing to invest. Two prominent

---

[12] Such price increases will have been larger, the greater the wage costs as a proportion of total cost and the lower the price elasticity of demand for the product concerned. Knight 1968.

examples, one from the last decade of the colonial regime and the other from the first years of independence, are the Groundnut Scheme and the Village Settlement Scheme. Both were examples of the 'transformation' approach to agricultural development, in which the local organization of production, in terms of land tenure, technology, crops, and 'attitudes' of producers, was to be radically changed in the context of large-scale undertakings. The ground-nut project, which was to affect over 2 000 000 acres, cost a total of £50 000 000. Nearly £9 000 000 was scheduled to be spent on the village development schemes during the first five-year plan.[13] Both projects suffered from excessive expenditure on infrastructure and both demonstrated that the capital-intensive technology of modern farming in the northern hemisphere does not automatically yield high returns in tropical conditions. Tractors employed on these schemes were little used and soon ruined by corrosion and poor maintenance; their productivity was often low because they were unsuitable for local soils and conditions. The schemes eventually had to be written off, when it became clear that they could only continue with large-scale, long-term government subsidy (Eicher *et al.* 1970). Similar errors in the allocation of development funds, leading to inefficient use of the scarce resources available in the rural sector, have been repeated on a smaller scale on numerous other occasions. Poor planning and project evaluation are among the factors keeping the growth rate of agricultural income below its maximum potential. Underestimation of the rationality and efficiency of existing peasant agricultural institutions and techniques was a weakness of the transformation approach. On the other hand, the necessary emphasis by low income producers on long-term security rather than short-term income maximization slowed the pace of adoption of worthwhile innovations in irrigation, fertilization, new crops, and new seed varieties (Lipton 1968).

Population growth is a further constraint on agricultural development. The rural population of Tanzania has increased by over 4 000 000 since 1948, at an average annual rate of 2·5–3 per cent. Although total land resources are plentiful, population densities on lands with good rainfall and soil conditions have increased sharply. As the population grows in regions such as Kilimanjaro people are being forced to accept plots of land smaller than those held by their

---

[13] Van Arkadie in Faber and Seers 1972.

fathers or to move on to less productive land. Ricardian diminishing returns have thus contributed to the low rate of increase of agricultural income during the post-war period.

3. WAGE TRENDS

The wage series presented in Table 2.8 is less than ideal. Though disaggregated in such a way that we can compare the trend in estate employment with that in urban wage employment, the data do not reveal the wage differences among workers of various levels of education and lengths of time in employment. The rural–urban income differential and rates of migration are compared in disaggregated form in succeeding chapters; for the moment, as we are analysing only the over-all rate of migration to the estates and urban areas, disaggregation of income differentials beyond the

TABLE 2.8

Trends in agricultural and non-agricultural real wages 1955–1970
(1958 prices)

Year	Non-agricultural real wages sh per month	Index	Agricultural real wages sh per month	Index
1955	86	91		
1956	97	102		
1957	95	100		
1958	95	*100*	36	*100*
1959	110	116	42	117
1960	114	120	56	156
1961	126	133	67	186
1962	154	162	80	222
1963	205	216	115	319
1964	227	239	120	333
1965	238	251	127	353
1966	248	261	133	369
1967	258	272	136	378
1968	262	276	129	358
1969	307	323	132	367
1970	290	305	142	394

Sources: Tanzania, Central Statistical Bureau various years;
Tanganyika, Labour Department various years; and
Tanzania various years.

receiving area dichotomy will be ignored.[14] Increases in wages have
been rapid in both non-agricultural and agricultural sectors. Non-
agricultural wages, adjusted for the rise in the consumer price index,
more than trebled in the twelve-year period after 1958. Wages in
agriculture rose at an even faster annual rate. Taking 1958 as base
year, the index of real wages stood at 394 in 1970. From 1958 to 1970
agricultural and non-agricultural wages increased at an average
annual rate of 12·1 per cent and 9·7 per cent, respectively, which is
extremely high by international standards.

Our primary concern is with the consequence of these rises for
rural–urban income differentials; what led to these rises will be
analysed in Chapter VIII. If, as we have established, non-wage rural
incomes stagnated during this period, then the income differential
between agricultural self-employment and employment for wages
must have increased at the same dramatic rate as the increase in
wages. Thus in 1970 the difference between non-agricultural wage
employment and agricultural self-employment was approximately
three times what it had been in 1958, while within agriculture the
difference between self-employment and wage employment was
approximately four times its earlier level. If we assume a rough
parity between income from agricultural wage employment and self-
employment in 1960, based on the fact that it was about this time
that labour scarcity ceased to be a problem to estate employers
(Tanganyika, Labour Dept. 1962), the implication is that in 1970
agricultural wages were approximately two and a half times income
from self-employment, and non-agricultural wages were five times
average agricultural self-employed income.

3.1 *The measurement of income differentials. Some qualifications.*

The remittance of a part of the migrant's wage income to his family
at home raises source area income and, more significantly, lowers
receiving area income, yielding an income differential considerably
less than that indicated by our measure. (The urban–rural remittances
of migrants will be examined in Chapter VII, when we assess the

[14] In our discussion of the rural–urban income differential we have omitted
consideration of the component of urban incomes generated by the self-employed.
The distribution of income of the urban self-employed is considered in Chapter VI
where we determine the extent to which self-employed incomes attract migrants to
the town and the extent to which they are a manifestation of the urban employment
problem.

strength of the relationship of the migrant to his home area.)
Although the amount of money sent home by migrants must qualify
our view of wage earners as leading a highly privileged existence, it
does not imply that we have overestimated the financial inducement
for rural residents to migrate. Urban–rural remittances suggest that
family income rather than individual income is being maximized.
As long as the wage earned in urban employment is higher than the
average product per family worker (or the marginal product,
whichever is higher) on the family farm, the incentive to migrate
remains.[15]

Different rates of inflation could lead to an overestimation of the
degree to which the rural–urban earnings gap has widened. There is
no rural price index for Tanzania and both the small-holder income
series for 1960–5 and the urban wage series are discounted by the
price index constructed for urban wage earners. If the rate of
inflation was higher in urban than in rural areas the result would be
an underestimate of the growth rate of rural income and an
overestimate of the income differential. The rate of increase in prices
of non-agricultural goods would be just as high in rural as in urban
areas, if not higher, because the few price controls in operation
would be more effectively enforced in large centralized markets than
in small dispersed ones. Though urban prices are likely to have risen
faster than rural prices, the difference is unlikely to have had more
than a marginal effect on the rural–urban income differential.

A further source of distortion is the fact that the differential does
not reflect the direct (transport and moving) costs or the indirect or
psychic costs of migration. If these costs are increasing, at least part
of the rise in wages goes to maintaining the difference in earned
incomes rather than to raising it. Here again the evidence is
somewhat thin. The rise in the fares of buses and trains is
counterbalanced by the post-war extension of services which has
reduced the time and energy involved in moving from place to place.
As Table 2.9 indicates, 81 per cent of all migrants in the seven towns
came by bus or train and only 3 per cent walked. In any case, the
direct money cost of the journey to town is a small proportion of

[15] Marginal product would, of course, equal average product under conditions of
constant returns to labour. If land is scarce and there is no change in technology, the
addition of another farm worker may only result in work-sharing, in which case
marginal product would be less than average product and the latter would constitute
the relevant opportunity cost of migration.

urban income and a one-time expenditure only, and is thus unlikely to reduce significantly the lifetime earnings differential between rural and urban residents. As Table 2.9 shows, nearly half of all migrants paid sh 10 or less for transport to town and only 6 per cent paid more than sh 60.[16] We can conclude that the widening of the rural–urban differential is not compensating for an increase in the cost of transport to town.

TABLE 2.9

Distribution of urban migrant population by means of travel and cost of journey to town

Means of travel	%	Cost of journey (sh)	%
Bus	60	Less than 10	47
Car or lorry	4	10–30	28
On foot	3	30–60	18
Ship	9	Over 60	6
Train	21	Total	100
Other	2		
Total	100		

Source: NUMEIST 1971

There are no direct measures of the non-economic costs and rewards of migration, important as these may be. The greater their preference for leisure, traditional goods, economic independence, and familiar social life, the less likely rural residents will be to move to an urban area in response to a given income differential. The supply curve of labour may, however, have become more wage elastic over time. The rapid increase in formal education for the rural population has spread new sets of values as well as new ideas; radios and newspapers which have proliferated over the past twenty years constantly emphasize the positive aspects of change and economic improvement. Belief in the positive aspects of change and the unity of the nation, in contrast to allegiance to the tribe, has clearly been enhanced by political independence and successful national self-government. Increasing numbers of people from the rural residents' own groups have changed their way of life and

---

[16] The low level of expenditure on the rural–urban journey of migrants currently living in town may reflect the fact that most migrants do not travel long distances. The relationship between rate of migration and distance, and the effect of transport costs as a deterrent to migration, are examined in Chapter III.

economic situation by raising cash crops or entering wage employment. The demonstration effect among rural residents has been reinforced by the greater variety and quantity of manufactured goods in rural shops. Traditional tribal ties have also been broken down by the diminished political status of tribal leaders and the change in patterns of land tenure. In some areas land scarcity has caused difficulty. Rural dwellers now appear to place a higher value on market products, and seem more willing to change their lives in order to acquire cash with which to buy them. It is unlikely, in the light of these changes, that the psychic costs of migration have increased sufficiently to outweigh the increased difference between wage and non-wage income.

3.2 Migration rates and income differentials

The widening difference between income from agricultural self-employment and urban wage employment income is consistent with a view of the increase in urban migration as determined primarily by economic factors. Relatively constant opportunity costs together with sharply rising returns to employment have increased the benefit of moving to town. The evidence of a widening income differential between self-employment and wage employment within the agricultural sector, however, appears inconsistent with the sharp decrease in the rate of migration to the estates in the north-east of the country. We would expect a wider differential to be associated with a higher rate of migration. Either another counteracting economic factor is at work or non-economic factors are dominant.

4. THE GROWTH OF WAGE EMPLOYMENT OPPORTUNITIES

The period from 1890 to 1948 witnessed the introduction and rapid expansion of wage labour in Tanzania. Over 395 000 people were in wage employment by the end of the period; yet over 80 per cent of the male labour force continued to derive their income from non-wage earning agricultural activity. In an economy with such a small proportion of the labour force in wage employment, if wage-earning opportunities grow only at the same rate as the labour force, the number of people who have to establish themselves in agricultural self-employment continues to increase. Even if we assume that wage employment opportunities are growing faster than the labour force (at 3 per cent and 2 per cent per year, respectively), an economy with

80 per cent of its labour force in agricultural self-employment will still have almost 70 per cent of its workers in agricultural self-employment after fifty years of growth, and its farm population still growing in absolute terms (Berg in O.E.C.D. 1971). Given the increasing scarcity of highly productive land, there is likely to be a considerable strain on the capacity of the rural sector to absorb labour even at constant per capita levels of income.

As Table 2.10 indicates, wage employment growth in Tanzania has not even kept pace with the expansion of the labour force. Indeed, one of the most striking features of the Tanzanian labour market over the past twenty-five years has been the absolute decline in the total number of wage employment opportunities; as a result the size and burden of the agricultural self-employment sector has increased in relative as well as in absolute terms. The proportion of the labour force in wage employment declined from 19 per cent in 1948 to 11 per cent in 1967.

TABLE 2.10
The proportion of the male labour force in wage employment 1948–1967

Year	Male labour force[a]	Total wage employment	Percentage of labour force in wage employment
1948	2 090 880	395 500	19
1957	2 452 680	430 470	17
1967	3 291 218	346 741	11

[a] Adult males.
Sources: Tanganyika Labour Department 1949–68; Tanzania Central Statistical Bureau 1968, various years; Tanzania Bureau of Statistics 1969–71.

We have noted that population growth has been a constraint on the growth of rural incomes. But even with a constant self-employment–wage-employment income differential and a constant rate of out-migration from rural self-employment, the growth of the non-wage sector would require an increasing number of rural residents to leave home and seek employment. Thus the outward shift of the supply curve of labour resulting from population growth and the inward shift of the demand curve for wage labour have certainly contributed to the shift in the aggregate balance from scarcity to surplus.

4.1 *Structural change and (sectoral) employment trends*

Table 2.11 shows that the decline in agricultural wage employment from its 1953 peak has proceeded at nearly twice the rate of the decline in over-all wage employment. In 1966 total employment on agricultural estates was only 54 per cent of what it had been thirteen years earlier.[17] Unlike the aggregate trend, which has shown some signs of recovery in recent years, agricultural wage employment has continued to decline, reaching a low point in 1970 of 46 per cent of its 1953 level.

While tea, coffee, and food-crop estates all reduced their number of wage jobs, the greatest decrease came in the sisal industry which had employed over 50 per cent of all agricultural wage labour throughout the colonial period. In 1953 there were approximately 152 000 wage earners in sisal; by 1959 this number had fallen to 138 000; and over the next three years there was a further contraction of over 20 000 jobs. The decrease in agricultural wage employment in Tanzania since 1945 has been offset somewhat by the growth of non-agricultural wage employment. The 70 per cent increase in non-agricultural employment during the post-1945 period stands in sharp contrast to the 43 per cent decline in agricultural wage employment. Employment in the transport, public utilities, construction, and service sectors has expanded, but most noteworthy from the perspective of the changing structure of the labour market has been the growth of employment in manufacturing and in government.

The development of manufacturing industry was constrained during most of the colonial period by the fact that the limited foreign investment in non-primary production in East Africa was concentrated in Kenya. It has been argued that the adoption of a common external tariff and the elimination of trade barriers among the East African partner states served to reinforce Tanzania's disadvantage.[18] The bias in foreign investment toward external orientation of the monetary sectors and primary commodity production was, however, a more fundamental cause of Tanzania's low level of industrialization. The channelling of investment into estate agriculture rather than manufacturing was rationalized by reference to the small size of the territory's market for manufacturers and to a labour force held

---

[17] As we noted earlier, virtually all agricultural wage employment was estate employment, though the small proportion of the agricultural wage labour force engaged by African small holders tended to be undernumerated.

[18] See Ghai 1964. For a persuasive refutation, see Hazelwood 1966.

TABLE 2.11
Sectoral employment growth 1952–70

Year	Total wage employment		Agricultural wage employment		Non-agricultural wage employment		Non-agricultural/ Agricultural Ratio
	Number	Index	Number	Index	Number	Index	
1952	443 597	100	235 106	100	208 491	100	47
1953	448 271	101·05	246 549	104·87	201 722	96·75	45
1954	439 094	98·98	237 111	100·85	201 983	96·88	46
1955	413 100	93·13	223 074	94·88	190 026	91·14	46
1956	424 209	95·63	229 073	97·43	195 136	93·59	46
1957	430 470	97·04	236 758	100·70	193 712	92·91	45
1958	430 547	97·06	236 801	100·72	193 746	92·93	45
1959	428 268	96·54	235 547	100·19	192 721	92·44	45
1960	404 106	91·10	222 258	94·54	181 848	87·22	45
1961	401 846	90·59	204 941	87·17	196 905	94·44	49
1962	397 028	89·50	202 484	86·12	194 544	93·31	49
1963	340 344	76·72	166 769	70·93	173 575	83·25	51
1964	351 257	79·18	165 091	70·22	186 166	89·29	53
1965	333 755	75·24	140 177	59·62	193 578	92·85	58
1966	336 497	75·86	127 869	54·39	108 628	100·07	62
1967	346 741	78·17	124 827	53·09	221 914	106·44	64
1968	351 711	79·29	109 030	46·37	242 681	116·40	69
1969	367 926	82·94	114 057	48·51	253 869	121·76	69
1970	375 635	84·68	108 934	46·33	266 701	127·92	71

Source: Tanzania, Central Statistical Bureau, various years.

unsuitable for disciplined factory employment because of the prevalence of circular migration. In the post-Independence period foreign investors have had a change of view and the number of manufacturing establishments in Tanzania has expanded rapidly.

That a low level of effective demand did not permit the establishment of plants of economically efficient size at an earlier time is contradicted by the case of the textile industry. Pre-1940 levels of imports exceeded the operating capacity of the first plant established in 1961, and investment in four more textile plants between 1961 and 1965 appeared economically justifiable (Rweyemamu 1971). Explanation of low levels of manufacturing investment based on 'the inherent unsuitability' of the African labourer for work in environments requiring a high level of industrial discipline are also inadequate. Labour productivity in non-agricultural enterprises has risen dramatically in Tanzania in recent years, and the rise can only partly be explained by increases in the capital intensity of production. The high level of instability of both the sisal and the urban labour force during the colonial period was a rational response to working conditions, rather than a specifically African behaviour pattern.[19] Changes in working conditions, independent of increased mechanization, have resulted in increases in stability and productivity.

If growth in market size and changes in the nature of African labourers do not explain the increase in manufacturing investment, what does? Four main factors seem to be responsible: much of the import substitution has been initiated by former suppliers such as Phillips Industries who, afraid of losing their export market in the face of increasing competition, chose to build subsidiary plants whose markets would be protected by tariff barriers. Other European firms with no previous stake in the Tanzanian market, such as TIPER petroleum, used direct investment as a means of gaining a market foothold (Rweyemamu 1971). Both these developments were reinforced by the policy of the newly independent government which encouraged foreign investment in manufacturing as a means of restructuring the economy[20] and decreasing dependence on primary product exports. Tax incentives, guarantees against nationalization, and the establishment of industrial estates were among the policies

[19] See Chapter VII.
[20] Similar factors appear dominant in the post-war industrialization of Nigeria. See Kilby 1969.

adopted. A fourth factor, particularly important for processing industries that depend on export markets, has been the lowering of trade barriers by potential importers.[21]

4.2 Structural change and rural–urban employment trends

Since the hope of finding work is an important motive for migration among rural residents, the location of productive enterprises employing labour will be an important element in determining the destination the migrant selects, and hence the migration pattern as a whole. A key factor in the pattern of migration during the colonial period was the concentration of employment opportunities in the rural north-east. Has there been significant relocation of the demand for wage labour in the post-war period, and, if so, what influence has this had on the direction of migration?

If we consider the agricultural sector alone, the decline in agricultural wage employment has entailed a decline in total rural employment. Whether there has been a rural–urban shift in wage employment opportunities thus depends on the distribution of the increase in non-agricultural employment. The evidence suggests that modern non-agricultural production activities have been predominantly urban based.

It is not difficult to understand why firms producing manufactured goods would choose to build in urban areas, and in the capital city in particular. A profit-maximizing firm in a competitive market will seek to locate in the area that minimizes total costs. Total costs can be divided into costs of production and transport costs. If we assume that costs of production are the same at all the alternative sites being considered, then the location decision becomes a function of transport costs alone. For most manufacturing firms in Tanzania, Dar es Salaam is the minimum cost location both in regard to shipping inputs from their source to the factory site and in regard to distributing output among consumers. In 1966 over 75 per cent of manufacturing value added and employment was concentrated in consumer goods industries, as compared to 45 per cent in Kenya (Rweyemamu 1971). There was no capital goods production; intermediate production thus accounted for the remaining 23 per

---

[21] In the 1930s the Secretary of State for the Colonies, noting unfair competition from low-paid African labour, imposed a 100 per cent duty on binder twine imported from Tanzania, forcing the closure of a factory established some years earlier. Rweyemamu 1971.

cent. This type of manufacturing structure entails a high import content and helps to explain why Dar es Salaam as the primary port of entry for Tanzania's imports has a significant cost advantage over other locations. It would appear that, since the additional mileage required to move goods from Dar es Salaam to a centre farther inland would be such a small proportion of total mileage for goods coming from Europe or China or Japan, the additional transport cost would be minimal. However, the structure of transport costs is such that monetary costs and the cost of delays and trans-shipment generally involve a more than proportional increase (Alonso in Alonso and Friedman 1964). Only in those cases in which local materials are a significant proportion of purchased current inputs would sites other than Dar es Salaam have an advantage; it is not surprising to find coffee-processing plants located in Moshi and Bukoba, the urban centres of the two regions with the highest level of coffee production.[22] Producers of intermediate goods with a high import content, such as Aluminium Africa, have a similar transport cost incentive on the input side to locate in Dar es Salaam. As a result, consumer-good producers that rely on a high proportion of locally produced intermediate good inputs often find Dar es Salaam an advantageous site.

As regards distribution, Dar es Salaam's advantage over other urban concentrations or rural areas derives from the size of the market that the capital city represents. It is large not just because of population size but also because a relatively high proportion of its population falls into income groups with high propensities to consume manufactures. The fact that so large a proportion of the national market is located in so confined a geographic area means that Dar es Salaam is, for most investors considering the location of a single plant to serve the national market, the site that minimizes distribution costs. This is particularly important for weight-gaining products, such as beer or soft drinks, for which transport of the final product can represent a significant proportion of total costs.

Because of the small size of the Tanzanian market the spatial concentration of industry is reinforced by scale economies internal to the firm. As with economies of scale, agglomeration economies lead to savings on costs of production when production is spatially

---

[22] The fact that these industries are weight losing, in the sense that the final product weighs less than the inputs, reinforces the material orientation in the location decisions of such plants.

concentrated. However, unlike economies of scale which are internal to the firm and can thus be taken advantage of in cities of all sizes and even in rural areas, agglomeration economies are external to the firm and related to the size, population density, and economic structure of the surrounding area. On the one hand there are the localization economies that result from close spatial association of like plants. These would include savings on specialized repair facilities, on the development of a pool of labour with specific skills, and on overhead costs (Balassa 1961). In Tanzania, where small market size and economies of scale combine to limit the number of firms in most product groupings, urbanization economies associated with the juxtaposition of unlike economic activities are likely to be of greater importance. Beyond pointing to possible savings in large-scale overhead facilities, such as electricity and water supply, and the possibility of administrative economies and gains in labour productivity associated with urban work habits and attitudes, it is extremely difficult to define in what ways increasing urban size decreases production costs for the individual firm (Tang 1958). Nevertheless, the fact that Tanzania has only three cities with populations in excess of 50 000, the minimum city size tentatively suggested for manufacturing activities, indicates that economies of agglomeration are a factor contributing not only to the urban location of industry but to its concentration in Dar es Salaam.

The decline in agricultural employment has entailed a decline in rural employment, while the increase in the manufacturing component of non-agricultural employment appears to have increased urban employment. Other non-agricultural activities also are urban centred because linkages between manufacturing and construction and service industries have led the latter to locate close to the former. In addition, government administration and commerce, which provided the original impulse for the development of urban areas during the German period, remain predominantly urban, and government services such as health and education are concentrated in urban areas. Only mining and quarrying, tied to a resource base in the same way as agriculture, appear predominantly rural.

What little data there are on the location of wage employment opportunities confirm the picture of non-agricultural employment concentrated in towns, hence a shift of all wage employment opportunities from rural to urban areas. In 1970, as Table 2.12 indicates, 70 per cent of all non-agricultural wage employment,

TABLE 2.12
The sectoral and urban–rural distribution of wage employment 1970

Total wage employment	375 635
Urban employment	187 300
Rural employment	188 335
Agricultural employment	107 368
Non-agricultural employment	268 267
Rural non-agricultural employment	80 967
Urban non-agricultural employment	187 300
$\frac{\text{Urban} \times 100}{\text{Total}}$	49·8%
$\frac{\text{Urban non-agric.} \times 100}{\text{Non-agricultural}}$	69·9%

Source: Tanzania. Central Statistical Bureau, various years.

TABLE 2.13
The growth of Dar es Salaam wage employment 1961–70

Year	Dar es Salaam wage employment	Index 1961 = 100	Dar es Salaam employment as a proportion of total wage empl.	Dar es Salaam employment as a proportion of non-agric. wage empl.
1961	38 007	100	9·4	19·3
1962	42 894	113	10·8	22·2
1963	44 204	116	12·9	25·2
1964	46 640	123	13·2	24·8
1965	54 604	144	16·3	28·0
1966	59 124	156	17·5	28·1
1967	65 246	172	18·8	29·2
1968	70 655	186	20·0	29·1
1969	71 788	189	19·5	28·1
1970	79 416	209	21·1	29·6

Source: Tanzania. Central Statistical Bureau, various years.

which had risen to 50 per cent of total wage employment, was in urban areas. A direct indication of the increase in the urban/rural employment ratio is found in Table 2.13, which shows the rapid growth of wage employment in Dar es Salaam. From 1961 to 1970 the proportion of total wage employment located in Dar es Salaam more than doubled, increasing from 9·4 per cent of the total to 21·1 per cent.

4.3 *Migration rates and changes in employment opportunities*

If rural residents considered only the difference in earnings between agricultural self-employment and wage employment, we would expect an increase in migration to the estates rather than the decrease that actually occurred. Given the contraction in wage employment opportunities in agriculture, this would have led to a supply of wage labour in excess of demand. Because of the institutional constraints on wage rate manipulation, this labour surplus would not have been eliminated by a compression of differentials between agricultural wage employment and self-employment. The decrease in the rate of migration in spite of a widening income differential shows that migrants respond to employment probability as well as to prospective higher wages. The probability of finding a job is only relevant to a rural resident's decision to move if it is less than one. The labour scarcity of the colonial period with its virtual guarantee of a wage job for anyone no longer existed in the 1960s. The risk of not finding a job, or of spending a considerable amount of time searching, was a real consideration for the first time in Tanzania. In response, migrants appear to have discounted the widening difference between wage employment income and agricultural self-employment income by estimating employment probability.

The hypothesis that the rural resident weighs employment probability against income size is supported by a comparison of employment growth rates with migration rates to the six urban centres and Dar es Salaam. Wage employment in Dar es Salaam doubled from 1959 to 1965 as a proportion of total non-agricultural employment; employment opportunities in Dar es Salaam were growing at a rate considerably faster than employment opportunities in other urban areas. The Dar es Salaam proportion of total non-agricultural employment remained constant after 1965, which implied that employment growth rates in the capital city and regional centres had equalized. This is consistent with our finding that population growth and net in-migration were higher for Dar es Salaam than for the regional centres before 1967, and roughly equal for the post-1967 period. As there is no reason to believe that interurban wage differentials have changed significantly over the 1960s,[23] the decrease in the rate of in-migration to Dar es Salaam would appear to be associated with the shift in employment growth rates and the consequent probability of finding a job.

5. SUMMARY

Despite impressive increases in non-agricultural inputs and cash crop exports, mostly owing to peasant rather than estate activity, per capita income of agricultural small holders remained stagnant for most of the post-war period. The beneficial effects of innovations and increased participation in the money economy were offset by rural population growth and Ricardian diminishing returns. At the same time, gains in the agricultural sector were negated by the government's policy of industrialization through import substitution. Incentives for industrial investment distorted the pattern of investment in favour of the non-agricultural sector, contributed to the deterioration of rural–urban terms of trade, and led to a government-administered net flow of development funds from rural to urban areas. Government decisions on projects, deterioration in the external terms of trade, the sheer size of the agricultural sector, and the conservatism of its participants imposed additional constraints on agricultural income.

While the opportunity costs of migration remained stable during this period, the returns to migration rose dramatically. Wages in both agricultural and non-agricultural employment increased steadily throughout the period, although at a faster rate after Independence. Growth of the rural labour force and the widening gap between income from agricultural self-employment and from wage employment increased the size of the migrant stream. While the flow of migrants to the towns rose, migration to the agricultural estates almost came to an end because employment on them was decreasing. This suggests that rural residents took employment probability into account when estimating expected returns to migration. The growth of urban employment was part of the structural shift in the wage sector of the economy. Increased investment funds for industrial development led to a rise in the urban share of total output.

[23] Tanzania, Central Statistical Bureau, various years.

III

DEMOGRAPHIC CHARACTERISTICS, ECONOMIC BACKGROUND, AND REGIONAL ORIGIN OF MIGRANTS

1. INTRODUCTION

DIFFERENT rates of migration for demographic and regional sub-groups of the rural population appear to be a virtually universal characteristic of migratory movements, internal or international, urban or rural, in industrialized or less developed countries, past or present. The phenomenon of migration selectivity is of interest here for two reasons. First, the composition of the migrant population affects the economic consequences of migration. For example, in the rural areas the consequences of out-migration for output and income will depend on whether those who move come from more or from less productive segments of the population. Similarly in the urban areas the welfare and resource allocation consequences of a large influx of rural residents will depend on whether the migrants are labour force participants and have employment experience that will enhance their value to the urban community. Moreover, the consequences of a move to town for the person migrating may vary dramatically, depending on whether the migrant is old or young, male or female, educated or uneducated.

Differences in the returns to migration among population sub-groups lead on to the second reason for our concern with the selectivity process. There are barriers, some rational, some arbitrary—the products of the operation of the labour market, inertia in traditional social institutions, and political manipulation—which limit the degree of mobility in the wage labour market. These barriers help to explain why potential migrants face different sets of returns to urban migration depending on their region of origin, sex, marital status, education, age, family background, employment and residential experience. Lack of perfect factor mobility is not limited to urban labour markets: attitudes and institutions in the rural areas also work to segment work roles, responsibilities, and rewards. The costs of migration—opportunity costs and psychic costs in particu-lar—are also likely to vary with the demographic and other characteristics of the sub-group. An analysis of the relationships between different rates of migration and different costs and returns among sub-groups will provide additional insights into the determinants of migrant behaviour, and will add another dimension to the picture of the influence of economic development and structural change on the migratory behaviour of the population.

2. REGIONAL ORIGINS OF PRESENT MIGRANTS

The migrant population of each of the seven towns is shown in Table 3.1 distributed by the regions in which the migrants were born. Table 3.2 summarizes the first Table. Ten per cent of all urban migrants come from outside Tanzania.[1] Only in Arusha, which is located near the Kenyan border and is the headquarters of the East African community, does the proportion of non-Tanzanians differ significantly from the mean. The distribution shows the dominance of Dar es Salaam among migrant receiving areas and the influence of distance on the decision of rural residents to move to town.

2.1 *Another perspective on Tanzania's urban hierarchy*

The final column of Table 3.2 gives for each town the number of regional areas providing more than 5 per cent each of the town's migrant population. While half the migrant population of Dar es Salaam is drawn from only three regions, Coast, Morogoro, and Mtwara, nine regions contribute at least 5 per cent to the city's total migrant population. By comparison, the other six towns average only four regions contributing at least 5 per cent of their migrant populations. Not only does Dar es Salaam, as the country's dominant urban economic centre, attract more migrants than other towns, it also draws on a wider hinterland. While the six towns are primarily regional centres, Dar es Salaam appears to have the entire country as its source area. Only Mwanza, with seven regions, each contributing more than 5 per cent of its migrant stream, is comparable to Dar es Salaam in this respect.

The relation between intra-regional migration and migration to

---

[1] Given the concentration of expatriates in trade and high-level man-power posts which are heavily concentrated in urban areas, it is not surprising that the proportion of non-Tanzanians in the total urban population, 7 per cent, is more than seven times what it is in the rural areas. It should be recalled that Europeans were not included in the sample. Thus these external migrants are either Africans or Asians.

TABLE 3.1

Regional origins of the seven-town migrant population

Region	Dar es Salaam % of total	Tanga % of total	Arusha % of total	Mwanza % of total	Tabora % of total	Dodoma % of total	Mbeya % of total
Outside Tanzania	9·69	9·35	22·88	10·90	7·00	—	—
Arusha	0·49	—	5·08	—	—	—	—
Coast	23·70	2·88	—	—	—	—	—
Dodoma	1·26	—	9·76	—	—	17·19	—
Iringa	2·20	—	—	—	—	—	14·84
Kigoma	0·90	—	—	3·25	7·00	—	—
Kilimanjaro	5·83	9·11	38·56	2·55	—	10·94	—
Mara	1·21	—	—	14·39	—	—	—
Mbeya	4·08	4·32	—	3·94	7·70	—	57·81
Morogoro	14·59	3·84	—	—	—	—	—
Mtwara	11·58	—	—	—	—	—	—
Mwanza	0·90	—	—	19·95	—	—	—
Ruvuma	4·76	3·36	—	—	—	—	—
Shinyanga	1·08	—	—	4·18	—	—	—
Singida	0·76	—	—	3·71	—	11·72	—
Tabora	3·73	2·64	—	14·39	40·55	17·19	—
Tanga	7·76	51·80	11·86	—	—	—	—
West Lake	1·84	—	—	15·32	—	—	—
Zanzibar	3·64	—	—	—	—	—	—
Other regions	—	12·70	11·86	7·42	37·75	42·96	27·35
Total	100·00	100·00	100·00	100·00	100·00	100·00	100·00
Total number	123 654	23 143	13 098	23 920	7 937	7 104	7 100

Source: NUMEIST 1971.

TABLE 3.2
Summary of findings on regional origins of migrants

Town	Percentage from outside Tanzania	Percentage of migrants from surrounding region	Largest percentage of migrants from another region	Number of regions contributing more than 5% each of town's migrants
Dar es Salaam	9	24	15	9
Tanga	9	53	9	4
Arusha	22	5	39	4
Mwanza	11	20	14	7
Tabora	7	41	12	3
Dodoma	5	17	16	4
Mbeya	5	57	15	2

Source: NUMEIST 1971.

TABLE 3.3
Regions with regional capitals in sample : urban direction of migration

Region	% of urban migrant stream directed to regional capital	% of urban migrant stream directed to Dar es Salaam	% of urban migrant stream directed to another urban centre	Total %
Arusha	43	39	18	100
Coast	98[a]	98	2	100
Dodoma	31	39	31	100
Mbeya	41	49	10	100
Mwanza	79	18	3	100
Tabora	30	41	29	100
Tanga	52	41	6	100

[a] Dar es Salaam is the capital of Coast Region.
Source: NUMEIST 1971.

Dar es Salaam is illustrated in Table 3.3. Here migrants from each of the seven regions whose capital cities are included in the sample are distributed according to urban destination. The regional and national capitals attract between 59 per cent and 94 per cent of rural out-migrants from each region. In none of the seven regions was another urban area as great an attraction as either Dar es Salaam or

TABLE 3.4
Inter-regional migrants: urban direction of migration

	To Dar es Salaam	To Mwanza	To five towns	Total
	%	%	%	%
All inter-regional migrants[a]	64	13	23	100
Inter-regional migrants from regions east of Singida[a]	75	2	23	100
Inter-regional migrants from Singida Region and west[a]	42	35	23	100

[a] Excluding Coast and Mwanza Regions.
Source: NUMEIST 1971.

the regional capital. In three of the six regions, more rural migrants went to Dar es Salaam than to the regional capital. Mwanza is the only region in which the regional capital attracts more of the urban migrant stream than Dar es Salaam: 79 per cent of rural out-migrants go to Mwanza town and only 18 per cent go to Dar es Salaam.

In the previous chapter, we established that a marked increase in migration in recent years (i.e. 1967–71) has caused Mwanza to grow at a faster pace than the other urban areas, replacing Tanga as Tanzania's second-largest urban area. In the regional heterogeneity of its migrants and the strength of its attraction for migrants from the surrounding region, Mwanza has greater similarities to the national capital than to the other regional centres. The growing role of Mwanza as the second national urban centre in Tanzania is illustrated by Table 3.4, in which inter-regional migrants from fifteen regions are distributed by urban destination. Dar es Salaam's position at the top of the urban hierarchy, its rapid growth, and its nationwide power of attraction are demonstrated by the move of nearly two-thirds of all inter-regional migrants to the capital city, while Mwanza receives 13 per cent and the other five towns together 23 per cent.

If we divide Tanzania by a line running north–south along the eastern border of Singida Region, which is approximately at the mid-point of the country, we find, not unexpectedly, that three-quarters of all migrants from the eastern half of the country have gone to the capital, while only 2 per cent have made the move west to Mwanza. In the western half of the country, which is closer to Mwanza, Mwanza nearly equals Dar es Salaam as a destination for inter-regional migrants. While 42 per cent of migrants from the western half of the country have gone to Dar es Salaam, 35 per cent made the move to Mwanza and only 23 per cent went to the other five towns. Mwanza, with a more rapid growth of economic opportunities in the 1960s than that of other towns, became a significant destination for rural–urban migrants. Although the analysis reinforces our earlier finding of high primacy in Tanzania's urban hierarchy, it shows that Mwanza is now becoming a second national centre.

2.2 The effect of distance on urban migration

Table 3.2 shows that, except in Arusha, a town's own region provides a greater number of migrants to the town than any outlying region. In six out of seven cases intra-regional migrants comprise a higher proportion of the total migrant population than inter-regional migrants from any of the remaining sixteen regions. This suggests that the direct and psychic costs, which vary directly with the distance between source and receiving regions, have a significant influence on the resident's estimate of net returns to migration. Unlike the other towns, which are located near the geographic centre of their regions, Arusha town is virtually on the border of Kilimanjaro Region, which in fact serves as its regional hinterland. This lends additional support to the distance hypothesis.

The predominance of the surrounding rural hinterland as a source of migration to the regional towns may be attributable as much to social homogeneity as to geographic accessibility. Certainly an urban migrant from the rural areas of Mbeya, the origin of 57 per cent of the migrants to Mbeya town, will find the near-by town more socially familiar than Tabora or Tanga, which respectively draw only 8 per cent and 4 per cent of their migrant population from Mbeya Region. An insight into this question is provided by Table 3.5 which compares the educational levels of long-distance and short-distance migrants. The Table shows that long-distance migrants tend to be better educated than short-distance migrants. The majority of migrants in Dar es Salaam from regions closer to Dar es Salaam than to the six regional capitals have 1–4 years of education (Std. 1–4) or no formal education, while the majority of migrants

TABLE 3.5
Proportion of Dar es Salaam and six-town urban migrants with Standards 1–4 or no formal education from near-by and distant regions[a]

	% of migrants to Dar es Salaam with no formal education or Std. 1–4	% of migrants to six towns with no formal education or Std. 1–4
Regions closer to regional capitals than to Dar es Salaam:		
Arusha–Kilimanjaro	19	23
Dodoma–Singida–Tabora	45	53
Iringa–Mbeya–Ruvuma	29	45
Kigoma–Shinyanga	28	56
West Lake–Mwanza–Mara	17	39
Regions closer to Dar es Salaam than to the six regional capitals:		
Coast	74	31
Morogoro	54	32
Mtwara	50	38

[a] Tanga region is excluded because of its nearness to both Dar es Salaam and Tanga town.
Source: NUMEIST 1971.

into Dar es Salaam from regions closer to regional capitals than to Dar es Salaam have more than Standards 1–4 education. Similarly migrants to the six towns from relatively near-by regions have, with one exception, a higher proportion with no formal education or Standards 1–4.

The fact that educated migrants tend to travel farther than uneducated migrants suggests that social distance lowers the propensity to migrate. If education lessens the parochialism of students, preparing them better for existence in unfamiliar social settings, then the social costs to the individual of migrating to more distant, more socially removed towns will diminish with increasing education. An alternative hypothesis is that the more highly educated migrants are willing to migrate longer distances because they can expect a larger increase in income by so doing. In unskilled, low-income occupations with informal hiring procedures, migrants from other regions, who have few local contacts and are unfamiliar with the workings of the local labour market, may have difficulty finding employment; whereas the more formal hiring procedures of occupations requiring a higher level of education may discriminate less against migrants from distant regions. Uneducated migrants would be less inclined to move long distances because they would be less likely than educated migrants to find employment the further they went from home.

The information in Table 3.6, however, does not support this hypothesis, as there appears to be no significant difference of income by region of origin in Dar es Salaam. Uneducated migrant males to Dar es Salaam from more distant regions fare just as well as migrants from the coast region. Similarly, in regard to the possibility of difference in ease of access to employment, column (c) shows that the proportion of inter-regional male migrants without a source of income is actually less than it is for coast region migrants.[2] The evidence suggests that it is the effect of education on psychic costs rather than on expected returns that makes educated migrants likely to travel farther than the uneducated.[3] This finding supports the more general hypothesis that psychic costs are, in addition to direct costs, a significant influence on the rural resident's assessment of net returns to migration.

3. AGE SELECTIVITY

The disproportionate number of 14–30-year-olds in the migrant stream is one of the first things noted by researchers on African urban migration (Caldwell 1969). Though the selection of younger people is not a 'universal', running through all patterns of migration selectivity, exceptions are not easy to find. One is the movement of a whole community or tribe, such as the migration of the Bantu peoples into East Africa in the eighteenth and nineteenth centuries or the Ngoni migration from southern Africa into what is now

[2] The distribution of unemployment rates may differ from the distribution above to the extent that participation rates among migrant males vary from region to region.

[3] It also implies the virtual absence of tribalism in the working of Tanzania's urban labour market. Since migrants from greater distances are likely to be from a different tribe than intra-regional migrants, the fact that distance travelled does not have an independent influence on the economic success of a migrant in town is evidence of absence of urban tribal discrimination. This is important for the Tanzanian development process, both in avoiding the obstacles to national unity produced by tribalism in so many African countries and in making efficient use of geographic mobility in allocating human resources among alternative activities.

TABLE 3.6
Dar es Salaam migrant males: average total income and proportion
without a source of money income by region of birth

Region of birth[a]	Average total income (sh) (uneducated migrants) (a)	Index (Coast-100) (b)	% without a source of income (all migrants) (c)
Coast	236	100	13
Dodoma, Singida, Tabora	248	105	13
Iringa, Mbeya	231	98	12
Morogoro	278	118	11
Mtwara	237	100·4	11

[a] Other regions are excluded from this table because of the small cohort size for uneducated migrants.
Source: NUMEIST 1971.

Tanzania in the mid-1800s (Oliver and Mathew 1963); in such a case, there is clearly no selection by age. An exception of greater contemporary significance is the concentration of older people among the migrants leaving urban employment to return to the countryside, a consequence of the longer stay of migrants in employment together with their continued dependence on rural areas for security in retirement.[4]

These examples are exceptions to the pattern of events in Tanzania. Young people were selected for the forced migration associated with slavery (Alpers 1967), and, as far as we can judge from the sketchy evidence, young people made up most of the post-1870 migrations to rural employment centres. Gulliver (1955), for example, noted that about two-thirds of the migrants from Songea to the northern employment areas were under the age of 30.

Before examining the current pattern of age selectivity, let us consider the explanations for these earlier age differences in migration rates. The logic behind the operation of the slave-traders is all too clear. The price their human commodity brought varied with strength, expected duration of service, and health, and these were all correlated with age. A crude productivity criterion also led to the selection of young men for the forced migrations associated

[4] See Chapter VII.

with the conscription of labour during the colonial period. The physical strength of the younger migrants remained important even after the migratory movements became more voluntary. As late as the 1930s many of those who travelled from the south-western areas to the estates in Tanga or the Northern Region, did so on foot; this would effectively discourage those without the necessary physical stamina (Tanganyika, Labour Department 1938). The gradual introduction of mechanized transport in the 1930s and 1940s eliminated the endurance element and thus the age differential from the direct costs of migration (Tanganyika. Labour Department, various years). The fact that migration in Tanzania continued to be the province of young people suggests that elements other than direct costs determine the higher rate of migration of the young.

One hypothesis suggests that if migration is permanent, so that it results not just in a short-term gain but an increased long-term stream of income, then there is a higher present value for younger people of future earnings because of longer life expectancy (Sjaastad 1962). According to this explanation, the difference in age specific migration rates is explained by different estimates by rural residents of the returns to migration. In the Tanzanian case, however, the fact that rural–rural migration in the colonial period was predominantly circular and short term implies that it was differences in short-term rather than long-term income between source and receiving area which prompted the migrant's decision. If so, the expected duration of the remainder of a migrant's working life would be an irrelevant consideration. Even if movements were short term, however, a migrant could permanently increase the level of his expected stream of earnings by investing the returns of migration in the source area. Though there are no precise indicators of the expenditure patterns of returning circular migrants, there is evidence that at least some of the sisal estates' wages bill was invested in seeds, hoes, etc. in migrant source areas, thus contributing to the spread of cash crop production in Tanzania (Tanganyika. Labour Department 1928). The hypothesis that younger rural residents were more likely to migrate because they had a longer period in which to receive a higher income is a partial explanation of age selectivity in colonial period migration.

Different returns to migration for different ages could also be caused by wage structures on the estates reflecting different levels of productivity. Since estate work was predominantly unskilled, deterioration in the strength and endurance of older men could result in remuneration declining with increasing age. In fact, employers did not make different payments to more or less productive labourers. The task system established a minimum level of work to be accomplished in order to receive the fixed daily wage, rewarding greater productivity with more leisure. This leisure was rarely transformed into additional income because of a scarcity of alternative employment opportunities. Opportunity and psychic costs also differed by age in Tanzania in the colonial period. Source area incomes, and thus opportunity costs of migration, tended to be higher for older than for younger men. Older rural residents were more likely to have an income from cash crops, both because older men were more likely to have migrated in the past and brought back money to invest at home, and because of the traditional land-tenure systems which frequently limited a son's right to his own land until he reached a certain age (Gulliver 1958). The psychic as well as the opportunity costs of migration increased with age. Older men with families and positions of social and political leadership were more likely to be in the position of 'succumbing to the pressures they feel from the obligations their kinsfolk demand of them or from the personal satisfaction they derive from holding positions of influence and authority in the rural social system' (Mitchel 1971, pp. 13–14).

It should also be noted that the need for cash was frequently greatest when a man was still quite young. With greater integration of rural residents into the money economy, such traditional institutions as the payment of bride-price were placed on a monetary basis for the first time. The demands of these institutions, which concentrated cash needs in the early years of manhood, imply that the psychic returns to migration would be higher for young men than old. In other words, a younger man would value the same expected income differential more highly than an older man. The difference in psychic returns would be reinforced to the extent that the change in preferences for cash versus traditional goods was generational. For younger people, who placed a greater value on money goods, the result would be a higher valuation of money income opportunities and a greater sensitivity to spatial income differentials. In this same category of differences in psychic returns to migration is the suggestion that among some tribes migration had become a form of initiation rite; for a young man to be considered a full adult, at least one journey to an area of wage employment was necessary. In such a case, young men would value the experience of migration, independent of money returns, more than older men (Watson 1958).

A comparison of curves *A-A'* and *B-B'* in Fig. 3.1 reveals that the age profile of all migrants currently living in Tanzania's urban areas is somewhat more skewed towards the younger age groups than the age profile for the rural source area population as a whole. While 45 per cent of the rural population is between the ages of 14 and 29, 55 per cent of the urban migrant population falls within that age group. The difference in the degree of skewness of the distributions of current ages, however, underestimates the current age selectivity of migrating to the extent that urban migrants remain in town for extended periods of time. A more appropriate measure of selectivity is age on arrival. The relatively greater degree of skewness of curve *C-C'* than of *A-A'* or *B-B'*, which indicates that nearly 75 per cent of all migrants arrived in town younger than 30, reflects the fact that over 50 per cent of urban migrants left their home area more than four and a half years before 1971. Table 3.7 disaggregates the age-on-arrival curve and reveals that neither the over-all mean age on arrival of 23·6 years nor the shape of the distribution varies significantly when calculated separately for Dar es Salaam and the six towns for males and females.

Even these figures underestimate the full degree of age selectivity among first-time migrants. Table 3.8 shows that while the majority

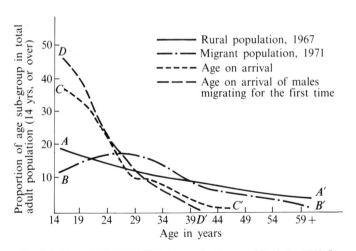

Fig. 3.1. From *NUMEIST* 1971; Tanzania. Bureau of Statistics 1969–71

TABLE 3.7
Migrant population: age on arrival
(%)

Age on arrival	Males			Females		
	Dar es Salaam	Six towns	Total	Dar es Salaam	Six towns	Total
14–19	37	34	36	46	40	44
20–4	31	29	30	27	27	28
25–9	14	14	14	9	15	11
30–9	11	14	13	9	9	9
40 or over	5	6	6	7	6	6
Total	100	100	100	100	100	100
Average age on arrival	24·1	23·4	23·9	23·4	22·9	23·1

Source: NUMEIST 1971.

of migrants came to the town of their current residence directly and did not participate in stage migration, the older a migrant male on arrival in town, the greater the likelihood that he had lived for a period of at least three months in a place other than his birthplace or his current town of residence. As a result, curve D-D' in Fig. 3.1, which charts the distribution of age on arrival of first-time migrants, is still more skewed than C-C'; over 90 per cent of all first-time migrants arrived in town before the age of 30. We can thus conclude that the current phenomenon or urban migration is characterized by a high degree of age selectivity.

TABLE 3.8
Migrant males: age on arrival by number of places lived in three months or more other than birthplace and current residence
(%)

Age on arrival	None	One	Two or more	Total
14–19	67	18	15	100
20–4	50	27	23	100
25–9	51	24	25	100
30–9	37	28	35	100
40 or over	39	26	35	100

Source: NUMEIST 1971.

TABLE 3.9
Migrant population: average age of arrival by year of arrival

Year of arrival	Males		Females	
	Dar es Salaam	Six towns	Dar es Salaam	Six towns
1971	22·2	26·4	25·1	23·4
1969–70	24·7	23·3	23·4	23·4
1967–8	24·8	23·8	21·8	23·0
1965–6	23·6	22·9	22·3	23·5
1963–4	23·3	22·3	24·6	22·2
1961–2	25·6	24·6	22·9	22·0
1956–60	25·5	22·3	23·4	21·5
1955 and before	23·8	22·9	23·0	22·4

Source: NUMEIST 1971.

In addition, Table 3.9, in which the average age on arrival is documented for migrants who arrived in town in various years, confirms our identification of age selectivity as a characteristic of past flows of migrants. There is no significant variation in the age of arrival of Dar es Salaam or six-town migrants, between those who arrived before 1955 and those who arrived in the later fifties, in the 1960s or in 1970–1.[5] While we will see that there have been marked shifts in the composition of the migrant stream over time along other demographic continua, we can conclude that the selectivity of young rural residents has been a stable characteristic of Tanzanian migration.

Have the determinants of age selectivity that we have analysed in the framework of our investment in human capital model remained stable over time as well? Differences in the opportunity costs and psychic costs of migration for different ages, rather than in the returns to migration, were the most significant factors at work in the past. That older rural residents feel the pressures of family and social responsibilities more acutely than young men is still likely to be true. However, as rural society has become more differentiated economically and socially, the structure of opportunity costs has become more complex. Our expectation that older rural residents will have

[5] While Table 3.9 does not reflect the age on arrival of those past migrants who returned to the countryside, there is no reason to believe that their age distribution on arrival differed from that of migrants who remained in town.

higher incomes than younger rural residents is no longer firm. To take an extreme example, a young Form 4 leaver who remained in the rural area in a government job would be earning more than a peasant twice his age. Within agriculture, a young peasant who inherits a sizeable plot planted with coffee will have a considerably higher income than an older man who has never sold crops for cash. However, in areas where land is scarce it is the young, with smaller or less well endowed plots than their parents, who still tend to have the lower incomes. Thus the structure of rural incomes by age no longer has a consistent influence on the age distribution of migrants.

While the influence of opportunity costs may have weakened, age differentials in the returns to migration have reinforced the existing pattern of age specific migration rates. Urban unemployment has introduced a new element of risk into the rural resident's decision to migrate. If, as one would expect, older Tanzanians are more averse to risk than young, then the shifting balance in the labour market has introduced a new dimension to the tendency for the returns to migration to be higher for younger rural residents. In addition, the stabilization of the labour force[6] means a longer expected period of economic activity for younger migrants. Also, to the extent that younger rural residents have greater access to educational opportunities and that education and expected urban incomes are correlated, the returns to migration will be higher for the young.

There is one new element in the structure of returns that does not, at first, appear to be consistent with the differentials in age specific migration rates. Table 3.10 shows that there is now a progressive decrease in the proportion of urban wage earners with a monthly income of less than sh 150 and a progressive increase in the proportion earning sh 1000 or more as one moves from younger to older workers. The fact that the incomes of those aged 50 and above deviate from this pattern, which is also reflected in average monthly wage figures, is due to the lower educational qualifications of this group. The positive relationship between age and urban income that has emerged in recent years appears to be working against the existing pattern of age selectivity in migration. This is not the case, however, because the fact that there are higher incomes for older workers does not imply higher returns for migrants who are relatively old on first arrival. We shall see in the discussion of factors contributing to the stabilization of the labour force (Chapter VII)

[6] See Chapter VII.

TABLE 3.10
Adult urban wage earners: wage income by age
(%)

Income per month (sh)	Age in years				
	14–19	20–9	30–9	40–9	50 and over
Up to 149	30·1	7·5	4·2	2·3	5·0
150–99	29·5	18·8	16·6	12·8	18·3
200–49	21·0	19·6	19·8	20·2	22·5
250–99	7·4	13·1	9·3	9·6	8·3
300–49	2·3	11·9	9·3	10·1	12·5
350–499	2·3	11·5	16·6	15·6	10·8
500–999	6·8	13·2	13·3	11·5	12·5
1000 and over	0·6	4·4	10·9	17·9	10·0
Total	100	100	100	100	100
Average monthly wage (sh)	233	383	491	586	462

Source: NUMEIST 1971.

that it is experience on the job and not age *per se* that is rewarded with higher income. The emergence of wage structures more complex than those of the colonial period has actually served to reinforce the pattern of age selectivity in migration, for the younger a migrant is when he takes his first step on an urban job ladder, the higher he can expect to reach in the course of his working life.

4. SEX SELECTIVITY

Migration in Tanzania has been predominantly male. Relatively few women made the trip to the north-eastern estates during the colonial period (Gulliver 1955) and Table 3.11 shows that 54 per cent of current urban migrants are males. However, the relative rates of urban migration of males and females have shifted significantly over the last two decades. Table 3.12, which documents the sex composition of the urban migrant population by year of arrival in town, reveals a sharp rise in the proportion of women in more recent years. Only one-third of the migrants who arrived in 1950 and before were females, while among those who arrived in 1970 and 1971 there was actually a majority of women.

Since this approach does not take into account migrants who

TABLE 3.11
1971 Migrant population: distribution by sex
(%)

	Male	Female	Total
Dar es Salaam	55	45	100
Six towns	53	47	100
Total	54	46	100

Source: NUMEIST 1971

TABLE 3.12
Migrant population: year of arrival by sex
(%)

Year	Male	Female	Total
1971	46	54	100
1970	49	51	100
1969–68	55	45	100
1967–66	58	42	100
1965–61	60	40	100
1960–51	64	36	100
1950 and before	67	33	100

Source: NUMEIST 1971.

came to town and returned to the country before 1971, it is possible that the higher proportion of women among recent arrivals is due to female migrants' shorter length of stay rather than to changes in the male and female rates of migration. If this were the case, however, we would not expect to find changes over time in the sex composition of the urban population. That the sex ratio in Tanzania's urban areas, as noted in Table 3.13, has changed significantly since 1948 confirms the increase in the proportion of women in the migrant stream.

TABLE 3.13
Dar es Salaam sex ratios: male/female

1948	141
1957	131
1967	123

Source: Tanzania. Central Statistical Bureau 1968.

In order to understand why this shift, which has far-reaching implications for the social structure of the towns as well as for urban labour utilization, has occurred, it is necessary to consider why female rural residents migrate. We have argued that the migrants' decision to move to town is largely a response to the difference in economic opportunities between rural and urban areas. This view of the migrant as an autonomous decision-maker must be qualified when the behaviour of female rural migrants is considered. The responses of male and female migrants to a question regarding their main reason for coming to town are noted in Table 3.14. A high proportion, 70 per cent, of the male migrants indicated that the search for employment was their main reason for coming to town; in sharp contrast, only 9 per cent of female migrants indicated that they came to town with the primary motive of participating in the urban labour market. Sixty-six per cent of the migrant women currently living in urban areas indicated that they came to town to live with their husbands as economic dependants.

The motives given by female migrants correspond to their behaviour in the labour market. A general picture of the role of women migrants in the urban economy can be obtained from Tables 3.15 and 3.16. Only 13 per cent of all adult female migrants have any form of wage employment, compared to 73 per cent of migrant males, and the proportion of women with non-wage money earning employment is only half of that for males. Only in those forms of employment that do not yield a money income, such as tending a

TABLE 3.14
Migrant population: main reason for coming to town by sex
(%)

	Male	Female	Total
To seek employment	70	9	42
To attend school	6	2	4
To live with parents or other relatives	6	7	7
To 'be with husband'		66	30
To visit	10	11	10
Other	7	4	6
Total	100	100	100

Source: NUMEIST 1971.

small plot of land or producing goods for home consumption, do we find a greater proportion of women than men. Fully 66 per cent of migrant women have no urban income at all, compared to 11 per cent of the men. Of particular interest is the fact that of the 80 per cent of the female migrant population in the seven towns with no money income, only 10 per cent were seeking work. Applying the conventional definition, we find that the participation rate for adult women in Tanzania's urban labour market is only 0·28, less than one-third the level for men. Even if the definition of participation is loosened to include among the employed those engaged in economic activities yielding non-money income, the maximum participation rate is 0·41, less than half of what it is for males. Not only is the participation rate for female migrants lower than the rate for males, it is also significantly lower than the rate, similarly defined, for females who have remained in the rural areas (Tanzania. Bureau of Statistics 1969–71).

TABLE 3.15
Migrant population: source of income by sex
(%)

	Male	Female
Wage employment	73	13
Non-wage	14	7
Non-money income	2	14
None	11	66
Total	100	100

Source: NUMEIST 1971.

Given this evidence of female economic dependency and lack of involvement in the urban labour market, we cannot simply explain the rising rate of female urban migration by changes in economic opportunities between source and receiving areas. Nor can we conclude that the rate of female urban migration is derived directly from the rate of migration among rural males, for such a hypothesis, while consistent with the increase in the rate of urban migration of females, leaves unexplained the increase in the proportion of females in the urban migrant stream.

Two sets of factors have contributed to the increase in the ratio of females to males in the migrant stream. The first and most important

TABLE 3.16
Migrant population: proportion seeking work and sex-specific participation rates

	Those with no money income	Those seeking work	Participation rates	
	% of sub-group total	% of those with no money income	Those with money earning employment + those seeking employment/total adult population	Those with money earning and non-money employment + those seeking employment/total adult population
Males	13	28	0·90	0·90
Females	80	10	0·28	0·41

Source: NUMEIST 1971.

set has been a rise in the proportion of male migrants bringing their wives to town to live. That wives no longer remain in the rural areas to tend the family's plot of land while husbands go off to sell their labour, is an effect, though in part also a cause, of the stabilization of Tanzania's wage labour force. The relationship of this stabilization to the migration of dependent women is analysed in Chapter VII.

The second set of factors has led to the increase in the rate of migration of independent women, who are moving in response to the difference in economic opportunities between rural and urban areas. Table 3.17, documenting the marriage status of migrants by year of arrival, provides evidence of the growing size of this sub-group of migrants. As expected, the proportion of migrants who are married on arrival is considerably higher for women than for men. More importantly the proportion of men who are unmarried on arrival has remained relatively stable over time. Most men come to town unmarried and marry only after they have established themselves economically, frequently returning home to do so and bringing their new wives back to town with them. For women this is not the case. While only 13 per cent of those women who came to town in 1952 or before were unmarried, the proportion had increased to 33 per cent of all female arrivals in 1970 and 1971, implying that the increase in the rate of migration of independent women was even faster than the increase in the rate of migration of dependent women.

The migration of these women can be explained as a response to spatial differences in economic opportunities. The widening rural–

TABLE 3.17
Migrant population: marriage status on arrival by sex and year of arrival
(%)

	Males			Females		
	Unmarried on arrival	Married on arrival	Total	Unmarried on arrival	Married on arrival	Total
1970–1	64	36	100	33	67	100
1964–9	67	33	100	25	75	100
1953–63	60	40	100	26	74	100
1952 and before	58	42	100	13	87	100

Source: NUMEIST 1971.

urban income gap thus appears to be one of the factors determining the increasing migration rate of female workers. Education appears to be another factor. Table 3.18 indicates that the higher a woman's level of formal education, the more likely she is to come to town to seek employment. The proportion of female migrants who came for reasons of employment increased from 4 per cent among those with no formal education to 18 per cent and 29 per cent for Standards 5–8 and Form 1–6 leavers respectively. During the colonial period the number of educational opportunities for females was only a small proportion of those open to men. The growth in educational opportunities for females, which has been even faster than that for males, is clearly one reason for the increasing proportion of economically independent educated women in the urban migrant stream.[7]

We have not established, however, why, of all women who come to town, a higher proportion of educated than of uneducated women do so with the intention of seeking work. One reason for this may be that formal education changes a woman's perception of her role in society (Mbilinyi 1970); another may be the fact that economic opportunities improve with education.[8] As Table 3.19 indicates, the lower the educational level, the greater the difference in earnings between men and women; uneducated females are among the most poorly paid urban workers in Tanzania.

This may provide a clue to the extremely low participation rate of women who have come to town to be with their husbands. Rates below those for women living in the rural areas may be due not to less desire for employment (associated perhaps with higher incomes of husbands in urban than in rural areas), but to a disadvantaged position in the urban labour market. Women may have withdrawn from the labour market because they cannot find work, not because of a preference for leisure and complete economic dependence. The higher participation rate of educated women with easier access to employment positions supports this hypothesis.

[7] In rural areas among 50–64-year-olds only 3 per cent of females have had any formal education, compared to 23 per cent of males. Among 15–19-year-olds 34 per cent of females have received some formal education, compared to 61 per cent of males. The implication is that over the last two to three decades educational opportunities for women have expanded faster than those for men. Tanzania, Bureau of Statistics 1969–71.
[8] Urban income differentials by educational level for men and women are documented in Chapter IV.

TABLE 3.18

Migrant females: main reason for coming to town by education
(%)

Education	To seek employment	To attend school	To be with parents or other relatives	To be with husband	To visit or other	Total
No formal	4	—	8	69	19	100
Std. 1–4	5	—	6	77	11	100
Std. 5–8	18	7	8	53	14	100
Forms 1–6 plus	29	11	7	45	8	100

Source: NUMEIST 1971

TABLE 3.19
Male and female urban wage index for educational sub-groups

Education	Males	Females
No formal	1·00	0·62
Std. 1–4	1·00	0·82
Std. 5–8	1·00	0·82
Forms 1–6 or more	1·00	0·95

Source: NUMEIST 1971.

5. SELECTIVITY BY SOCIO-ECONOMIC BACKGROUND

Here we consider the occupation of the migrant's father, and the rural employment experience of the migrant himself, both on his own plot of land and in wage employment, characteristics of the migrant's socio-economic background which might distinguish them from those who remain in the rural areas.

5.1. *The family background of urban migrants.*

The position of a family in the rural hierarchy may influence the younger generation's propensity to migrate. We would expect a migrant from one of the few rural families in which the father was an educated, high-income white-collar worker to face costs and returns to migration different from those faced by a migrant from a peasant background. The expected returns to migration might be higher because of better and more widespread urban contacts or because of greater ease of access to educational opportunities. Psychic costs of migration to an urban area might be lower because of the similarity of rural white-collar households to urban households. These factors suggest that migration would be selective of rural residents from a non-peasant background, though differences in the opportunity cost structure of migration would influence the difference in net returns.

In Tanzania's rural areas approximately 83 per cent of economically active males are engaged in peasant farming (Tanzania. Bureau of Statistics 1969–71). Table 3.20 shows that the occupational distribution of the fathers of migrants is virtually the same as that for the rural population as a whole: 80 per cent of all migrant males had fathers who were self-employed in agriculture. But, before we conclude that selectivity by family background is not significant in the Tanzanian context and reject the hypothesis of lower psychic costs and higher returns for migrants from non-peasant backgrounds, it is necessary to disaggregate the migrant population by education as well as by father's occupation. Urban migrants with Standards 5–8 or more education are more likely to come from non-peasant backgrounds, than those with little or no formal education. This suggests that children from non-peasant backgrounds are more likely to complete primary school and gain access to one of the extremely scarce places in secondary school. There is evidence from a number of developing countries that even when access to secondary school is competitive, candidates from middle-class backgrounds fare much better than candidates from working-class or peasant backgrounds (Bhagwati 1973).

TABLE 3.20
Rural-born migrant males: father's occupation by migrant's educational level
(%)

Education	Peasant farmer	White collar	Manual worker	Business trade	Total
No formal	89	3	3	5	100
Std. 1–4	87	4	5	4	100
Std. 5–8	79	8	8	5	100
Forms 1–6 or higher	65	19	7	9	100
Total	80	8	6	6	100

Source: NUMEIST 1971.

5.2. *Prior self-employment of urban migrants*

Rural–urban migration in Tanzania, as in other developing countries, can be perceived as a shift from the agricultural to the non-agricultural sector. This, however, does not necessarily imply that migrants are peasant farmers who lay down their hoes and abandon their land to move to the city. An alternative hypothesis is that the different growth rates of the agricultural and non-agricultural labour forces are due to the choice of work by new workers rather than to the shift of farmers or agricultural wage employees. Confirmation of this hypothesis would require evidence that most urban migrants have no prior employment experience. Although 80 per cent of urban migrants come from a peasant economic background, Table 3.21 shows that 63 per cent of them had no first-hand experience of agricultural self-employment. Only 14 per cent of all urban male migrants had ever grown cash crops on their own *shamba,* while another 23 per cent had a *shamba* on which they grew produce for family consumption.

This finding is clearly associated with the pattern of age selectivity. Most migrants leave their home areas before they have received their own land; if they are old enough to have their own land, they leave before starting to cultivate their *shamba* and becoming economically tied to their rural residence and way of life. If the youth of migrants is the reason for their inexperience in agricultural self-employment, we would expect to find among older migrants a greater proportion who have worked their own *shamba.* The bottom row of Table 3.22 indicates this: 65 per cent of those who arrived under the age of 30 did not have their own *shamba* while among those older than 30 on arrival, the proportion without experience of agricultural self-employment declined to 50 per cent.[9] In addition, more older than younger migrants with their own *shamba* grew cash crops.

Table 3.22 also shows that, regardless of age, the more educated migrants have less experience of agricultural employment. Fifty-five per cent of migrants under 30 without formal education did not have their own *shamba* before leaving their home area, while 69 per cent of those with Standards 5–8 and 91 per cent of those with Forms 1–6 or more had not had *shambas.* Among those over 30, the situation is the same: 38 per cent of those with no formal education did not have a *shamba*; as the educational level rises to Standards 1–4, Standards 5–8, and Forms 1–6 or more, the proportion of migrants

---

[9] Disaggregating further reveals that 71 per cent of those who arrived between the ages of 14 and 19 had no *shamba,* declining to 43 per cent of those 40 or over. However, if age is the predominant factor explaining that lack of experience of agricultural self-employment, 43 per cent without experience among the oldest group would appear inordinately high. In part, this is explained by the relationship in Table 3.8 between age on arrival and number of other places lived. Nearly 60 per cent of all migrants 30 or older had lived somewhere besides their home area and current residence. Thus many older arrivals had actually left their home areas at a considerably younger age. Older migrants leaving the rural areas for the first time are likely to have a higher proportion with agricultural self-employment experience. *NUMEIST* 1971.

without a *shamba* rises to 39 per cent, 57 per cent, and 81 per cent respectively.

Education delays the age of labour force entry and cuts the rural resident off from the land, at least while he is in school. Going to school and working one's own *shamba* are usually mutually exclusive. Most migrants, educated and uneducated alike, migrate to town when they are between 14 and 25. If the time before migrating is spent in school, then the new arrival is less likely to have worked his own *shamba*. If, as we have seen, the more educated are more likely to migrate, then most migrants will be people without previous experience in agricultural self-employment. This cannot be taken as an indication that those who are moving to town are land-scarce rural residents.

5.3. *Prior wage employment of urban migrants.*

Given the evidence for the limiting effect of age and education on agricultural self-employment, we would expect to find an equally low level of experience in agricultural wage employment. Wage employment opportunities comprise approximately 15 per cent of all male rural employment and the proportion of rural males who have at one time or another held a rural wage job is considerably higher. Nevertheless, as Table 3.23 indicates, only 8 per cent of male migrants had ever held an agricultural wage job. What is most significant is that only 6 per cent of migrants had ever worked on the sisal estates. Given the dramatic recent decline of over 100 000 jobs in the sisal industry, most of which were held by migrants, it would

TABLE 3.21
*Migrant males: agricultural self-employment
prior to migration*
(%)

	Had own *shamba*: grew cash crops	Had own *shamba*: did not grow cash crops	Did not have *shamba*	Total
Dar es Salaam	17	18	65	100
Six towns	11	27	62	100
Total	14	23	63	100

Source: NUMEIST 1971.

TABLE 3.22
Migrant males: agricultural self-employment prior to migration by age and education
(%)

	Under 30 on arrival				30 or older on arrival			
	Had own *shamba*: grew cash crop	Had own *shamba*: did not grow cash crop	Did not have *shamba*	Total	Had own *shamba*: grew cash crop	Had own *shamba*: did not grow cash crop	Did not have *shamba*	Total
No formal education	16	28	55	100	28	33	38	100
Std. 1–4	19	32	49	100	26	35	39	100
Std. 5–8	14	17	69	100	17	24	59	100
Forms 1–6 or more	3	6	91	100	6	13	81	100
Total	13	20	65	100	21	28	50	100

Source: NUMEIST 1971.

TABLE 3.23
Migrant male population: agricultural wage employment prior to coming to town
(%)

	Worked on relative's shamba			Worked on another peasant's shamba			Worked on non-sisal plantation			Worked on sisal estate		
	No	Yes	Total	No	Yes	Total	No	Yes	Total	No	Yes	Total
Dar es Salaam	86	14	100	98	2	100	97	3	100	94	6	100
Six towns	96	4	100	100	0	100	99	1	100	95	5	100
Total	90	10	100	99	1	100	98	2	100	94	6	100

Source: NUMEIST 1971.

have been reasonable to expect an influx of ex-sisal workers into the towns. Given the rising incomes and employment opportunities in the towns, it is of some interest that this did not occur. The explanation appears to lie in the fact that sisal workers were for the most part uneducated and unskilled, while, as we will see, urban employment opportunities were increasingly becoming the province of the educated.

6. SUMMARY

Examination of the regional origins of migrants reveals that, in terms of the number of regions serving as source areas, only Dar es Salaam, which draws migrants from all areas of the country, can be considered a national centre. We also found that distance acts as a constraint on the mobility of potential migrants. The analysis of the regional origins of urban migrants revealed a positive relationship between educational level and distance travelled. Since this could not be explained by an increase in the returns to educational sub-groups with increased distance, the propensity of the educated to move longer distances appears to be due to education's reducing of the psychic costs of migration. Implicit in this is the conclusion that, in general, increasing distance increases the psychic as well as the direct costs of migration.

The migrants who moved from the labour source areas to the agricultural estates in the north-east of Tanzania during the first half of the twentieth century were predominantly young people. The annual stream of migrants from the countryside to the towns which has expanded so dramatically over the past twenty-five years has also been composed predominantly of young people. While the selectivity of the young has remained a stable characteristic of migration in Tanzania, there have been shifts in the factors responsible for lower returns to urban migration for older rural residents. On the one hand, the introduction of modern transport has eliminated the necessity of walking to town and with it the difference in direct costs of migration between young and old. Similarly, increased economic differentiation in the rural areas has weakened the positive relationship between age and the opportunity costs of migration. On the other hand, the stabilization of the urban labour force has meant that income differences between source and receiving areas no longer yield benefits for a short period only, but for the remainder of the migrant's working life, with the result that the returns to migration are now higher for younger rural residents. The introduction of relatively complex urban wage structures which reward experience on the job has increased the incentives for migration at an early age.

The stabilization of the labour force has become an important factor in sex selectivity in migration as it has resulted in an increase in the proportion of migrants who bring their wives to town. While the high proportion of women coming to town as economic dependants must qualify our view of the role of economic factors in the decisions of rural residents, it is worth noting that part of the increase in women migrants is due to the increased number of independent job-seeking women. One reason for the low involvement of women in the urban labour market appears to be the paucity of economic opportunities for them. The fact that the increase in the rate of migration of female labour force participants has come from among educated rural women, for whom urban employment probabilities and incomes are higher, supports this hypothesis.

Education is also a factor in the selection of migrants by family background. While the migrant stream overall does not select migrants from non-peasant rather than peasant backgrounds, the more highly educated portion of the migrant stream is selective of non-peasants. For the time being the small size of this group limits the significance of this pattern of selectivity. The migrant selectivity of rural residents without employment experience is largely derived from the age selectivity pattern and is reinforced by the pattern of educational selectivity, the detailed analysis of which we are about to consider.

IV

MIGRATION, EDUCATION, AND URBAN SURPLUS LABOUR

EDUCATION and migration appear to be complementary human capital investments; a strong positive relationship between the propensity of rural residents to migrate and their level of formal education has been observed in a variety of countries (Byerlee 1974; Todaro 1971). Differences in migration rates, opportunity costs, and economic returns for rural residents with different levels of education are documented here. This information, in summary form, is one dimension of a migration function that is also estimated across regions and urban areas and over time. The function is used to test, more rigorously than in our previous discussions, hypotheses as to the influence of income differentials, employment probabilities, and non-economic factors on the propensity to migrate; it also provides the basis for assessing the quantitative impact of changes in government policy.

1. EDUCATION AND THE PROPENSITY TO MIGRATE

The propensity of rural residents to migrate increases with their level of education. Table 4.1 indicates that rural residents with Standards 1–4 are nearly three times as likely to migrate as those with no formal education. Standard 5–8 leavers are nearly four times as likely to move as rural residents with one to four years of

TABLE 4.1

Comparison of rate of rural–urban migration and urban wages for four education groups: Tanzanian males

Education level	Migration rates[a] (per 100 rural dwellers)	Urban wage rates (sh per month)
No formal	0·011	271
Std. 1–4	0·032	280
Std. 5–8	0·123	359
Post primary	0·249	870

[a] See Appendix B for a definition of the migration rates used throughout this study.

education, and the propensity of post-primary leavers to migrate is nearly twice that of those with a primary education; more than twenty times that of those with no education.

An economic explanation for this relationship is depicted in Fig. 4.1. The income of rural workers who have just completed their formal education and begun to work is lower than that of uneducated workers whose experience as agricultural producers is greater. Their greater training and natural ability, however, combined with better contacts with those in control of the supply of credit, enables the educated to use their resources more efficiently, to be more innovative, and thus to raise their income above that of the uneducated.

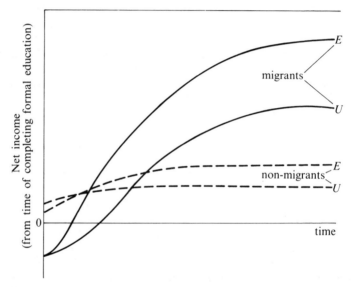

FIG. 4.1. Relation of net income to time by education and migrants' status

The net income of migrants is negative at first, as direct costs of migration must be borne during the period of moving and searching for a job. The income of the educated becomes positive before that of the uneducated and rises more steeply and to a higher level, reflecting their greater access to urban wage employment, higher starting wages, and the more numerous job ladders in the preferred occupations open to them.

Given the migrant's personal rate of discount of future earnings, i, the present value of a stream of returns $(Y_1, Y_2, \ldots)$ less costs $(C_1, C_2, \ldots)$ for T periods into the future is:

$$\text{P.V.} = \sum_{t=1}^{T} \frac{(Y_t - C_t)}{(1+i)_t}.$$

The present values of the net incomes in Fig. 4.1 are illustrated in Fig. 4.2 over a range of discount rates. For the uneducated the present value of urban income exceeds that of rural income only at relatively low discount rates, below i_u. For the educated, the economic advantage of migration is more obvious; the present value of urban benefits dominates the rural stream at all except high discount rates, above i_u. If the mean discount rate is the same for the educated and the uneducated, then expected net returns to migration will be higher for the educated. The Line F in Fig. 4.3 illustrates the relationship between the migration rate and the difference in present values of expected rural and urban incomes. If economic factors alone influence the migration decision, then the higher differential for the educated, V_2, than for the uneducated, V_1, would be

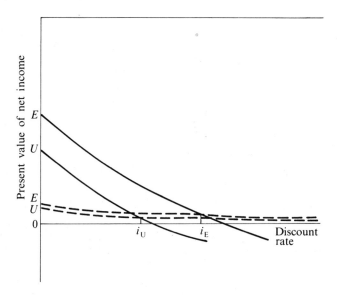

Fig. 4.2. Relation of present value of net income to discount rate

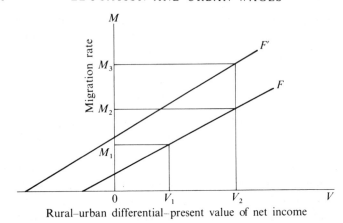

Rural–urban differential–present value of net income

FIG. 4.3. Relation of present value of net income to migration rate

associated with a higher rate of migration, M_2, among the former than among the latter, M_1.

Analysis of the relationship between migration rates and education is complicated by the difficulty of separating economic from non-economic costs and returns. The educational system may select individuals who are relatively open to change or come from families having 'urban oriented' values on occupation and consumption. Alternatively, education may alter the rural resident's utility function, increasing his preference for urban jobs and an urban mode of living. Differences in the psychic costs and returns of migration to groups with different amounts of education may make educated rural residents more willing to move. For example, in Fig. 4.3 if the difference in the present values of economic benefits is V_2 for both educational groups, the migration rate for the educated would be M_3 and for the uneducated M_2. Of course, a higher rate of migration among the educated may be due to both movement along a migration function and a shift in the function, as is the case with the differential between M_1 and M_3. We begin to improve the specification and assess the relative importance of economic and non-economic causes of the positive relationship between educational level and the rate of migration by examining the educational structure of urban wages and rural incomes.

2. EDUCATION AND URBAN WAGES

The relationship between urban wages and education is largely determined by that between occupation and education. Table 4.2 shows the average monthly wage and the proportion of workers above sh 500 is higher in those jobs requiring higher levels of skill. Approximately three-quarters of the white-collar workers are in the two upper income brackets, earning more than sh 300 per month; production workers are concentrated in the two middle wage groups, 73 per cent earning between sh 200 and sh 499; while 75 per cent of unskilled and 89 per cent of service workers earn less than sh 300.[1] The difference in average income between the various major groups is substantial: taking the income of service workers as an index of 100, unskilled workers earn 115, production workers 167, and white-collar workers 301. If the sub-groups of public servants and sales personnel, 'atypical' in that they cover a wider range of jobs and do not fit neatly into any major occupational group, are omitted from the white-collar and service categories, the differential between these two categories increases from 301:100 to 375:100.

Educational attainment is the principal criterion by which jobs are distributed among competing applicants. Most highly paid positions in Tanzania are accompanied by fairly rigid requirements, and experience on the job is rarely regarded as a substitute for formal education (Resnick in Resnick 1968). The educational distribution of wage earners by occupation illustrated in Table 4.3 confirms the importance of educational attainment even in occupations not filled by high-level manpower. The number of workers with no formal education or post-primary education is significant in only three occupational sub-categories. In ten of the thirteen sub-categories more than 95 per cent of all employees are in the top three or bottom three educational categories.[2]

White-collar jobs are the province of workers with a high level of education, while skilled and semi-skilled jobs are mainly filled by those with primary school education. The association between education and occupation is relatively stable within the four major occupational groupings. If the occupational sub-categories are ranked according to the average number of years of education

[1] Both the 'service workers' and the 'unskilled' are workers in jobs requiring little or no skill. The distinction between them is that the former are engaged in personal services while the latter are in production.
[2] The 'skilled workers' and 'machine operators' sub-categories do not appear selective of workers with particular educational qualifications, because wage earners hired in different years are aggregated in Table 4.3 and because educational requirements have been rapidly upgraded in these sub-categories.

TABLE 4.2

Urban[a] adult wage earners: occupation by income, 1971
(%)

OCCUPATIONS

Wage income sh per month	White collar					Production					Service					Unskilled
	Prof./tech. Mngr/Admin.	Semi-technical	Clerical	Public Service	TOTAL	Skilled	Drivers	Craftsmen	Machine operators	TOTAL	Cleaner Messenger	Sales	Hotels bars	Domestic service	TOTAL	
up to 199	5·4	6·0	7·3	24·6	8·7	8·5	3·5	15·7	25·4	13·7	41·6	47·0	9·0	2·4	58·6	34·5
200–99	5·4	19·3	20·7	27·5	18·5	33·0	32·9	44·9	48·4	40·1	52·8	20·2	12·4	14·6	30·2	41·0
300–499	8·1	18·1	33·5	30·4	26·4	33·0	50·6	34·3	19·7	33·2	62·7	27·0	8·7	1·6	7·5	21·7
500 & over	81·1	56·6	38·5	17·4	46·3	25·6	12·9	5·1	6·6	13·0	79·4	19·1	1·5	—	3·7	2·8
	100	100	100	100	100	100	100	100	100	100	100	100	100	100	100	100

[a] The urban areas covered are Dar es Salaam, Tanga, Mwanza, Arusha, Dodoma, Mbeya, and Tabora.
Source: NUMEIST 1971.

TABLE 4.3

Urban adult wage earners: occupation by education 1971
(%)

| Education level | White collar | | | | | Production | | | | | | Service | | | | Un-skilled |
	a Prof. management	b Clerical	c Semi-technical	d Public service	Total white col.	e Skilled	f Machine operator	g Craftsmen	h Drivers	Total production	i Domestic	j Messenger Cleaner	k Hotel Bar	l Sales	Total service	m Unskilled
No formal	2·5	3·0	4·2	4·0	3·2	10·8	18·0	20·0	26·8	17·7	33·1	42·3	34·6	22·4	34·4	35·4
Std. 1–4	5·0	3·5	7·3	4·0	4·4	19·7	18·0	34·0	36·1	26·4	46·5	26·1	25·6	27·6	31·5	27·4
Std. 5–8	20·8	38·4	33·3	72·0	38·3	55·2	55·6	44·0	34·0	48·5	20·4	29·0	36·8	35·7	29·9	34·1
Post-primary	71·7	55·1	55·2	20·0	54·1	14·3	8·3	2·0	3·1	7·4	—	2·8	3·0	14·3	4·2	3·0
Total	100	100	100	100	100	100	100	100	100	100	100	100	100	100	100	100

Source: NUMEIST 1971.

received by members of the group, we find that the four sub-categories making up the white-collar category rank 1–4; the four sub-categories comprising skilled and semi-skilled workers rank 5, 6, 8, and 9; and the service and unskilled jobs are all in the lowest places, with the exception of sales in seventh place. Given these rankings, the use of aggregate occupational categories in the subsequent analysis does not entail much loss of precision. Table 4.4 summarizes the propensity of employers to hire people of a given educational level, and it shows clearly that the higher the 'skill level' of the occupation, the higher the educational requirement.[3]

TABLE 4.4

Urban adult wage earners: index* of propensity of occupational groups to employ people of certain educational levels 1971

Education	White collar	Skilled & semi-skilled	Service	Unskilled
No formal	0·2	0·9	1·7	1·8
Stds. 1–4	0·2	1·2	1·5	1·3
Stds. 5–8	1·3	1·6	1·0	1·1
Post-primary	2·7	0·4	0·2	0·2

* The index is computed by dividing the proportion of Occupation X that has Education Y, by the proportion of all wage earners that have Education Y. In other words if 30 per cent of all service workers have Std. 5–8 education and 30 per cent of all wage earners also have Std. 5–8 education then the index is 1·0. An index greater than one means that that particular education level is more heavily represented in that occupation than among wage earners in general. An index smaller than one means the opposite.
Source: NUMEIST 1971.

Given the positive relationship between wages and occupation, and occupation and level of education, there is a strong presumption that wage income is positively related to level of education; Table 4.5 shows that this is the case. The average gross returns to an additional year of education for urban wage earners in 1971, estimated crudely on the basis of increase in monthly earnings, rise from sh 4·4 to sh 26·7 to sh 85·3 for Standards 1–4, Standards 5–8,

---

[3] The similarity of propensities in the service and unskilled categories justifies the grouping of service workers with unskilled workers in the analysis used to derive the urban wage series, see Appendix B.

TABLE 4.5

Urban adult wage earners by sex, education, and wage income 1971
(%)

Wage income: sh per month	Females				Males				Total			
	No formal educ.	Std. 1–4	Std. 5–8	Post-primary	No formal educ.	Std. 1–4	Std. 5–8	Post-primary	No formal educ.	Std. 1–4	Std. 5–8	Post-primary
Up to 149	48.4	28.9	12.3	—	8.7	11.4	5.0	1.2	15.1	13.0	6.1	1.0
150–99	37.1	34.2	25.4	2.6	24.3	25.5	17.8	2.4	26.4	26.3	18.9	2.4
200–49	9.7	21.1	20.2	3.8	27.4	25.3	24.1	4.8	24.5	24.9	23.5	4.6
250–99	1.6	7.9	7.0	9.0	13.7	10.6	14.6	5.7	11.7	10.4	13.5	6.4
300–49	—	5.3	12.3	11.5	12.1	8.8	11.4	9.1	10.2	8.5	11.5	9.5
350–499	1.6	—	12.3	12.8	10.0	12.5	14.7	12.4	8.6	11.4	14.4	12.5
500–999	1.6	—	10.5	34.6	2.8	4.8	8.8	35.6	2.6	4.3	9.1	35.5
1000 and over	—	2.6	—	25.6	0.9	1.1	3.6	28.7	0.8	1.2	3.1	28.1
Average monthly wage(sh):	100	100	100	100	100	100	100	100	100	100	100	100
	168	226	295	825	271	280	359	870	251	269	349	861

Source: NUMEIST 1971.

and post-primary education, respectively.[4] The dramatically higher private returns to post-primary education, which help to explain the excess demand for secondary school places and slack demand for primary school places discussed below, are accentuated by the fact that, while the social cost of education increases rapidly as a student rises through the educational system, the private costs rise more slowly, resulting in a wider gap in net than in gross returns between primary and post-primary education. At the secondary level, school fees, books, room and board, and a personal allowance to compensate for forgone earnings are covered by the government (Cameron and Dodd 1970).

TABLE 4.6
Average wages by education and age: 1971

Education

Age	No formal education		Std. 1–4		Std. 5–8		Post-primary	
	Average wage	Index	Average wage	Index	Average wage	Index	Average wage	Index
14–19	179	100	159	100	221	100	445	100
20–9	216	121	223	140	291	132	679	157
30–9	256	143	313	197	447	202	1266	284
40+	326	182	383	241	614	278	1391	313

Source: NUMEIST 1971.

Though wage earners with post-primary education are concentrated in the high income categories, nearly 25 per cent of them earned less than sh 350 per month, because income increases with age for all groups. Ninety-five per cent of those with post-primary education earning less than sh 350 were below the age of 30. Table 4.6 brings out the wage relationship between age and education more clearly. In a society where there is considerable respect for traditional values, higher incomes for older workers could be a pure reward for age. In the wage or 'modern' sector of the economy it is more likely that age is a proxy for experience and that employers increase wages with seniority as an inducement to stability and a reward for the higher productivity of experienced workers. Also,

[4] This assumes an average of 6 years of additional education for post-primary leavers. As more people leave the educational system after Form 4 than go on to university, this figure may be an overestimate, making the average returns figure for this sub-group something of an underestimate.

since younger wage earners are more recent entrants into the urban labour market, the age–wage relationship could be partly due to a decline in the private returns to education associated with the phenomenon of 'filtering-down', which we define below as the decline over time of the occupational levels of new labour force entrants with a given level of education. It is clear from the Table that income differences by education are wider for older age groups. The more education an individual has, the greater the likelihood that his employment will be secure and will offer promotion and seniority-scaled wage structures. Also, the continued scarcity of post-primary leavers means that opportunities for upward mobility by job changes will be greater for those with more education.[5]

3. EDUCATION AND RURAL INCOME

Income data are inadequate for the precise specification of the relationship between income and level of education in rural areas. Nevertheless, the available evidence is sufficient to determine whether rewards for education are higher in urban than in rural areas, an issue of central importance to our analysis of the education selectivity of migration. The wages of unskilled, uneducated urban workers exceed average rural incomes. If we can establish that urban differences by education exceed rural differences, it will follow that the difference between urban wage earners and rural workers is wider for the educated than for the uneducated.

Higher wages among the educated may be a reward for higher productivity. Alternatively, educational differences between occupations may be 'exaggerated', in the sense that the wage difference between occupations is wider than the difference in marginal productivity because educational qualifications for high income occupations are 'excessively high', excluding competent workers

---

[5] The high proportion of young workers among the post-primary leavers with low incomes is consistent with the hypothesis that filtering-down depresses the income of new entrants to the urban labour market. For this to affect the relative slopes of the trend lines, the effect of filtering-down on income would have to be more significant for those at the top of the education scale than those at the bottom. The fact that the uneducated have always been heavily concentrated at the lower end of the urban wage distribution substantiates the hypothesis, as it implies that filtering-down has not had a significant effect on the income of those uneducated who succeeded in finding employment. (This does not imply that for the uneducated there has been no decline in urban expected income, as expected income also depends on the level of employment probability.)

with less formal education.[6] In Tanzania's urban areas both production and institutional factors contribute to the explanation of the positive relationship between wage and education levels. The necessity of some formal education for civil service or clerical jobs requiring literacy illustrates the first type of determinant.[7] That occupational wage differences did not narrow significantly when Africans—with a dramatically lower supply price than the colonialists they replaced—gained access to high level jobs is evidence of the second type of determinant.

Is the influence of productivity and institutional determinants of incomes likely to be greater in urban than in rural areas? In rural areas there are few jobs in which higher incomes are received on the basis of a presumed difference in productivity rather than on the basis of performance. Furthermore, nowhere in Tanzania can a school leaver gain preferential access to an already high-yielding plot of land by virtue of his education alone. The efficiency of the educational system in selecting the more able or in transmitting knowledge or skills that increase productivity, must be proved in every instance, rather than simply assumed, as is frequently done in urban areas.[8]

The contribution of education to productivity is likely to be lower for rural than for urban workers because the content of the curriculum is less appropriate to their occupations. The debate about the proper amount and content of education for the long-run welfare of the African community in Tanzania dates back to the 1920s. Throughout the colonial era, however, government schooling was determined more by the short-term manpower needs of the colonial

[6] Even where wage and productivity differentials between educational groups are the same, institutional factors may still have an indirect influence on the wage structure. For example, the productivity differential may be exaggerated as a consequence of a scarcity of educational opportunities, the supply of which is not determined solely by private demand, or the productivity differential may be affected by institutional influence on choice of technique. If 'excessively' capital intensive techniques are utilized and there is a positive relationship between the K/L ratio of an industry and skill (or educational) intensity then the higher productivity of the educated is in part due to the inappropriate technology and resulting higher levels of complementary capital with which the educated work.

[7] To hypothesize an extreme situation where institutional factors alone determine the education–occupation relationship it must be assumed that skills necessary for high income jobs are learned on the job rather than in school and that those with formal schooling are no more successful at learning the skills than those without.

[8] The generalization regarding the lack of institutional influence on the rural structure of income must be qualified where rural credit is rationed, and the educated have preferential access for reasons independent of efficiency in the use of innovations.

élite than by any theory. The first government schools were established by the Germans at a time when administrative consolidation in East Africa required increasing numbers of clerks, tax-collectors, interpreters, accountants, and artisans. The system was operated within a strict manpower planning framework: the output of Africans with the requisite skills was to expand only as fast as government requirements. Education as a means of bringing about integrated rural development was considered beyond the scope of government action (Cameron and Dodd 1970).

The British, having had problems with the rapid expansion of academic education in India and Sri Lanka (Ceylon), felt that education beyond low-level village schools, mostly controlled by missionaries, 'should be rigidly limited in output to the estimated capacity of the country's power of absorption' (Tanganyika. Education Department 1961). The British policy of indirect rule added another dimension to the role of government schools, the training of a local élite in the ways of 'modern' political leadership. Tabora School, opened in 1924 for chiefs and the sons of chiefs, closely followed the model of the English public school, providing the student with an education to 'fit him to fulfil his duty to the State and towards his own people as their leader and educator' (Thompson in Resnick 1968).

In accordance with the recommendation of the Phelps-Stokes Commission (1924) and the 1925 Advisory Committee on Educational Policy in British Tropical Africa (Great Britain 1925), the British in Tanzania adopted a new policy of adaptation in their educational approach. Education, while still fulfilling its specific role of providing trained manpower, was also to be an agent of local community development and 'natural' growth, operating within the framework of village life and helping it to adapt to changing economic and political circumstances. This policy was to counter the danger that education 'might contribute more to the disintegration and bastardization of that society than to its stable evolution by producing a privileged elite divorced from and out of sympathy with the communities from which it has sprung' (Thompson in Resnick 1968).

What actually happened was that the goal of community education became an abstract ideal, while the educational system remained substantially the same. There were three reasons for this: first, in times of economic stringency education was one of the first areas in which cuts were made, with the result that community education felt the pinch before the other 'more important' aspects of the system (Cameron and Dodd 1970). Secondly, community education involved the development of an entirely new curriculum; since no models existed and little systematic thinking had been done about the future shape of the Tanzanian society and economy, this proved beyond the capabilities of the local and expatriate staff. Thirdly, because returns to the individual from traditional education were so much greater than those from the new community education, Africans protested against community or agriculturally-oriented education, in the belief that it was part of an attempt to keep them down (Saul in Mbilinyi 1976).

At Independence, Tanzania inherited a system of education that had been highly successful in meeting the colonial government's needs for a small élite group of urban non-manual workers; from the wider perspective of the new government, however, the system was inadequate because it reached only a very small percentage of the population and benefited only the urban areas. Furthermore, it was elitist because the selection process, the educational content, the privileged existence of students, and the higher earnings of the educated, all combined to make people view education as a means of personal advancement, rather than a way of developing society.

The new government concentrated on the quantitative inadequacy. Its leaders were aware that rapid expansion of the educational system would compel school leavers to integrate themselves into the rural economy, if only because educational output would outstrip the number of new jobs in the wage economy. Indeed, the education of the rural population was one of the government's goals. Nevertheless, the expanded educational system virtually duplicated the content of colonial literary education, particularly at the lower levels. In *Education for Self-Reliance,* written six years after Independence, President Nyerere (1965) argued that change in education must have a qualitative as well as a quantitative dimension. Education must

prepare young people for the work they will be called upon to do in the society which exists in Tanzania—a rural society where improvement will depend largely upon the efforts of the people in agriculture and in village development . . . It must produce good farmers and education must inculcate a sense of commitment to the total community, and help the pupils to accept the values appropriate to our kind of future, not those appropriate to our colonial past.

In practical terms he suggested such diverse policies as raising the age of entry from 5 or 6 to 7 or 8 so that primary school leavers would be old enough to go into farming on completing their education; integrating schools and farms in such a way that children could learn modern practices and become aware of the fact that their living standards and those of the nation as a whole depended on agriculture; rearranging the school calendar so that students could help their fellow villagers at times of peak labour demands; and generally altering the curriculum so as to emphasize subjects more directly relevant to rural development (Nyerere 1965).

The restructuring of the school system encountered the same problems that had impeded the development of community education during the colonial era. The development of primary and secondary curricula in tune with both the economic and social goals of Tanzania and the market for wage labour will take some time. The right blend of vocational and literary subjects and the content of each has yet to be found. The educational system has an inherent inertia; radical change in education imposes new demands on teachers who are often only semi-skilled and not particularly open to changes which they see as a threat to their status in the local community. Changes in teacher training and retraining programmes for older teachers have been introduced, but it will take time for the effects to be felt (Cameron and Dodd 1970). The biggest obstacle to effective change remains the clash between private and social gains inherent in an economic system in which education is virtually the only means of access to positions of power and wealth. Primary education is valued only as a means of gaining access to secondary schools, not as a means of improving one's life in the rural areas:

In practice especially in the higher standards all efforts are at present directed toward success in the general entrance examination which opens the door to the secondary school. Secondary school education has become the chief object of parents, children and teachers in the primary schools. The teachers and the school tend to be judged according to the percentage of 'passes' in the general entrance examination. Yet only about 15 per cent of the pupils can actually be admitted to a secondary school or to one of the few vocational schools still open to primary school leavers.

Hardly anyone is willing to consider the possibility of his failing, until the day the results of the general entrance exams are known. This is the real tragedy of the G.E.E. The prize to be gained is too big to think of anything else. This is not only true of the children. The parents themselves expect the school to prepare their child not for life in the villages, but for success in the G.E.E. (Heijnen 1968).

The academic orientation of the curriculum suggests that the contribution of formal education to the productivity of small-scale farmers is likely to be marginal at best. Neither the government nor any other institution intervenes in rural areas in any way that would favour the income of the educated. It is therefore reasonable to conclude that if there are income differentials among rural educational sub-groups they are narrower than those among urban wage-earners and that the difference between rural and urban incomes is wider for the educated than for the uneducated. This conclusion supports our economic interpretation of the positive relationship between educational level and the propensity to migrate.

4. A PRELIMINARY ESTIMATE OF THE MIGRATION FUNCTION

We can now estimate a migration function which, when fully elaborated, will allow a more rigorous assessment of the relationship between migration, education, and the different economic opportunities of rural and urban areas. Most econometric studies attempting to incorporate the influence of education into the standard regional cross-section migration model do so by introducing the average level of education of the source area population into the estimating equation as an independent variable.[9] This procedure, however, limits the precision of the analysis, as there is no way to determine whether the greater propensity to migrate among the educated is due to greater responsiveness to an expected rural–urban income difference or to wider income differences for the educated.[10] By disaggregating the model by educational sub-groups, we can assess the economic and non-economic hypotheses put forward in explanation of the association between educational level and propensity to migrate (Levy and Wadycki 1974, Bowles 1970).

The first function estimated is:

$$M_{ruea} = F(W_{urea}, DIST_{ru}, UP, E_{reau})$$

where the notation is as in the Introduction and e is education group,

[9] For example, see Beals et al. 1967, Sahota 1968, and Schultz 1971.
[10] These studies also have a problem with the specification of the independent variable. A significant association between regional average educational levels and migration rates is not sufficient to confirm that the educated have a higher propensity to move to town than the uneducated. The relationship may be due to higher mobility among all members of the regional population, educated and uneducated alike, with education serving as a proxy for an unspecified independent variable with which it is highly correlated.

a current age or year of arrival in town,and *UP* is population of the urban receiving area.[11] The wage variable is defined as the algebraic difference between urban wages and average rural incomes, i.e. $W_{urea} = W_{uea} - W_{rea}$. There are 108 observations, with each observation corresponding to the migration rate between a given region and a given urban area associated with a given educational level and a given age or year of arrival.[12]

The stratification by age requires explanation. While the greater readiness of younger rural residents to migrate is recognized as a virtually universal characteristic of migratory movements,[13] earlier applications of human capital theory to migrant behaviour have tended to treat age differences in migration rates in a way that introduced a systematic bias into the analysis. The source of the bias is that, in estimating responses by age to economic and non-economic factors, migration rates derived from a current age profile of the migrant population in a given year are related to the same set of independent variables. But age selectivity implies that the older the urban resident who was born and raised elsewhere, the longer he has been in town. Rural–urban differentials and employment probabilities change. Since it is likely that migrants form their expectations on the basis of levels of cost and returns at the time of migration (or, if there are communication lags, during some period prior to migration), using observations of the economic variables from years after the date of migration will yield biased estimates.[14] When only contemporary data on the economic variables are available, only recent migrants should be included in the numerator of the migration rate. The procedure adopted here minimizes the

[11] The sources of data and method of generating the variables for this and all subsequent regressions are discussed in detail in Appendix B.
[12] There are three rural regions, three urban areas, four educational groups, and three age or year of arrival groups.
[13] The age structure of rural–urban migrants in Tanzania is documented and its determinants analysed in Chapter III.
[14] This potential bias is ignored by Sahota 1968 and Schultz 1971. In their econometric studies they attribute the relatively higher coefficients on the economic variables for young migrants to factors, such as longer remaining time in remunerative activities, which constitute explanations for a higher degree of responsiveness among young rural residents. However, as a consequence of age selectivity, the young age groups of the urban stock of migrants are predominantly earlier arrivals. But in these studies age-specific migration rates are all related to economic variables from the same year. Therefore a wider gap between gross and net migration rates among relatively early arrivals and a widening of income differentials over time may be a more significant explanation of the differentials in coefficients.

bias by interpreting age-specific migration rates from a time series perspective and disaggregating the independent variables by time periods. This allows age-specific migration rates to be linked with observations on the dependent variables from the appropriate time period.[15]

Employing ordinary least squares to estimate a simple linear form of the migration function,[16] we obtained

$$M = -0.014 + 0.00039 - 0.00073 DIST + 0.0027 UP$$
$$(-0.54) \quad (7.89) \quad (-1.97) \quad (6.22)$$
$$(1.76) \quad (-1.13) \quad (0.70)$$

$$\bar{R}^2 = 0.48 \quad \text{d.f.} = 104.$$

The first figure below each coefficient estimate is the t statistic for the null hypothesis that the coefficient value is zero, while the second figure is the elasticity calculated at mean values of the variables. All the coefficients are of the expected sign and are, at a minimum, significant at the 5 per cent level using a one tailed t test. The strength of the wage variable is indicated by the high t statistic, 7.89. When the equation is re-estimated[17] with the omission of this variable the proportion of the variation in the migration rate explained by the regression falls from approximately 0.50 to 0.17. The elasticity of the wage variable (1.76) can be further broken down into separate figures for urban and rural wages. Assuming that all variables remain constant while only the wage in question varies, an elasticity of 2.0 for urban wages and −0.3 for rural wages is calculated. These quantitative results should be used cautiously because the elasticities cannot be expected to be valid except near the mean of the variables. Nevertheless the strength of the results emphasizes that urban–rural wage differentials, especially for higher educational groups, are an important factor in the variation in migration rates.

[15] See Appendix B for a detailed explanation of how the relationship between the current age of migrants and year of arrival was specified.

[16] A double log form of the function and other specifications of the wage variable, including a wage ratio $w = W_u/W_r$, were tried. For the log function zero observations were replaced by small numbers. In all cases the estimates were consistent with the reported regression.

[17] See Barnum and Sabot 1975.

5. THE ESTIMATED MIGRATION FUNCTION WITH ADDITION OF EMPLOYMENT PROBABILITY

Given full employment in the receiving area, a migrant who comes to town can be sure he will find a job after a minimal period of searching. When there is surplus labour in the receiving areas and wages are not downwardly flexible, expected economic returns to migration will depend not only on the difference between urban and rural income, but also on the probability of finding a job within a specified period. Here the presumption is that the rural resident will discount the potential returns to migration by the probability of finding a job or will add to the total direct costs of migration the opportunity costs, measured in terms of rural income forgone, and the additional costs of maintenance involved in living in town, while waiting for a job. The expectation of doubled earnings arising from the move from agricultural self-employment to urban wage employment may be an inadequate inducement to migrate if the probability of finding employment within the period that a rural resident is prepared to spend searching for a job is less than half. There is surplus labour in Tanzania's urban areas and it has been increasing during the period with which we are concerned. Moreover, as we have seen, rural–urban wage differentials have not been adjusted downwards as a consequence but have on the contrary been rising. Since the crucial assumptions hold, the theory suggests that migration rates will be influenced by employment probabilities.

The probability of a rural resident with educational level e finding a job in time period a is defined as:

$$P_{ea} = \frac{\gamma_{ea}}{u_{ea}/(1 - u_{ea})}$$

where γ_{ea} is the net rate of growth of employment for the sub-group and u_{ea} is the sub-group's rate of unemployment. Before introducing employment probability (or urban expected income) into the migration function, we consider the differences among educational groups and the time trends of each of these components of the variable. The rate of growth of employment for an educational sub-group can be viewed as a function of the rate of growth of occupations employing the sub-group, weighted by the distribution of the sub-group among these occupations, and of changes in the education–occupation relationship. (See Appendix B.)

As we have seen, the post-war period has been one of rapid

structural change, reflected in changes in industrial and occupational wage-labour demand. Agricultural wage employment declined, largely as a consequence of higher wages and a change in the system of labour use on the sisal estates, but also because investment shifted from the rural to the urban areas. Employment in the transport, public utilities, construction and service sectors has expanded, but the most noteworthy growth of employment opportunities has been in manufacturing and government. In the sectors in which employment has expanded most rapidly, labour demand has been relatively skill-intensive. Table 4.7 shows the change in the distribution of urban employment among three occupational categories. From 1955 to 1971 the proportion of unskilled workers in the urban African wage labour force declined from 56 to 36 per cent, the proportion of skilled workers declined marginally, and the proportion of white-collar workers increased sixfold, from 5 to 30 per cent. Since the highly skilled occupations employ the most highly educated workers, the changes shown here mean that employment growth rates are higher for the educated, a pattern reinforced by changes in the relationship between education and occupation levels. As we show in the next chapter, the rapid expansion of the school system resulted in an oversupply of educated workers relative to demand in high level occupations. The educated consequently filtered down into lower level occupations, displacing the uneducated and progressively squeezing them out of the urban labour market.

TABLE 4.7
Occupational distribution of urban African labour force in Tanzania 1955–71

	Unskilled	Skilled	White-collar
1955	0·56	0·39	0·05
1957	0·56	0·39	0·05
1960	0·52	0·38	0·10
1962	0·49	0·37	0·14
1964	0·46	0·37	0·18
1966	0·42	0·36	0·21
1968	0·40	0·35	0.25
1970	0·37	0·34	0·28
1971	0·36	0·34	0·30

Source: See Appendix B.

Table 4.8 indicates that in each of the three sub-periods with which
we are concerned the rate of growth of employment has consistently
been higher for higher educational levels. In addition, the difference
in growth rates between the educated and the uneducated has
increased: while the rate of growth of employment for Standards 5–
8 and Forms 1+ leavers was higher in 1966–70 than in 1955–60,
employment growth rates for Standards 1–4 and the uneducated
declined.

The pattern of employment growth rates does not necessarily
imply a similar pattern of employment probabilities. If unemployment rates are higher for groups with rapid rates of employment
growth, the probability of employment for these groups may be no
lower than for groups with lower rates of employment growth. In
Tanzania's urban areas the unemployment trends partially counter-
balance the time trends in employment growth rates, increasing
among primary and post-primary leavers and decreasing among the
uneducated (Barnum and Sabot 1976). Nevertheless as Tables 4.9
and 4.10 show, urban employment probabilities and expected wages
increase with educational level. During the period 1955–70 the
average probability of finding an urban job was 1·4, 4·0, and 7·1
times that of rural residents with no formal education for Std. 1–4
leavers, Std. 5–8 leavers, and post-primary leavers, respectively, and
their average expected wage 1·6, 5·7, and 13·9 times that of rural
residents with no formal education. The hypothesis that the
probability of finding an urban job is an independent influence on
the migration decision is supported by the educational structure of
employment probabilities. More substantial support comes from the
econometric analysis.

TABLE 4.8
Estimated urban wage employment growth rates by education 1955–70

Period	Average annual growth rates (%)			
	No formal education	Std. 1–4	Std. 5–8	Forms 1+
1955–60	1·3	2·5	3·1	2·9
1960–6	0·9	2·0	3·5	3·8
1966–70	0·7	1·9	3·4	3·5

Source: See Appendix B.

TABLE 4.9

Average probability of finding an urban job (within four months) for four education groups in three time periods: Tanzanian males

(%)

Date	No formal education	Standard 1–4	Standard 5–8	Form 1 and up	Aggregated over education
1955–60	0·12	0·22	0·78	1·0	0·25
1960–6	0·16	0·21	0·71	1·0	0·34
1966–70	0·10	0·19	0·47	1·0	0·33
Aggregated over time periods 1955–70	0·14	0·20	0·56	1·0	0·30

Source: See Appendix B.

TABLE 4.10

Estimated urban expected wages by education 1955–70

Period	Monthly expected wages (employment probability × average wages)							
	No formal education		Std. 1–4		Std. 5–8		Forms 1+	
	Sh	Index	Sh	Index	Sh	Index	Sh	Index
1955–60	13	100	26	100	117	100	200	100
1960–6	29	223	40	153	176	150	336	168
1966–70	23	177	46	177	150	128	448	224
1955–70	25		39		142		347	

Source: See Appendix B.

With the income variable redefined as the difference between the expected urban wage and the average rural income, i.e. $\bar{W}_{urea} = (P_{uea})(WU_{uea}) - WR_{rea}$, where P is employment probability, the re-estimated equation is:

$$M = 0·043 + 0·003\bar{W} - 0·00074DIST + 0·0022$$
$$(1·90) \quad (9·36) \quad (-2·12) \quad (5·48)$$
$$(0·57) \quad (-1·14) \quad (0·58)$$

$$\bar{R}^2 = 0·55 \quad d.f. = 103.$$

A comparison of this result with the equation in which the wage variable is the actual wage differential shows that the use of expected wages has resulted in an increase in the $\bar{R}^2$ from 0·48 to 0·55 and a higher t statistic on the wage variable. On the assumption that all variables remain constant except the one in question, an estimated

elasticity of 0·7 is obtained for probability and the urban wage and
−0·25 for the rural wage. These may seem modest values for the
elasticities, but when one recalls that they apply to the migration
rate measured with a rural base it is clear that they are substantial.
Because Tanzania has a predominantly rural population, even a
small change in the migration rate results in a substantial increase in
the number of migrants as a proportion of the urban labour force.
These findings emphasize the importance of job probability in
determining the flow of rural–urban migration.

6. PSYCHIC COSTS AND RETURNS AND THE MIGRATION FUNCTION

There appears to be a strong association between migration rates
and differing economic returns to migration for educational sub-
groups of the rural population, but the possibility that non-economic
(or psychic) returns also vary with level of education must not be
overlooked. Although the distinction is to a large extent arbitrary,
for heuristic purposes we can consider psychic costs and psychic
returns separately.

One hypothesis is that rural residents with formal education have
a lower level of psychic costs because those who attend school are
often pre-selected by the openness to change of their parents, their
village, or their tribe. The regional distribution of education varies
widely in Tanzania, from 13 per cent of the adult population with
some education in Shinyanga to 50 per cent in Kilimanjaro. These
differences reflect variations in past levels of mission and government
activity and in levels of cash income, which determined the
feasibility of local educational development. The higher level of
education in the Kilimanjaro region may also reflect the fact that the
Chagga were more receptive than other tribes to the changes in
methods of child-rearing and in the approach to the acquisition of
knowledge and to socialization. It is likely that people who had
adapted to the changes associated with western formal education
would also be able to make the adaptations to their traditional
modes of behaviour that migration required.

The educational process itself contributes to the formation of
values and of attitudes towards change and traditional society;
indeed, this was one of the explicit aims of education during the
colonial era. Missionaries wanted to produce 'sincere, educated
Christians, of whom the more the merrier', the emphasis being on

'Christian' rather than 'educated' (Cameron and Dodd 1970). For teachers, increasing the student's potential control over his environment as a means of improving material conditions was often less important than inculcating the values of the alien society the teachers represented, if only because they identified Christianity with western civilization and tended to view it as a necessary condition of progress. Government schools did not try to distinguish between education as a means of increasing an individual's store of knowledge and developing his rational thought process and education as a means of adapting Africans to a fundamentally alien way of life.

The socialization aspect of education is to a certain extent inevitable. The economic transformation desired by the current nationalist leadership implies a reordering of values and social *mores.* Although Africanization of the curriculum has meant the substitution of African history and culture for such absurdities as memorizing the names of English kings or reciting lines of *Romeo and Juliet,* for most children education is still an introduction to a new world. In many regions in Tanzania, most of the children in school have parents who received no schooling whatever, and for them the leap is greatest. The student is exposed to a world in which obligations and commitments are different from those with which he is familiar. In so far as education makes it easier for the student to move out of his familiar environment and extract himself from the web of traditional relationships and obligations, it reduces the psychic costs of migration. Similarly, psychic costs are reduced to the extent that education eases the adjustment to the unfamiliar environment that the city represents. Education may do this simply because the student has already, in going to school, faced a social transition and been introduced to urban behaviour.

Because education reduces the psychic costs or increases the psychic returns (for example, by teaching the student to place a higher value on manufactured than traditional goods) associated with migration, we would expect a higher rate of migration for educated than for uneducated rural residents. There is an insignificant urban wage difference between Standards 1–4 leavers and the uneducated; the probability of finding urban employment is much the same for both groups; and there is no reason to believe there are significant differences in rural income between the completely uneducated and the lowest educational group. A rate of urban migration among Standards 1–4 leavers three times that among the uneducated suggests that education influences the rate of migration through non-economic as well as through economic factors.

By disaggregating the dependent and independent variables by educational sub-groups we are able to use estimates of the migration function to see whether education inclines rural residents to migrate independently of its effect on economic opportunity. The two regressions estimated above constrained the coefficients on the independent variables to be the same for each education sub-group, implying that the response of rural residents to the hypothetical determinants of migration is independent of education. Alternatively the disaggregated data can be used to estimate separate equations for each sub-group and to examine the relationship between the coefficients of the individual equations to see if they are statistically different. For convenience we put the two lower educational categories (no formal education and Standards 1–4) together as one group, with the two upper categories Standards 5–8 and Forms 1 and above) in a second group. Because the range of wage data for these two groups does not overlap but shows a distinct gap at a rural–urban expected wage differential of approximately sh 25, we examine the behaviour of the estimated migration function at this point. The problem is illustrated in Fig. 4.4, where the slope is determined by the coefficient of the expected wage variable and the vertical intercept is calculated by using the mean values of the non-wage variables times their coefficients. Are the migration functions for the two groups best expressed by the straight line AC, the kinked line ABD, or the discontinuous segments AB and EF or EG?

Re-estimating the migration function with the data pooled into the two educational groups, the null hypothesis that the wage response of the two educational groups is the same was accepted and the null hypothesis that the two segments intersect at $\bar{W} = 25$ was accepted. The estimated equation is:

$$M = 0.07 - 0.420 + 0.0002\bar{W} - 0.0005 W{\cdot}D$$
$$(2{\cdot}47)(-1{\cdot}04) \qquad (1{\cdot}93)(-0{\cdot}15)$$
$$- 0.0011 DIST + 0.0008 DIST{\cdot}D + 0.0043 UP - 0.0038 P{\cdot}D$$
$$(-2{\cdot}63)(1{\cdot}27) \qquad\qquad (8{\cdot}54)(-4{\cdot}98)$$

$\bar{R}^2 = 0.66$ d.f. $= 100$

where D is the dummy variable taking the value of 1 if the observation is in the lower educational group and 0 if the observation is in the higher educational group. This equation effectively allows

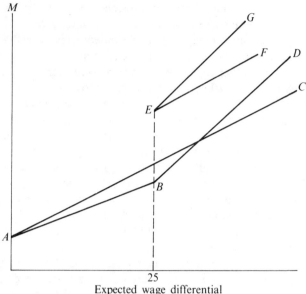

FIG. 4.4

the recovery of the two separate equations. A hypothesis of constant slopes on the wage variable was accepted with an F statistic of 0.023 (at a 5 per cent significance level the critical value is $F_{1100} = 3.94$, where the subscripts indicate the relevant degrees of freedom). A hypothesis of uniformity, between educational levels, for the non-wage coefficients was rejected ($F = 12.01$, F_3, $100 = 2.70$). Finally the intersection of the two segments in Fig. 4.5 was rejected and the hypothesis of discontinuity was accepted ($F = 4.80$, $F_{1100} = 3.94$). The accepted shape of the migration function is drawn in Fig. 4.5, which indicates the discontinuous jump in the migration rate for the upper educational group. This confirms the third alternative illustrated in §1 above, in which the differential in migration rates between educational sub-groups is due both to movement along a migration function reflecting differentials in economic opportunities and a shift in the function, reflecting the influence of non-economic factors. These results lend support to the hypothesis that, in addition to its effect on expected income differentials, education influences the rate of migration through its influence on the utility function of rural residents. The analysis does not support the hypothesis that

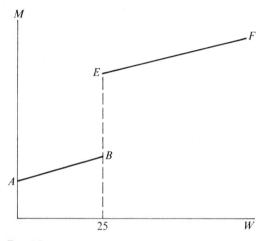

FIG. 4.5

education influences the response of rural residents to differing economic opportunities in a way related to the size of the difference, for example through differences in the efficiency of labour market communications networks.

7. SUMMARY

The propensity of rural residents to migrate to urban areas increases with their level of education. We have shown that the two, economic and non-economic, explanations for this relationship, generally presented as competitors, are actually complements.

On the one hand, the selection by relatively high-paying occupations of relatively highly educated workers, and hence the positive association between urban wages and education level, together with the mismatch between the academic content of the curriculum and a vocation in small-scale agriculture and the absence of government or other discrimination in favour of educated peasants, strongly suggest that the difference between rural and urban incomes is greater the higher the level of a worker's education. Furthermore as a consequence of the increasing relative demand for skilled labour, a corollary of structural change, and an increase in educational requirements for even low-level jobs, the rate of growth of urban employment over the period 1955–71 is positively related to educational attainment, as is the ratio of job openings to job seekers.

Not only does the regression analysis support the hypothesis that differences in economic returns to migration contribute to the explanation of the variance in migration rates, but also, with regard to the migration function, the significance of the independent variable measuring the probability of urban employment is a successful test of the inter-sectoral misallocation model of urban unemployment.

On the other hand, the likelihood that the education process contributes to the formation of values and attitudes that are urban oriented and that the school system is selective of children from families more receptive to change suggests that the educated rural residents are more responsive to spatial differences in economic opportunities than the uneducated. The regression analysis supports the hypothesis that the higher rate of migration among the educated is due in part to a shift of, rather than simply movement along, the migration function.

V

EDUCATIONAL OPPORTUNITIES, OCCUPATION, AND MIGRATION

THE quantitative analysis lends confirmation to the hypothesized positive relationship between the rural–urban income differential and the migration rate. When we consider the time trends of these variables disaggregated by educational group, however, an anomaly is apparent. The growth of educational opportunities and the increase in the supply of educated workers compared to employment opportunities in white-collar and skilled occupations explain the relatively low increase in the migration rates of uneducated rural dwellers, despite similar rates of increase in the rural–urban income differential for all education groups.

1. URBAN WAGE CHANGES AND MIGRATION RATES

There is no *a priori* reason to expect the rates of increase of wages to be the same for the four educational sub-groups. Assuming that wages are fixed according to the job and not according to the credentials of the workers, the average wage for each educational sub-group can be viewed as a function of its distribution among occupations and of the occupational wage structure. Since, as noted in the previous chapter, different factors influence wage levels in the lower and upper segments of the occupational scale, variation in wage increases among educational groups is to be expected. There may be mechanisms in Tanzania that preserve the occupational structure so that the initial point of impact is irrelevant to the rate of wage increases; even so, changes in the occupation–education relationship could result in variations in the rate of increase of wages among different educational groups. Table 5.1 indicates that, despite expectations to the contrary, the rate of increase in wages between 1955–61 and 1962–6, and between the latter period and 1967–70 was roughly the same for all educational groups. Thus we would expect roughly similar increases in migration rates for all groups.

Table 5.2 indicates that while among rural residents with post-primary education the rate of urban migration in the period 1967–70 was 1·8 times what it was in the 1955–1961 period, an increase

TABLE 5.1
Index of average wages for educational sub-groups 1955–1970

Period	Index of Average Wages			
	No formal education	Std. 1–4	Std 5–8	Form 1 +
1955–61	100	100	100	100
1962–6	170	160	165	168
1967–70	217	204	215	224

Source: See Appendix B.

TABLE 5.2
Rates of rural–urban migration for four education groups in three time periods: Tanzanian males
(%)

Current age	Arrival[a] period	No formal education	Std. 1–4	Std. 5–8	Form 1 and up
35 and above	1955–61	0·012	0·030	0·106	0·180
25–34	1962–6	0·013	0·038	0·144	0·399
20–4	1967–70	0·014	0·067	0·277	0·318

[a] Period in which the majority of migrants in the age sub-group arrived in town.
Source: See Appendix B.

consistent with the evidence of widening rural–urban income differentials, there is a significant variation in the rate of increase in different educational groups. Among primary leavers the rate of migration was 2·6 times as high in the more recent period. The increase in the migration rate for those with a Standard 1–4 education is 1·6 times that of the earlier period. Uneducated rural residents do not follow the pattern of rapidly increasing rates of migration. The migration rate of the uneducated in the period 1967–70 was only 1·2 times what it had been in the period 1955–61, and further disaggregation reveals a number of regions in which the rate of migration actually declined (Barnum and Sabot 1976).

Changes in the opportunity costs of the two groups do not seem to provide an explanation for the different responses of primary leavers and the uneducated to the same increase in urban wages. There is no evidence that uneducated rural dwellers increased their income faster than educated ones, or, given the stagnation of average rural incomes, of the corollary absolute decline of the incomes of rural educated workers. Before dismissing changes in economic opportunities as an explanation of changes in migration rates, consider the following model of the urban labour market. In this model the migration rate of the uneducated declines relative to that of the educated, despite a constant rural–urban income differential for the uneducated. The decline is caused by the expansion of the supply of educated workers at a faster rate than demand in high-level occupations and the consequent filtering-down of the educated into lower level jobs, which results in the displacement of the uneducated from these jobs and, ultimately, from the urban labour market.

2. FILTERING-DOWN AND DISPLACEMENT: THE MODEL

Changes in the occupational structures of urban wages and in the rates of growth of urban employment have straightforward implications for expected urban wages and hence for migration rates. When wages for the skilled occupations of educated workers rise in comparison with those for lower level occupations, expected net returns to migration increase for educated rural residents. The expectation is that the difference in migration rates between the two groups will also increase. Similarly, a relatively rapid increase in employment opportunities in skilled occupations will increase the probability of finding a job, and hence the expected returns to migration of educated rural residents. The impact of an increased supply of educational opportunities, and thus an increase in the number of school leavers, on expected returns and migration rates is not obvious. Despite the probable narrowing of the difference in urban wages between the educated and the uneducated, we would expect such increases to contribute to a widening of the difference in migration rates between the two groups.

To demonstrate this, it is necessary to extend the simple model of migration and unemployment to include two urban sectors, the skilled and unskilled, and two types of labour, the educated and the uneducated.[1] The skilled, unskilled, and agricultural sectors are

---

[1] A model similar to the one presented here was developed independently by Fields (1974) as a means of analysing the response of private demand for education to increases in the supply of educated workers.

characterized by rigid wage differentials such that $W_s > W_u > W_a$. It is also assumed that education is the criterion used to ration jobs between competing job seekers; that employers reserve skilled jobs for the educated and give preference to the educated even when hiring for unskilled jobs; that any expansion of the educational system occurs in the rural sector; and that holding either an agricultural or an unskilled job precludes effective search for a skilled job. Figure 5.1 relates the expected wage for school leavers and the uneducated on the vertical axis to the number of educated members of the labour force on the horizontal axis.

Let us first consider the consequence of an increase in the number of educated workers for the expected income of school leavers. Assume that there is a shortage of educated workers in skilled jobs and the expansion of the educated labour force is confined to the range $0-L_1$, the number of skilled jobs. Thus the probability of employment in a skilled job, p_s, defined as the ratio of job openings to job seekers, is one and the expected wage, $p_s \cdot W_s$, remains constant at the level of the skilled wage, and all educated workers enter skilled employment. Any increase in the number of school leavers beyond L_1 results in a surplus of educated workers. The probability of an educated worker finding a skilled job declines to a level below unity. However, the initial surplus of educated workers will 'voluntarily' enter unemployment as the expected wage in skilled employment still exceeds the wage prevailing either in unskilled or

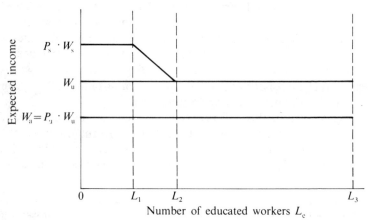

FIG. 5.1

in agricultural employment, where the probability of an educated worker obtaining employment is unity. L_1–L_2 is the number of unemployed educated workers necessary to depress p_s sufficiently that $p_s . W_s = W_u$. In the range L_1–L_2 any increase in L_e is associated with a decline in p_s and hence in the expected wage for educated workers. If the educated labour force expands beyond L_2, then income is maximized for the additional educated workers by their 'filtering down' into unskilled employment and receiving W_u. As long as there are more unskilled jobs than educated workers, the expected wage is W_u, as the probability of an unskilled worker obtaining a skilled job is, by assumption, zero and employment in the unskilled sector is assured. Up to the point, L_3, where the educated fill all the urban jobs, all the educated participate in the urban labour force only. The average wage of employed educated workers is reduced as filtering-down and displacement proceed.

Now let us consider the consequence of an increase in the supply of educated workers for the expected urban income of an uneducated resident. The increase in the supply of educated workers in the range 0–L_2, where all the educated enter either skilled employment or unemployment, has no impact on the expected wage of the uneducated; nor does the filtering-down affect the expected income of an uneducated worker. Even when only the uneducated are employed in unskilled jobs, given the difference between W_u and W_a, the supply of uneducated workers exceeds the number of urban employment opportunities. When this is so, the unemployment of the uneducated has so far reduced the probability of an uneducated worker finding an unskilled job, p_u, that the expected urban wage equals the agricultural wage $p_u . W_u = W_a$. Beyond L_2 the filtering-down of educated workers into unskilled employment reduces the number of urban jobs available to uneducated workers. However, there is no further decline in the expected wage of the uneducated (p_u remains constant) because, for the uneducated workers who are 'displaced' from the urban labour force, it is income-maximizing behaviour to return to the agricultural sector. The number of urban uneducated unemployed is reduced as L_e increases, so that $p_u . W_u$ remains constant.

Figure 5.2 illustrates the effect of an increase in the number of educated workers on migration rates, defined as the ratio of workers in town to workers in the countryside (where total labour force and employment are constant and all jobs are presumed to turn over

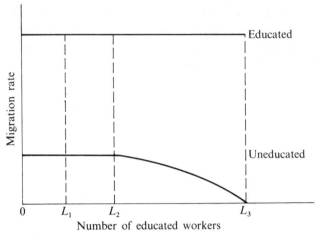

Number of educated workers

FIG. 5.2

every period). When educated workers exceed skilled jobs, beyond L_1, expected urban income for the educated declines from the skilled to the unskilled wage. However, since the unskilled wage exceeds rural income, all educated workers continue to move to town, that is, the migration rate remains constant at unity as the number of educated workers increases throughout the process of filtering down. It is only beyond L_3, when the educated have filled all the unskilled jobs, that a proportion of the educated will enter rural employment. For the uneducated, the number of unskilled jobs available is reduced once filtering-down begins, beyond L_2, and the number of educated in unskilled jobs increases. This in turn lowers the number of urban job seekers necessary to maintain the equilibrium condition $p_i W_u = W_a$ and the urban migration rate of uneducated workers declines. Thus, while educational differentials in average wages are reduced, the educational differential in migration rates is widened by an increase in educational opportunities. As the supply of educated workers expands and progressively encroaches on the unskilled labour market, the uneducated are squeezed out.

3. THE GROWTH OF EDUCATIONAL OPPORTUNITIES

We begin our assessment of the relevance to Tanzania of the filtering-down and displacement model by examining the expansion of the educational system. The high demand for educational opportunities during the colonial period was derived from the demand for the extremely scarce white-collar urban employment opportunities. Sending a son to school meant giving him a chance of a standard of living previously beyond reach of all but a few aristocrats and traders. Families of children who went to school and then to town probably fared better than families whose sons settled down to a peasant's life or went off periodically to the sisal estates. The demand for education increased as high wage employment opportunities grew, in step with the number of people leaving school in any year. A primary school certificate was virtually a guarantee of an urban wage job and, often, of one that required no manual labour. A secondary school education offered the sure promise of a place in the lower levels of the Civil Service or a job at an equivalent level (Iliffe in Kimambo and Temu 1969).

Before 1907, tribal societies in Tanzania had responded to the German intrusion with what Iliffe (1969) has termed a 'local compromise'. Though they had been defeated in military conflict by the Germans many times since 1870, the tribes preserved their traditional organization and maintained relations with Europeans in terms of existing political practice. There was no 'Christian Revolution' as among the Ganda and Lozi, no emergence of a modernizing section of the aristocracy, and no great enthusiasm for western education. During the Maji Maji uprising of 1905, intertribal rivalries were set aside and a final attempt was made to expel the ever more pervasive colonial presence. All military opposition ceased in 1907, after two years of war that involved a large part of Tanzania and cost some 75 000 lives (Iliffe 1969). The situation was now radically altered: traditional leadership was seriously under-mined and the technological inferiority of African society dramati-cally emphasized. The attitude toward European institutions changed: overt resistance and diplomacy were replaced by a willingness to adapt and the recognition of the need for internal change. Western education was now seen as the means by which Africans could change their society in order both to 'improve' it and to be able to deal with Europeans on their own terms (Iliffe 1969). In the immediate post-World War II period the need for increased educational opportunities became a rallying-point of the nationalist movement. 'We Africans want more opportunities; the Administer-ing Authority [Great Britain] tells us that we have not the necessary educational qualifications. But who holds the key to our proper

education? The Administering Authority itself.' (Gwassa in Kimambo and Temu 1969.)

The growing demand for education is an important factor in the
dramatic expansion of the educational system over the past decade
and a half. In Tanzania, as in most other developing countries, the
provision of education is predominantly the responsibility of the
government. The educated sons of the men who first recognized the
value of western education led Tanzania to Independence and
assumed control of government policy. Their personal success and
the political benefits that accrued to the nation as a whole were
associated with their investment in education, and they were
sensitive to the political volatility of confined excess demand for
school places.

The decision to expand the supply of educational opportunities
was supported by economic and social arguments. Investment in
Tanzania's human capital was expected to bring significant returns
by enhancing the productive capacity of workers and preparing
larger numbers of Africans for administrative and professional jobs.
Acute shortages of African personnel in a wide range of skilled
occupations and the consequent need to import expatriates to fill the
gaps reinforced this view. The returns to the government investment
would be not only economic: education would also contribute to a
sense of national identity, spread the ideology of development,
improve the functioning of democratic institutions, and remove the
constraints placed on progressive change by illiteracy and ignorance.

No attempts were made to quantify the social benefits or costs of
education. The latter include the value of resources used for the
construction and maintenance of school facilities and the training of
teachers; the value of output forgone by employing highly-educated
labour in teaching; the output forgone by having people old enough
to participate in the labour force in school; and, if the government
faced a rigid budget constraint, the output forgone from other
government projects sacrificed to the need for subsidies to fill the gap
between school fees and the actual costs of education. However,
there appeared to be little doubt that the returns would justify the
costs. Following Independence, Tanzania joined with other African
nations at Addis Ababa in setting a target for universal primary
education by 1980 and set an independent goal of self-sufficiency in
high-level manpower by 1984.

This entailed a large increase in the resources for primary

education, and even greater increases in expenditure on secondary schools. Enrolment in colonial government schools and expenditure on education per capita were considerably lower in Tanzania than in other British African colonies (as indicated in Table 5.3), which made the task of the new government even greater. As Table 5.4 indicates, education appropriations have been a growing proportion of a fast-growing budget.

4. FILTERING-DOWN AND DISPLACEMENT: THE EVIDENCE

The increase in educational output at all levels upset the balance between educated workers and employment opportunities. The extent of the adjustment problem for the urban labour market can be crudely assessed by a comparison of the relationship between the number of school leavers and employment opportunities in 1964 and 1970. Table 5.5 indicates that during this period university output increased by over one-third, outputs from Forms 4 and 6 nearly

TABLE 5.3
Education in three African colonies 1935

Category	Gold Coast	Northern Rhodesia	Tanganyika
per capita expenditure (£)	0·37	0·09	0·05
per cent of school-age children in government and government-aided schools	7·50	9·00	2·80

Source: Stephens 1968.

TABLE 5.4
Government expenditure on education 1938–69

Year	Money expenditure on education (£m)	% of total expenditure
1938	0·094	4·0
1947	0·269	4·8
1953	1·390	8·5
1961	5·010	15·4
1968/69	11·900	17·5

Sources: Stephens 1968, Knight 1966.

doubled, while Standard 7 output increased sevenfold. The total number of students receiving Standard 7, Form 2, or Form 4 certificates or university degrees increased from 13 933 in 1964 to 76 335 in 1970. Not all these students entered the labour force. A significant proportion of those below university level went on to higher levels of education. This proportion declined from 59 per cent in 1969 to 13 per cent in 1970, and is largely accounted for by the increased competition for secondary school places. The more rapid expansion of the primary than the secondary system resulted in a decline from 45 per cent to 11 per cent in the proportion of Standard 7 leavers able to gain access to Form 1. The broadening of the base of the educational pyramid implies a decrease in the average number of years of education of school leavers entering the labour force and a higher rate of growth of the latter group—a nearly eightfold increase in six years—than of the total outputs from Standard 7, Forms 2 and 4, and University.

The virtual constancy of the annual increase in non-agricultural wage employment is in sharp contrast to the rise in the number of school leavers entering the labour force. In 1964 the ratio of educated labour force entrants to net employment expansion was 0·65. By

TABLE 5.5

The balance between educational output and non-agricultural wage employment opportunities 1964 and 1970

	1964	1970
University output (East African and Overseas)	421	679
Form 4 output	761	1 389
Entered university	506	758
Entered labour force	255	631
Form 2 output	3 630	6 713
Entered Form 5	780	1 584
Entered labour force	2 850	5 129
Standard 7 output	9 121	65 624
Entered secondary school	4 196	7 372
Entered labour force	4 925	58 252
Total entered labour force	8 451	64 691
Primary leavers entered labour force	4 925	58 252
Post-primary leavers entered labour force	3 326	6 439
Increase in non-agricultural employment	12 856	13 229

Sources: Tanzania, Bureau of Statistics 1971a; Tanzania, Central Statistical Bureau, various years.

1970 the ratio had increased more than sevenfold; there were 4·8 educated labour force entrants to every new wage job created. Whereas in 1969 the ratio of post-primary entrants to the total increase in wage employment was 0·26, by 1970 it had increased to 0·48. In 1970 white-collar jobs comprised only 33 per cent of urban wage jobs and the annual increment was unlikely to go significantly higher. Thus a white-collar job for secondary school leavers and an urban wage job for primary school leavers could no longer be assured.

Since rapid employment creation and short-term changes in rural–urban income differentials were not feasible, there was only one means by which the urban labour market could adjust to the excess supply of school leavers. Scarce employment opportunities were rationed among competing job seekers, with the level of education as the principle criterion. The educational level attained by migrants arriving in different years and moving into different levels of employment provides direct evidence of filtering-down and displacement. Table 5.6 allows us to assess the extent to which the education requirements of the three broad occupations have changed over time.[2]

White-collar jobs are at the top of the occupational preference ranking. The best-educated have always been concentrated in this category, and thus cannot be displaced by better-educated job applicants filtering down. We would expect, however, that the increase in post-primary education would result in some displacement of the less well educated from these jobs. This has in fact occurred. Fourteen per cent of all migrants in white-collar occupations in Dar es Salaam who arrived in 1955 or before had no formal education or Standards 1–4. Among 1971 arrivals in these occupations, only 1 per cent had no formal education and 5 per cent had Standards 1–4; Standard 7, secondary, and university leavers had corresponding increases in their share of white-collar employment. Government adoption of manpower planning for the high and medium level administrative, technical, and professional posts comprising a significant portion of white-collar jobs has limited the change in their educational composition. Rather than allow demand

[2] Upward mobility among migrants limits the usefulness of year of arrival as a proxy for time series data on the relationship between education and occupation for labour force entrants. However, the evidence on the employment history of current wage employees indicates that job changes are infrequent and rarely entail inter-occupational mobility.

TABLE 5.6

Migrant population: educational distribution of occupations by year of arrival
(%)

Year of arrival	Unskilled					Semi-skilled and Skilled					White collar				
	No formal educ.	Std. 1–4	Std. 5–8	Forms 1+	Total	No formal educ.	Std. 1–4	Std. 5–8	Forms 1+	Total	No formal educ.	Std. 1–4	Std. 5–8	Forms 1+	Total
1971	40	30	27	3	100	20	29	45	6	100	1	5	36	58	100
1970–69	40	30	27	3	100	21	28	46	5	100	2	5	36	57	100
1968–67	43	29	26	2	100	23	30	42	5	100	2	5	38	55	100
1966–65	46	28	24	2	100	26	31	38	5	100	2	8	35	55	100
1964–63	49	28	21	2	100	32	34	31	3	100	3	7	35	55	100
1962–61	50	29	19	2	100	32	34	31	3	100	4	8	33	55	100
1960–56	53	28	17	2	100	32	34	31	3	100	4	8	31	57	100
1955 & before	61	28	10	1	100	37	34	27	2	100	4	10	31	54	100

Source: NUMEIST 1971.

for secondary school places to determine supply, as has been the effective policy for primary schools, the government geared secondary school expansion to the labour requirements of medium and high level occupations. In the white-collar category the labour market was not required to adjust to a supply of secondary and post-secondary leavers grossly in excess of demand. In consequence, secondary school places were rationed, rather than high level employment positions, and the excess demand for secondary school places increased as primary education continued to grow.

Post-primary school leavers have tripled their share of employment in the semi-skilled and skilled category over the period 1955–71. If man-power planning had been completely effective, there would not have been such an increase. The rise is consistent with the evidence from Table 5.5 that the number of secondary school leavers entering the labour force annually exceeds the increase in white-collar employment opportunities. The most significant shift in the semi-skilled and skilled category has been the rise of primary school leavers from 27 to 45 per cent and the decline of the uneducated from 37 to 20 per cent. Increasing numbers of primary leavers are filtering down from white-collar occupations, displacing the uneducated from skilled and semi-skilled manual jobs. A similar phenomenon has characterized the unskilled occupations. The proportion of primary and post-primary leavers in this category has nearly tripled while the share held by the uneducated decreased from 61 to 40 per cent. A few years earlier a primary school leaver would not have accepted an unskilled labourer's job; in 1971 27 per cent of recent entrants to this category had completed a primary education.

Filtering-down and displacement occur only if the expectations of school leavers are flexible. Unemployment among school leavers in Asian countries is frequently explained by their rigid expectations. In Tanzania, school leavers appear to have adjusted their expectations when it became clear that the lower wage and prestige jobs now open to them paid better than the alternative jobs available.[3] School leavers are realistic; they are not refusing to do work which is 'beneath their dignity'.[4] Tanzanians also appear to be adjusting

---

[3] This finding of a high degree of flexibility of expectations in Tanzania in regard to occupations is consistent with evidence from Uganda and Ghana. See Hutton 1971.
[4] This does not imply that there is no unemployment among the educated. If employment in a lower job constrains the effectiveness of search for a better job, it may be economically rational to remain unemployed for a time in hope of obtaining a high wage job. See Section 2.

their expectations of the returns to primary education. The devaluation of a primary certificate in the urban labour market, together with the low probability of gaining a place in secondary school and the high opportunity cost of education, means that for many parents it is no longer worthwhile sending their children to school. For the first time a significant proportion, approximately 12 per cent nationwide, of seats in the classrooms of primary schools are empty.[5]

The filtering-down and displacement model provides an economic explanation for the lower response of uneducated than of educated rural residents to the same proportionate increase in the difference between rural and urban incomes. The different occupational distribution of migrants with the same level of schooling who arrived in different years supports the hypothesis that a dramatic increase in educational opportunities for a given occupational level produced an increase in the number of years of formal education required for that level. The increase in the difference in employment growth rates between the educated and the uneducated documented in Table 5.7 is also consistent with the model. While the rate of growth of employment was higher in the period 1966–70 than in the period 1955–60 for Standards 5–8 and Forms 1+ leavers, employment growth rates for Standards 1–4 leavers and the uneducated declined over time.[6]

Furthermore the model predicts that a significant increase in the supply of educated workers will result in a decline in the probability of obtaining a skilled job and in expected urban income. For the uneducated it predicts that an increase in educated workers and the filtering-down of the educated into unskilled occupations does not influence either the probability of obtaining an unskilled job or expected urban wages. However, the model assumes that the income difference between workers employed in the rural and urban sectors remains constant. A steady widening of the difference, as in Tanzania, is associated with an increase in the equilibrium level of unemployment, hence a decline in employment probability and, if there is a lag in the adjustment of the migration rate, an increase in expected urban income. This suggests that, if the educated labour

[5] Tanzania, Ministry of Economic Affairs and Development Planning, unpublished data.

[6] The shift in labour demand toward higher level occupations documented in Table 4.7 also contributed to the increase in the difference between the educated and uneducated in employment growth rates.

TABLE 5.7

Estimated urban wage employment growth rates by education 1955–70

Period	Average annual growth rates (%)			
	No formal education	Std. 1–4	Std. 5–8	Forms 1 +
1955–60	1·3	2·5	3·1	2·9
1960–6	0·9	2·0	3·5	3·8
1966–70	0·7	1·9	3·4	3·5

Source: See Appendix B.

force is growing faster than skilled jobs and filtering-down and displacement are occurring, if rural incomes are constant and wages in skilled and unskilled jobs are increasing at the same rate, the probability of employment for the educated would fall faster and expected urban income rise more slowly than for the uneducated. Tables 4.9 and 4.10 show that this is so. For uneducated workers the probability of employment declined by 0·02 from 1955 to 1970 while expected wages increased by 77 per cent. For Standard 5–8 leavers the probability of employment declined by 0·31 while expected wages rose by only 28 per cent.[7] Finally, the model predicts that the expected wage of the uneducated will equal the rural wage, and a comparison of Tables 4.10 and B.2 reveals that this is roughly the case.

5. SUMMARY

The gap between rural and urban incomes widened at about the same rate between 1955 and 1970 for the educated as for the uneducated and yet it was only educated rural residents who responded by increasing their rate of migration to urban areas. The explanation for this difference in behaviour, which runs counter to the prediction of the simple inter-sectoral misallocation model, lies in the government's decision, fundamentally political in nature though rationalized with economic arguments, to increase dramatically the number of educational opportunities. The consequent increased supply of educated labour force entrants was in excess of the demand in occupations that previously hired workers with such credentials. As a result while some relatively highly educated

[7] Note that the group Form 1 and above are outside the terms of the model because their probability of finding a job is unity.

workers remained in unemployment while waiting for preferred jobs, others filtered down into lower level occupations, in the process displacing workers with less years of schooling. The implications of this increase for changes in the distribution of income from generation to generation will depend largely on the incomes of households from which students are selected relative to incomes of households of the children who do not gain school places, information which is not yet available. The implications of this increase for the distribution of urban employment opportunities are, however, quite clear. Previously an uneducated worker could sustain some hope of gaining access to a relatively high-paying urban wage job because others like himself succeeded in the urban labour market. Now a child who does not gain entrance to primary school, and perhaps quite soon, entrance to secondary school as well, knows with virtual certainty that he is excluded from the islands of privilege that urban areas have become. Whether this change is for the good or is merely politically divisive depends in part on the degree of equity in the distribution of school places. A more important factor in the resolution of this issue is likely to be the extent to which the rise in average education levels in urban occupations represents capital deepening in the sense that workers with more education are more productive. In some occupations, at least, there is reason to doubt that this is the case.

VI

THE SOCIAL COSTS OF URBAN
SURPLUS LABOUR

THE resource costs of unemployment, the output forgone as a consequence of leaving idle part of the labour force, has an obverse side in the subjective cost, the loss of satisfaction which would have been derived from the consumption of the goods and services not produced. Assertions that urban surplus labour constitutes a grave social problem in developing countries are often based only on indirect evidence of migration from rural areas before there is growth of demand for labour in urban modern sectors. References to the direct measurement of unemployment are generally limited to the aggregate data collected by censuses or conventional labour force surveys, despite the importance of details of wealth, access to transfer payments, and length of time without work for an assessment of the subjective costs to the unemployed.[1] An equally serious defect is that such an approach generally abstracts from alternative models of how the labour market functions, or in this case malfunctions, despite the fact that the resource and subjective costs of a given quantum of unemployment can vary dramatically, depending upon the cause of the problem. In this chapter we assess the welfare costs of urban unemployment in Tanzania on the basis of an examination of the number and composition of the unemployed and in the light of the intersectoral misallocation model.

The measure of labour market imbalance devised in the industrial countries which entails the division of the total population into three distinct and mutually exclusive categories—those not in the labour force, the employed, and the unemployed—does not capture the full extent of the problems. In the labour markets of developing countries employment cannot be treated as a discrete homogeneous category, but, despite considerable analysis of what is meant by employed

---

[1] Pigou (1933) emphasized the relationship between the distribution of the loss of satisfaction and the subjective cost: '. . . the non-appearance of their [the unemployed] product involves a much greater loss . . . if it means that these men are reduced to the verge of starvation than if it means merely that the superfluities of some rich men are cut a little to finance the unemployed.'

surplus labour in rural areas (Kao *et al.* in Eicher and Witt 1964),
little has been done to clarify the concept in the context of urban
labour markets. The number of workers engaged in low income,
labour-intensive activities is sometimes used to demonstrate the
magnitude of the phenomenon; but in at least some segments of
urban 'informal sectors' the relatively low capital/labour ratios may
be due to relative factor prices different from those in the formal
sector, rather than to the absorption of excess supplies of labour.
The simple documentation of the proportion of workers with
incomes below a certain poverty level, as is done in most measures
of 'invisible underemployment', is not in any case a measure of
labour market imbalance, as it leaves unanswered the fundamental
question of the relationship between the income criterion applied
and the excess supply of urban labour. In this chapter we attempt to
clarify the definition of employed surplus labour and to measure its
magnitude by specifying an income criterion which gives underemployment the same normative implications with regard to labour
allocation as open unemployment.

1. OPEN UNEMPLOYMENT

Generally the unemployed, those involuntarily without paid employment, are identified with reference to some positive action which
they themselves have taken during a given period, such as going to
a government employment office, waiting in a job queue at a factory
gate, or writing a letter to a potential employer. Table 6.1 reveals
that when this criterion of active job search is applied, the aggregate
rate of open unemployment is only 8 per cent of the 'labour force'.

When the level of unemployment is low, the result only of labour
market friction, the direct costs of seeking a job do not influence the
decision whether or not to do so. With a significant level of urban
surplus labour and downwardly inflexible wages, however, the cost
of job search is likely to be introduced as a component of the labour
supply function. For some urban residents, though the wage of those
in employment will exceed the reserve price of their labour, the
expected net returns to active job search, the wage minus the
expected cost of job search (the latter increasing with the level of
surplus labour), will be less than their reserve price. This implies
that more people are willing to work at the going wage than are
engaged in active job search.

In order to adjust for the discouraged worker phenomenon and the consequent 'hidden unemployment', row 2 of Table 6.1 presents estimates of the rate of open unemployment based on a 'passive job search' criterion—an individual is considered a labour force participant if he (or she) indicated in the survey that he was looking for paid employment regardless of whether or not he had engaged in active job search within the reference period. The expression of the intention to work is a better indicator than active job search for willingness to work at the going wage, both because the former reflects the response to the cost of job search while the latter does not and because in African labour markets the job search process does not necessarily involve the formal channels noted above. Individuals frequently secure jobs on the basis of information from members of the family or from friends who are employed. Relaxing the job search criterion increases the aggregate urban unemployment rate in Tanzania by one-half to a total rate of 12 per cent.

TABLE 6.1
Rates of open unemployment in urban Tanzania in 1971 under alternative job search criteria and definitions of employment

	Males[a] %	Females[b] %	Total %
1. $100 \cdot \dfrac{Ua}{E+Ua}$	4·5	20·9	8·0
2. $100 \cdot \dfrac{Ua+Up}{E+Ua+Up}$	5·8	32·5	12·0
3. $100 \cdot \dfrac{Ua-Sa}{E+S+Ua}$	4·2	15·2	7·1
4. $100 \cdot \dfrac{Ua-Sa+Up-Sp}{E+S+Ua+Up}$	5·4	20·0	9·9

where Ua = Numbers without money income actively seeking paid employment
Up = Numbers without money income 'passively' seeking paid employment
E = Numbers in paid employment
S = Numbers producing goods for home consumption or barter
Sa = Numbers producing goods for home consumption or barter actively seeking paid employment
Sp = Numbers producing goods for home consumption or barter 'passively' seeking paid employment.

[a] 52·3% of total sample.
[b] 47·7% of total sample.
Source: NUMEIST 1971

The unemployment estimates in rows 1 and 2 are based on the assumption that all adults other than those who earn a cash income either are not in the labour force or are unemployed. Production for the market is thus the criterion for distinguishing between economic and non-economic activity for those not earning a wage. Although production for home consumption or barter is far less important in towns than in rural areas, 2 per cent of all adult urban males and 14 per cent of women grow crops to feed their families, or produce non-agricultural goods that never reach the market (*NUMEIST* 1971). Earners of low money incomes are counted among the employed and there is no apparent reason why producers of goods for home consumption or barter should be treated differently. Therefore in Table 6.1 rows 3 and 4, of those who produce goods for home consumption or barter, those who have been seeking work are transferred from among the unemployed to the employed, while those who have not been seeking work are transferred from 'out of the labour force' to the employed. For males the effect on their rate of unemployment is insignificant, for females the rate of unemployment decreases from 33 per cent to 20 per cent, lowering the aggregate rate of urban open unemployment in Tanzania from 12 per cent to 10 per cent.

2. THE COSTS OF UNEMPLOYMENT

What are the implications in terms of national output forgone of having one out of ten members of the urban labour force without work? In a situation of Keynesian demand deficiency the resource cost of unemployment is the difference between the gross national product in the recession period and what it would have been had GNP advanced smoothly from the pre- to the post-recession level. In the industrialized countries, estimates indicate that, because of a rise in the under-utilization of employed labour in a downturn, output in any year could be increased by more than the proportion that 'full employment' would have borne to actual employment. In Tanzania the resource cost of urban unemployment is considerably less than 10 per cent of national output for two reasons. Given the low level of urbanization and the absence of rural unemployment, the urban rate translates into a national rate of under 2 per cent. More fundamentally, there is no presumption of an accompanying under-utilization of capital or other factors where unemployment is the consequence of an intersectoral misallocation of labour. The social opportunity cost of an unemployed worker is given by the marginal product in the sector in which the surplus labour would be employed if optimally allocated; given the low level of productivity in rural areas the total increase in national output resulting from such a shift to full employment is likely to be considerably less than the ratio of full employment to the prevailing level of employment, which suggests that the resource cost of unemployment in Tanzania is 1 per cent or less of national income.[2]

This estimate rests on the assumption that an unemployed worker bases his decision to queue for a high wage job rather than accept employment at a lower income on an objective assessment of fixed and known alternatives, to each of which is attached known consequences. The implication is that the worker has *certain* knowledge not only of the structure of wages and the urban job opening rate, but of the number of competing job seekers as well. A more realistic assumption is that subjective knowledge is not a precise reflection of the objective situation and that the individual is searching for, rather than in possession of, complete and certain information regarding the labour market. If acquisition of information is like other economic activities in that specialization increases efficiency, then it can be economic for an individual to refuse low income employment and seek job information while unemployed. If all unemployment were of the search rather than the queuing variety, the unemployed would in fact be self-employed in information collection and, since such activity is necessary if labour is to be transferred from less to more productive uses, could be optimally allocated (Alchian in Phelps *et al.*). We cannot determine the proportion of search in total unemployment, but there is cetain to be some, and the higher it is, the lower the resource costs of unemployment are likely to be. In the industrialized countries unemployment has been viewed as a social as well as an economic problem largely because it is concentrated among groups upon whom the loss of income imposes relatively high 'subjective' costs. Thus we suspend judgement regarding the seriousness of the problem in Tanzania until we consider how the costs are distributed.

There are few wealthy workers, and those who have succeeded in

[2] Since it is rural rather than urban productivity that is relevant to measurement of the output forgone as a consequence of unemployment, the high proportion of the unemployed, 69%, who are educated does not significantly raise our assessment of the resource costs. For a more detailed discussion see Sabot 1977b.

TABLE 6.2
Percentage distribution of urban unemployed by age and sex

Age	Male	Female	Total
14–19	46	37	40
20–4	22	29	26
25–34	15	22	19
35–49	19	12	13
50–64	4	1	2
65 and over	—	—	—
Total	100	100	100

Source: *NUMEIST* 1971

accumulating savings sufficient to finance their consumption for anything more than a brief period of unemployment are likely to be in the older age group. Yet Table 6.2 indicates that 66 per cent of the unemployed are 24 or less. In order, therefore, to maintain the consumption of food, housing, clothing, and health services at the levels necessary to avoid serious deprivation there must be a

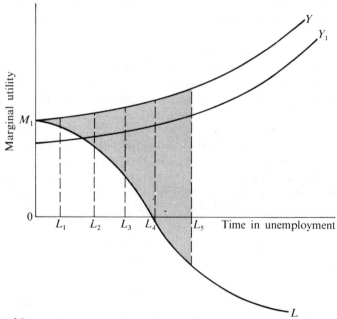

FIG. 6.1

redistribution of costs from the unemployed to the employed. Since there are no government relief systems to effect such a redistribution, unemployed workers must frequently rely on transfer payments from family members. It is reasonable to suppose that the subjective costs of a given pool of unemployed are negatively related to the ease with which such transfers can be arranged, and to their level.

For a given annual total of man-years of unemployment the social cost will be a negative function of the number of workers among whom that time is distributed. This relationship can be clarified with reference to Fig. 6.1, in which marginal utility is measured on the vertical axis and time in unemployment on the horizontal. The curve Y is the marginal utility of income forgone. The longer a worker is unemployed, the greater the total income forgone, the lower his annual income received, and thus the greater the utility of the marginal dollar forgone. Curve L is the marginal utility of leisure. Though it is involuntary, over a short period leisure is likely to yield benefits that are significantly positive. However, workers become demoralized and frustrated as the time in unemployment lengthens, which implies a decline of the utility of enforced leisure, so that at the margin it may become negative.[3] As Lewis (1966) has emphasized, extended periods of enforced leisure may even make the worker unfit for arduous and disciplined work:

A young man finds one day's work here; gets no work tomorrow; codges a meal next day from his aunt; finds another job for a few hours; steals something while the owner is not looking; shares a meal with a friend; borrows a few cents from a patron; and so on. After one has lived this life for two or three years, one becomes unemployable and could not do eight hours' work a day for five days a week even if it were offered—for psychological no less than physical reasons.

In such cases the decline in the marginal utility of leisure would reflect a reduction in expected future income as a consequence of current unemployment.

---

[3] This curve also reflects what Sen (1975) calls the recognition aspect of employment whereby, independently of its financial rewards, employment contributes to self-esteem and esteem by others. Just as for groups such as the 'leisured class', this aspect is likely to be less significant than for others, so the impact on welfare of forgoing this aspect of employment is likely to vary with length of time in unemployment. The increasing importance of the recognition aspect as time in unemployment lengthens may be seen as a factor contributing to the negative relationship between the marginal utility of leisure and time in unemployment.

In Fig. 6.1 it is assumed that a worker in full employment, depicted at M_1, is a price taker, sells the use of as much time as he desires at a fixed wage, and, at that given wage, equates the marginal utility of the income from an additional day's work with the marginal utility of an additional day's leisure. The welfare cost of unemployment is the area under the M_1–Y curve minus the area under the M_1–L curve. For a short period in unemployment, e.g. 0–L_1, the benefits of increased leisure offset a considerable proportion of the reduction in utility associated with diminished income. As the length of time in unemployment increases there is a disproportionate increase in welfare costs. An average annual rate of unemployment of 10 per cent, if evenly distributed amongst the entire labour force, would mean enforced idleness without pay for a little over five weeks per year per worker. If, at the other extreme, the unemployment was concentrated among 10 per cent of the labour force, then each unemployed worker would remain idle for the entire year. In Fig. 6.1 it is clear that the social cost of unemployment is significantly less in a situation where 100 workers are each without work for an average period of 0–L_1 than in a situation where 20 workers are idle for an average period of 0–L_5.

Taking account of transfers may weaken the relationship between subjective cost and length of time in unemployment, but it does not negate it. If relatives or friends make up a portion of the income of the unemployed, curve Y shifts down to curve Y_1. While the gains from leisure might initially outweigh the loss of satisfaction owing to reduced consumption, with increased length of time in unemployment the subjective costs would increase. If the contribution of labour time to the household is required as compensation for the transfer payment, curve L might also shift down, leaving the relationship between costs and length of time in unemployment virtually as it was initially.[4]

Though we do not have measures of the value of transfers or of the length of time in unemployment, there are indirect indications of

[4] Independently of the question of compensation for transfers, L may shift down if the activity of job search, which is likely to engage some of the unemployed workers' 'free' time, entails disutility in a manner similar to work for wages. Once again this may weaken but will not negate the relationship between length of time in unemployment and welfare costs. When there are transfers, the total welfare cost must include that borne by the workers contributing to the support of the unemployed throughout the entire period. For them as well there is likely to be some relationship between length of time in unemployment and welfare cost.

whether the unemployed are assisted financially by their families
and whether they have been without work for short or long periods.
A head of household, by definition, provides for his own economic
needs and frequently is responsible for the well-being of others. A
wife or child or other non-head of household is generally an economic
dependant, and income that she or he earns is rarely the primary
source of support for the family. Since a primary earner is likely to
have greater needs and less access to transfer payments than a
secondary earner, his unemployment involves more serious deprivation for himself and his family than that of a secondary earner.
Thus the higher the proportion of heads of households in the pool of
unemployed, *ceteris paribus,* the greater the aggregate subjective
costs are likely to be. Table 6.3 indicates that only a small proportion,
24 per cent, of the unemployed are heads of households,[5] a situation
largely accounted for by the predominance of women among the
unemployed.

TABLE 6.3
*Percentage distribution of unemployed[a] by status in household and
sex*

Status in household	Male[b]	Female[c]	Total
Head of household	40	15	24
Spouse of head	—	48	31
Other	60	37	45
Total	100	100	100

[a] Job Search Criterion 2.
[b] 37% of total unemployed.
[c] 63% of total unemployed.
Source: NUMEIST 1971.

The chronic nature of urban unemployment in Tanzania does not
imply that workers suffer longer periods of enforced idleness than
they would in a context where the phenomenon is cyclical. The
available evidence, though rather sketchy, suggests that for most
males periods of unemployment are relatively short, while for
females they are relatively long. Table 6.4 indicates that 40 per cent
of all migrant male unemployed workers had arrived in 1971, within

[5] A reflection of the preponderance of young workers: only 26% of the male
unemployed are married, which indicates that 40% or more of the unemployed heads
of household who are males are not responsible for the support of a family.

TABLE 6.4
*Percentage distribution of migrant unemployed by sex and year of
arrival*[a]

Year of arrival	Male	Female	Total
1971	40	19	27
1970	29	28	28
1968–69	14	23	20
1966–67	3	10	7
1961–65	9	10	10
1951–60	5	10	8
Total	100	100	100

[a] Job Search Criterion 2.
Source: NUMEIST 1971.

six months of the survey. An additional 29 per cent had arrived in
1970, implying a maximum of eighteen months for 69 per cent of the
unemployed male migrants. Forty-eight per cent of the unemployed
women migrants had arrived within eighteen months of the survey.[6]

Figure 6.2 summarizes our findings on the subjective costs of
urban unemployment in Tanzania. Given the preponderance among
the unemployed of young workers who would not have significant
savings, we have assumed that subjective costs are primarily a
function of access to transfer payments and length of time in
unemployment, which are measured on the horizontal and vertical
axes, respectively, the former declining from left to right. Curves *a*
and *b* are iso-subjective cost curves; with curves farther from the
origin representing higher costs. Curve *b* denotes the necessarily
somewhat arbitrary point beyond which the deprivation associated
with unemployment becomes particularly severe. For any given
length of time in unemployment a worker requires a certain
minimum total of transfer payments to provide him with the
consumption goods necessary to avoid deprivation. The longer the
time in unemployment, the larger the required total transfer.

There appear to be two distinct groups of unemployed workers,
one of which is clustered around point *y*, the other around point *x*.
The former, and larger, group comprises workers who have access

[6] Length of time in town sets an upper limit to length of time in unemployment, as a
worker may have previously held a job or been a labour force non-participant. The
earlier the year of arrival, the more likely that the worker had not been in continuous
unemployment.

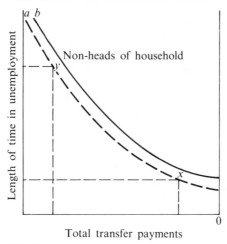

FIG. 6.2

to relatively large transfer payments and who continue to search, if only passively, for relatively long periods, namely household members who are the wives and children of the primary earners. The latter comprises household heads, predominantly older males, who have less access to transfers and who search for only short periods. As drawn, neither of these groups suffers particularly severe deprivation as a consequence of its joblessness. This supposition is not based on an examination of the consumption patterns of unemployed workers, but is suggested by our understanding of the labour market mechanism by which unemployment is generated in Tanzania.

In contrast to unemployment caused by demand deficiency, unemployment that is due to intersectoral misallocation is not characterized by a scarcity of employment opportunities relative to labour supply in the national aggregate.[7] For anyone willing to work at the going 'wage' there are employment opportunities in the rural areas. This state of affairs could be read as meaning that urban unemployment is voluntary, as of course in a sense it is. It is not,

---

[7] Of course even in a demand deficiency situation there are likely to be geographic areas or sectors where labour markets are tight. However, in the aggregate job seekers will outnumber job openings. It was Beveridge (1931) who, recognizing that in a dynamic economy there will always be 'frictional' unemployment, first suggested the converse as a criterion for identifying a situation of 'full employment'.

however, voluntary in the sense in which a wealthy *rentier* seeking employment is voluntarily unemployed if the wage at which he is willing to work is some multiple of prevailing rates. Where the individual retains the right to set the reserve price below which he will not sell his labour, the goods and services which the *rentier* or students and housewives, who are also capable of work but do not want it at prevailing wages, would have produced if economically active do not represent resource costs to the society. Nor can it be said that such workers suffer subjective costs as a consequence of their voluntary unemployment. For Keynes (1961), a continued surplus of job seekers relative to employment opportunities following a small decline in the real wage, is sufficient evidence of involuntary unemployment, as it would be manifest that unwillingness on the part of workers to accept lower wages is not the cause of imbalance. Where unemployment reflects an intersectoral misallocation, a marginal decline in the urban wage may reduce, but is unlikely to eliminate, the excess supply; unemployment of this nature may persist even where the reserve price of the unemployed is less than the wage prevailing in *rural* areas.

Fellner (1946) perceived that unemployment owing to wage rigidities is 'a hybrid consisting of "voluntary" and "involuntary" elements. This type of unemployment frequently is involuntary if it is taken for granted that the individual unemployed is limited to a specific segment of the labour market (geographically, or as to the nature of the work that is sought); yet he may voluntarily so limit himself.' When viewed *ex ante*, joblessness may be seen as imposing no subjective costs on the unemployed in a situation of intersectoral misallocation. In such a situation, expected urban income exceeds rural income for all urban job seekers and the presence of the unemployed worker in town is evidence that income forgone, even if above the worker's reserve price, is more than compensated for by the psychic benefits of the probability of obtaining a high wage job. But *ex ante* expectations, though they may influence behaviour, cannot be used to buy bread. Economic welfare is assessed by observing actual income or consumption, not by consideration of alternatives that become irrelevant once a decision is reached. Since, in a segmented labour market, employment opportunities are rationed by means other than the adjustment of wages, those who succeed in finding a job overfulfil their expectations while the unsuccessful underfulfil theirs. As in other situations in which there

THE COSTS OF UNEMPLOYMENT

are winners and losers, the welfare consequences of unemployment should only be assessed *ex post*.

The voluntary aspect of urban unemployment in Tanzania does not negate subjective costs but it has implications for their level. Although rural income is greatly exceeded by expected urban income, a rural resident is unlikely to migrate unless he can support himself while he looks for a job. Capital markets are notoriously imperfect for this type of investment and individuals vary in savings levels and access to transfers. The ability to finance a period of job search is likely to be a determinant of the variation in migration rates, and hence in unemployment rates, among sub-groups of the rural population.[8] A corollary of this is that an unemployed worker who exhausts his resources will take advantage of Tanzania's informal 'social security system' and either enter rural employment or take one of the low income jobs readily available in urban areas. If the short-terms costs become excessive the worker can always opt out of the lottery for high wage jobs, an option not generally open to unemployed workers in a situation of demand deficiency.

While unemployment in Tanzania can be viewed as a result of excessive rural–urban migration, it should not be inferred that the unemployed are all migrants. In fact, the unemployment rate among non-migrants is twice that among migrants; and non-migrants comprise 49 per cent of the urban unemployed. What evidence there is, however, indicates that the difference in unemployment rates is due less to constraints on mobility than to differences in access to transfers and in psychic and direct costs. In contrast to some Asian and Latin American countries where a substantial proportion of the population has lived in urban areas for a number of generations, most of the urbanization in Tanzania has occurred within the lifetime of urban adults. Fifty per cent of all workers classified as non-migrants were actually born in the rural areas but moved before the age of 14; the fathers of 50 per cent of all non-migrants were peasant farmers. Fifty-eight per cent of non-migrants visit relatives in rural areas and 28 per cent send remittances. When asked whether land was readily available for them in the rural areas in which their

---

[8] The dramatically higher rate of unemployment among females (see Table 6.1), despite their disadvantaged position in regard to wages and employment probabilities, is but one example. A corollary of the high psychic returns to migration discussed in Chapter III is the greater ease with which females as economic dependants can finance job search.

relatives were living, 40 per cent answered positively (*NUMEIST* 1971). While non-migrants are likely to be at some disadvantage in establishing themselves in rural areas, the strength of their ties with these areas indicates that non-economic barriers to mobility are far less severe for them than for urban dwellers removed by several generations from the countryside. This suggests that non-migrants are not much more likely than migrants to suffer serious privation as a consequence of unemployment.

The resource and subjective costs of urban unemployment in Tanzania, while not insignificant, are not of sufficient magnitude to give cause for grave concern or a policy of intervention. That only 10 per cent of the urban labour force is unemployed, however, does not imply that the other 90 per cent is fully employed. A final assessment of the social costs of surplus labour requires the determination of the proportion of employed surplus labour in the urban labour force.

3. CONVENTIONAL MEASURES OF EMPLOYED SURPLUS LABOUR

If employment is viewed as a continuous rather than as a discrete and homogeneous variable, then in developing countries there are numerous urban jobs that are closer to the unemployment than to the full employment end of the continuum. To assess the magnitude of total urban surplus labour in Tanzania we require a criterion for determining the dividing line between 'adequate' and marginal employment, or (the same thing viewed from the perspective of the labour force) the dividing line between employed workers who are 'surplus' and those who are not.

The gap between the rates of growth of wage employment and of urban population or labour force is sometimes used as an indicator of the trend of the urban labour market imbalance (Frank 1968, Todaro 1971). Adjusting this method to measure surplus labour at any given time entails assuming that all own-account workers are surplus labour and all wage earners are non-surplus or fully employed. Under this assumption a total of 30 per cent of the urban labour force in Tanzania is surplus labour: 10 per cent unemployed and 20 per cent employed surplus labour. The appropriateness of this approach, however, depends on the realism of the rather strict assumption of an identity between employed surplus labour and own-account workers. Reynolds (1969) has described the marginal jobs in which employed surplus labour is likely to be found:

Entrance to the occupations in question is open. Most of them require little or no skill, and also little or no capital. They thus provide a natural entry point for migrants from the country, who win a precarious foothold in the urban economy by crowding into petty trade, services and other small-scale activities. Overmanning of these activities contributes to low output and income per worker.

In order to assess the realism of the assumption of such an identity elsewhere we have examined the activities of own-account workers, their stability in employment, and their incomes.[9] Among the various activities of own-account workers, only the street-trading and cultivation categories, which employ respectively 21 per cent and 27 per cent of the total, appear to be uniformly small scale judged by the criterion of whether the capital required is sufficient to pose a significant barrier to entry. The transport sub-group includes taxi- or lorry-owners and others who own more than one vehicle and hire drivers, as well as menial porters. Among shopkeepers, although some have only a small stall, others have stores large enough to require the assistance of hired or family labour. Although luxury housing has been nationalized and most *rentiers* let only a room or two, some have several eight-room 'Swahili' dwellings at their disposal. The hotel and bar category includes those who own modern establishments in the centre of the city as well as workers who sell native beer at a stand under a palm tree in the 'suburbs'. Skill requirements frequently pose an additional barrier to entry, particularly in manufacturing, where tailors, cabinet-makers, bakers, and brewers are in the majority, and in contracting, which includes masons, roofers, carpenters, electricians, and plumbers.

Whether own-account work is an important point of entry to the urban labour market was determined by an examination of the data on the means of support of the current stock of migrants during their first months in town.[10] Only 6 per cent of new arrivals supported themselves entirely or in part with some form of self-employment. When those who found a wage job within a month after arrival or who had come to town for reasons such as education are excluded, the proportion of self-employed new arrivals is still only 11 per cent. If own-account work is used primarily as a stepping stone to other forms of urban employment, we would expect most of the current

[9] These paragraphs are summaries of findings presented in greater detail in Sabot 1977a, 1977b.
[10] Males were the basis of the inquiry because few females come to town to seek work.

self-employed migrants to have arrived in town recently and to have been in their current occupation for a short time. Yet only 6 per cent of all non-wage earners had arrived in town within six months of the enumeration; an additional 8 per cent had been in town six to eighteen months. Sixty per cent of all migrant own-account workers and no less than 50 per cent of each activity's participants had lived in town for over five and a half years. Only 15 per cent of the migrant self-employed had worked in their activity for less than one year, and 68 per cent over-all, and no less than 51 per cent of the participants in any one activity had been engaged for three or more years.

Entry to own-account work is not always open, nor is such work used primarily as a means of access to the urban market for wage labour. Furthermore, the incomes of the self-employed are not uniformly low; in fact the income of non-wage earners is unambiguously less equally distributed than that of wage earners. Nearly half of all the self-employed earned more than the minimum wage, which in 1971 was approximately sh 170;[11] comparison of the aggregate distributions of self-employed and wage-employed incomes revealed higher proportions of the former group in the highest income bracket (sh 1000 and over) as well as in the lowest income bracket (sh 100 and under). We can conclude that in Tanzania the seriousness of the problem of urban surplus labour cannot be determined from an examination of aggregate wage employment and labour force data, as there is no justification for assuming an identity between the self-employed and employed surplus labour.

Visible underemployment, the proportion of the employed with short working hours owing to a lack of desired additional work opportunities, is a conceptually sound component of surplus labour. However, by definition visible underemployment is a phenomenon of the wage sector. Since there is no demand for labour *per se* in the self-employed sector, it cannot constrain the number of hours worked. If self-employed workers work short hours they do so voluntarily, either because the return to additional hours of work declines below the supply price of labour at a low level of hours worked per week, or because time is devoted to job-search activities in the high-wage sector. In the former case the worker has withdrawn from the labour force; it is only in the latter instance that he could be

---

[11] The minimum wage varied among towns and sectors of employment.

considered unemployed for part of the work week, although since the worker is not looking for more of the same work but for a different job, he cannot be considered visibly underemployed. In the wage sector it is estimated that less than 5 per cent of the participants are visibly underemployed. Even among employees working less than 40 hours per week, the proportion seeking additional work is equally low; moreover, there is no evidence that visible underemployment contributes to the explanation of low monthly wage incomes. The phenomenon appears to be of little significance in Tanzania (Sabot 1977b).

Invisible underemployment, the proportion of the labour force whose incomes are 'abnormally low' even though working hours may be long, is not relevant to our investigation because no consideration is given to excess urban labour supply or efficiency in the allocation of labour among sectors when selecting the income criterion to be applied. Generally a poverty datum line or the minimum wage is applied, with the result that the unique problem of urban surplus labour is confused with that of low levels of per capita income and its distribution. In the next section, an income criterion with normative content in resource allocation terms is defined and the level of employed urban surplus labour in Tanzania is measured. The distribution of the labour force between rural and urban areas and the role of migrants in the urban labour market are central to the definition.

4. AN ALLOCATIVE EFFICIENCY CRITERION FOR THE MEASUREMENT OF URBAN SURPLUS LABOUR

In our discussion of the relationship between migration and urban labour market imbalance we have ignored the existence of a low income sector in which incomes are flexible. Others have assumed that the unemployed and self-employed can be aggregated without loss of precision in the analysis. A closer examination of the role of the flexible income sector in the urban labour market can yield the income criterion we need for the measurement of employed surplus labour. The distribution of the national labour force among three sectors and its implications for the returns to labour in each sector, for the maximization of national output, and for the definition of urban surplus labour can be illustrated by means of Fig. 6.3.

'Regular employment' in the urban areas is depicted in Fig. 6.3 (a). By the term 'regular employment' we denote all those employees

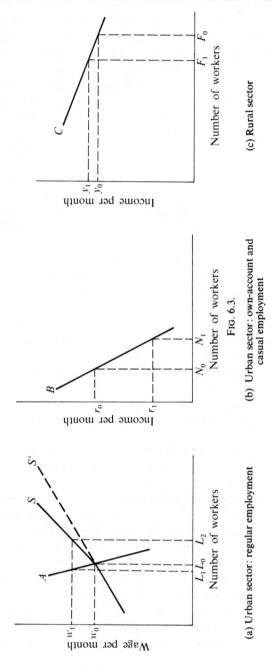

FIG. 6.3.

(a) Urban sector: regular employment

(b) Urban sector: own-account and casual employment

(c) Rural sector

in receipt of a regular monthly wage or salary. The wage labour force is measured on the horizontal axis and the real wage in shillings per month on the vertical axis. This sector is characterized by a mechanism of wage-determination which is not competitive, i.e. the interaction of supply and demand alone is insufficient to result in a wage that will 'clear the market'. The demand curve for labour in this sector, labelled D, reflects the technical relationship between the marginal product of labour and employment, with a fixed capital stock. The curve is assumed to slope downwards owing to diminishing returns, implying that the higher the wage, the lower will be the most profitable level of employment.[12]

The supply curve of labour to the urban regular employment sector is labelled S. The supply of labour at higher wages is assumed to be mostly the consequence of migration from the rural sector, but also, in some circumstances, of the transfer of labour from the second urban sector. It is assumed that intersectoral mobility proceeds in response to the expectation of positive net economic returns. If a wage is established above the equilibrium level, urban jobs are 'rationed' among competing applicants by a sort of queuing mechanism implying that potential migrants must weigh the costs of waiting in the queue for urban jobs against the benefits of eventually receiving a higher income. This means that at wages above w_0 there is only a probability, not a certainty, of finding a job; and this is in contrast to the situation below w_0. Thus, at w_0 the supply curve of labour becomes less elastic, causing the curve to be kinked at its intersection with the demand curve. If the demand curve for labour remains fixed, the supply curve of labour is given by S. However, if the demand curve for labour shifts upwards to the right, the labour supply curve will be as the dashed line S' (a straightforward continuation of the supply curve below w_0).

The second urban sector is depicted in Fig. 6.3(b). By the term 'own-account employment' we denote those income earners who do not receive a wage income. The term 'casual employment' refers to wage earners not in receipt of a regular monthly income, who are generally hired and paid on a daily basis.[13] The number of workers

---

[12] The underlying assumption is that there is some degree of *ex-post* substitutability between capital and labour.

[13] This sector is not synonymous with the 'informal sector' as defined by the I.L.O. (1972a), as a significant proportion of casual workers are included in government surveys of establishments. However, if the formal–informal sector dichotomy is based

in the sector is measured on the horizontal axis, and real income per month on the vertical axis. Though it is not appropriate to call curve B a demand curve for labour, it does indicate the technical relationship between employment and marginal product with a constant stock of capital. Figure 6.3(c) illustrates the rural sector, which we take as mainly consisting of small-scale agriculture. The number of workers is measured on the horizontal axis (with some licence as to its length relative to the other two sectors). Real monthly income is again measured on the vertical axis. It is assumed that the own-account and casual employment urban sector and also the rural sector are distinguished from the urban regular employment sector by the absence of institutional or other constraints on competitive income determination.[14]

Let us consider a situation in which the wage in regular urban employment, w_0, is set at the level which clears the market so that all the L_0 workers who offer themselves for employment are employed. Let us also assume that N_0 workers are engaged in urban own-account work or in casual employment, and that the remainder of the national labour force, F_0 workers, are in the rural sector. The monthly regular wage, the monthly income from own-account and casual employment, and the monthly income from rural employment are, on these assumptions, all the same: $w_0 = r_0 = y_0$. Since income equals the marginal product of labour, in this situation there is no possibility of obtaining any addition to total output simply by altering the disposition of the total labour force among the three sectors.

Now let us consider the situation that appears to characterize the Tanzanian labour market. Whether the cause is the introduction of minimum wage or other labour legislation, pressure from trade unions, the action of employers for whom an increase in the wage rate means proportionately greater increases in labour productivity, or some combination of these factors, the wage in urban regular employment is raised above its market-clearing level to w_1 and is held at that level. As a consequence, the supply of labour in this sector increases to L_2 and the number of regular-employment jobs

on a structural difference in the wage determination mechanism such that wages are 'protected' from market pressures in the former and 'unprotected' in the latter, then the flexible wage sector can be identified with the informal sector.

[14] Activities carried on in rural areas where the legal minimum wage applies, such as plantation agriculture and government employment, are thus excluded from the analysis.

declines to L_1.[15] The net result of the increase in the wage rate is an excess supply of labour in the urban sector of L_1-L_2.[16]

The proportion of this excess supply remaining in open unemployment and the proportion entering the own-account and casual employment sector depend on the degree to which employment in the latter sector places a constraint on job-search behaviour in the regular employment sector. At one extreme, participation in the own-account and casual employment sector is equivalent to participation in the rural sector. It is assumed that rural employment entirely precludes effective seeking for urban jobs. All the excess supply is thus likely to remain in open unemployment.[17] The withdrawal of labour raises the marginal product and incomes of workers remaining in the own-account and casual employment sector and the rural sector by only small amounts. Given the assumption of competitive income determination, monthly incomes in the two sectors remain equal. It is important to recognize that the unemployed do not return to the countryside even though remunerative work is available there. Those without jobs remain in town because the positive probability of obtaining a high-wage job implies that their long-run expected income is higher in urban than in rural areas.

At the other extreme, participation in the own-account and casual employment sector does not interfere at all with job-search activity in the regular employment sector. In this case none of the excess supply of labour remains openly unemployed. The costs of waiting in the job queue can always be reduced by participation in the own-account and casual employment sector. The increase in the number

[15] As drawn, the elasticity of curve A (the proportional change in labour output in the regular employment sector divided by the proportional change in marginal product) is less than unity. It has been shown that when the elasticity exceeds unity, a rise in the wage, while still leading to excess supply, will entail a backward-sloping supply curve and thus a decrease in the number of workers in the urban sector and an increase in rural sector labour and output. See Corden and Findlay 1975.

[16] A rise in the urban real wage is likely to entail a change in the 'terms of trade' between the regular-employment sector and the other two sectors in favour of the former. This should cause an inward shift of the marginal product curve in the latter. These shifts may be somewhat offset by increases in output demand resulting from the changes in the terms of trade and the increase in the urban population. The consequences of alterations in prevailing relative prices and in the pattern of sectoral demand interactions are peripheral to the main analysis and are ignored here.

[17] In this case some of the L_0L_2 labour attracted by the high-wage employment opportunities is drawn from the own-account work and casual employment sector as well as from the rural sector.

of workers in the sector, N_0N_2, will be equal to the loss of employment in the regular sector, plus the number of additional migrants, a total of L_1L_2. The consequence of this increase is that competitive pressures, from which the sector is unprotected, push down monthly incomes from r_0 to r_1. All the increase in the urban sector labour force, L_0–L_2, comes from the rural sector, raising incomes there somewhat, from Y_0 to Y_1. Thus, in this situation, we obtain both a relatively high-income urban sector and a relatively low-income urban sector, with incomes in the rural sector falling in between the extremes of w_1 and r_2. Once again it is important to recognize that this configuration of w_1 and L_1, with r_1 and N_2 and Y_1 and F_1, is 'stable' in that it can persist over a long period. The 'rigidity' of w_1 means that the wage for regular employees does not fall; the positive probability of obtaining a high-wage job retains the N_1 workers in the urban own-account and casual employment sector despite the low remuneration there and despite the higher incomes obtainable in agriculture. It is economically quite 'rational' to work in this sector at an income below the rural opportunity cost of migration.[18]

It is unlikely that either of these extreme cases applies. In the urban areas of Tanzania a significant proportion of the employed are engaged in active job search. Employment and job search are not necessarily mutually exclusive activities. The significant level of open unemployment is evidence that the perceived probability of

[18] Furthermore, the level of unemployment does not equilibrate the flow of urban migrants. An increase in rural out-migration decreases incomes in the own-account and casual employment sector relative to rural sector incomes, thus increasing the cost of job search per period. By increasing the level of excess urban supply, migration also decreases the probability of finding a high-wage job, and this increases the number of periods necessary to wait in the low-income urban sector before finding a job in the regular employment sector. Therefore expected total costs of job search rise with the increase in migration. This introduces an additional complication regarding the determinants of the slope of S relative to S'. When participation in the own-account and casual employment sector does not constrain, or only partially constrains, a person's ability to look for a job in the sector of regular employment, the additional labour forthcoming from the countryside is likely to be greater than L_0L_2 and the total excess supply will be greater than L_1L_2. This is because, on the assumption that the disutility of work and job search are the same, income from casual or own-account employment reduces the costs of job search per period relative to the situation in which a job seeker must be unemployed, thus increasing the expected net returns to migration for a given rural–urban income differential and implying an increase in the slope of S. In the case where employment places no constraint on job search, income in the own-account and casual income sector declines to a level somewhat below r_1 owing to the addition of more workers while income in agriculture rises to a level somewhat above y_1 with the migration of more workers to the urban sector.

finding a job is higher for the unemployed than for those in own-account or casual employment. In Tanzania, the ratio of the probabilities of obtaining a high-wage job for the employed and for the unemployed appears to be neither 1 nor 0.

In this case the excess supply of urban labour resulting from the high wage in the regular employment sector divides itself between open unemployment and low-income employment in the own-account and casual employment sector. How workers allocate themselves is determined by the ratio of the probabilities. It can be demonstrated rigorously that the closer the ratio is to 1 and the less own-account or casual employment constrains the effectiveness of job search, then, for a given rural–urban income differential: (a) the greater is the total excess supply forthcoming; (b) the greater is the proportion of the total excess supply in own-account or casual employment; (c) the lower is the equilibrium rate of unemployment; (d) the lower is the equilibrium income level in the own-account and casual labour sector; and (e) the greater is the gap between marginal product in that sector and in the rural sector (Sabot 1977b).

In the initial situation described there was no redistribution of the national labour force among the three sectors that could increase total output. In the situation that results from the increase in the urban wage this is not so. Clearly, any urban unemployed could be more productively engaged in the agricultural sector; in addition, as long as employment does not entirely preclude job search, there is a proportion of workers in the own-account and casual employment sector whose transfer to the rural sector would increase total output. The possibility that such a change in the allocation of the labour force could lead to increased over-all output provides both the rationale for calling the urban unemployed 'surplus' and also the basis of an income criterion for the measurement of employed surplus labour.

In order to define this income criterion precisely we need to clarify the relationship between marginal product in the rural sector and the disposition of the national labour force. In Fig. 6.4 marginal product is measured on the vertical axis. The number of workers is measured on the horizontal axis, but, in contrast to Fig. 6.3, measurement is from right to left, from $0'$, and the rural marginal product of labour curve slopes downwards from right to left. The total labour force, $00'$, is divided between the urban areas (both sectors) and the rural areas. When a given number of workers, e.g.

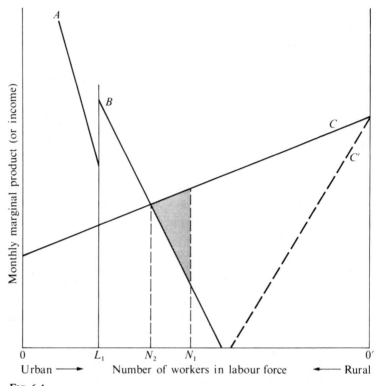

FIG. 6.4

$0'N_1$, are employed in the rural sector, the marginal product in that sector can be read from the corresponding position on the vertical axis according to curve C.[19] When no workers are present in the urban areas (i.e. when all workers are in the rural sector), the marginal product may be positive, as at the intercept of the curve C on the vertical axis above 0. Of course, the marginal product in agriculture may decline, as does curve C', to zero before all workers are absorbed in the rural sector, and we consider the implications of this later. For the moment let us assume curve C as given.

In Fig. 6.4 the marginal product curve of the own-account and casual employment sector from Fig. 6.3 may be superimposed on the marginal product curve in the rural sector, making due allowance at

[19] Alternatively we can say that when OO′ *minus* the given number of workers present in the urban sector, e.g. ON_1, is taken the marginal product in the rural sector can be read according to curve C.

the left-hand side of the diagram for the workers in urban regular employment (at wage w_1); that is to say, the measurement of labour in the own-account and casual employment sector starts from L_1 *not* from 0. The L_1N_1 workers in Fig. 6.4 equal the N_1 workers in Fig. 6.3. Let us assume the situation in which own-account work or casual employment does not effectively constrain job search, so that the own-account and casual employment sector acts as a sponge soaking up the excess supply of urban labour. It is obvious from Fig. 6.4 as drawn that the transfer of N_1N_2 workers from the urban own-account and casual employment sector to the rural sector would yield a net gain to total output equal to the shaded area. Urban surplus labour, N_2N_1, thus comprises workers whose marginal productivity is less than it would be in rural areas. That is to say, urban surplus labour, *must be measured with respect to the marginal product of workers in agriculture.*[20]

Curve C' implies that with rural labour force $0'N_2$ there is disguised unemployment in the traditional sense that labour can be withdrawn from the sector without any loss to output, marginal product $= $ o, which can only occur under restrictive assumptions regarding the indifference map between work and leisure of rural labour (Berry and Soligo 1968). From the above definition it is obvious that if Curve C' applies, there is no unique problem of urban employed surplus labour. No matter how low the income is in the own-account and casual employment sector, if the marginal product of labour is greater than zero, allocative efficiency is increased and there is a net gain to total output associated with the movement of rural labour into the sector.[21] In this situation the unemployed still constitute urban surplus labour, if transferring them to own-account

[20] Only if the demand for labour in the regular employment sector is invariant with respect to the wage rate will N_1N_2 in Fig. 6.4 equal L_1L_2 in Fig. 6.3(a) and N_1N_2 in 6.3(b)—the total excess supply of labour. If the wage increase decreases the demand for labour, then the number of workers whose transfer from the own-account and casual employment sector to the rural sector would increase total output is somewhat less than the total excess supply. This implies that the high urban wage imposes a cost on the economy not only by resulting in urban surplus labour as defined but also by leading to excessive capital intensity in production in the regular employment sector. Even if N_1N_2 is transferred to the rural sector, total output could be further increased by employing additional labour in the regular employment sector.

[21] Alternatively rural disguised unemployment can be said to exist when the income of an additional worker exceeds rural marginal product. This can occur together with urban employed surplus labour if the marginal product in the own-account and casual employment sector is not only lower than rural income at the margin but also lower than rural marginal product.

or casual employment would not reduce marginal productivity in that sector to zero.

The income criterion necessary for the measurement of employed surplus labour should now be clear. It can be taken as the marginal product prevailing in the rural sector with the existing disposition of the labour force. Owing to diminishing marginal productivity, such a measure will yield an overestimate of employed surplus labour. It treats the B curve as being horizontal in the vicinity of N_1, but, in Africa at least, this may not be too far removed from reality.

An estimate of the magnitude of urban employed surplus labour in Tanzania is presented in Table 6.5. The level of rural income per labour force member is the criterion applied to the distribution of urban income. Rural inter-regional income differentials, which persist in Tanzania partly because of intra-rural constraints on labour mobility, are a potential source of bias in the measurement of employed surplus labour. This is reduced by grouping the migrant population by region of origin. For each of the seventeen regional groups a separate income criterion is applied to measure surplus labour. The average of the regional criteria is used to measure the surplus only for non-migrants. Of the total urban labour force, 10·3 per cent is classified as employed surplus labour. As expected, given the differences in the distribution of income between wage earners and own-account workers, the proportion of the latter group categorized as surplus labour is nearly four times that of the former.[22] Adding the 9·9 per cent of the urban labour force that is openly unemployed yields an estimate of 20·2 per cent as the total proportion of the urban labour force that is surplus.[23]

Some qualifications are in order. If workers in the own-account and casual employment sector do not differ in regard to degree of monopoly power, they all receive an income equal to the productivity of the marginal worker and the rural marginal product criterion yields an overestimate, as all of ON_1 in Fig. 6.3 or L_1N_1 in Fig. 6.4

[22] Because of the relatively large size of the wage sector, the absolute numbers of surplus labour in that sector are only marginally less than in the non-wage sector.
[23] Variation among individuals in embodied human capital and hence in potential productivity, and in dependency status and access to alternative sources of income and hence in the deprivation they will suffer through unemployment or low-income employment, implies that an index of resource or welfare costs would require the urban labour surplus to be assessed at a relatively high level of disaggregation. This is beyond the scope of the current paper: hence the term 'aggregate magnitude of urban surplus labour' refers to the proportion of the labour force that comprises the problem as defined.

TABLE 6.5
*Percentage of surplus labour in urban Tanzania in 1971 among
employment sub-groups and the total labour force*[a]

Category	Proportion of the sub-group	Proportion of the urban labour force
Employed surplus labour		10·3
among wage earners	5·1	
among own-account workers	19·8	
Unemployment		9·9
Total surplus labour		20·2

[a] Weighted average of the proportions of the urban stocks of migrants from each of 17 regions earning less than average product in rural region of origin and the proportion of non-migrants earning less than average rural product.
Source: *NUMEIST* 1971

would be included as surplus. The dispersion of incomes among own-account workers indicates that differences in skills, levels of complementary physical capital, desirability of business locations, market information, and so forth contribute to varying degrees of monopoly power among sector participants. Nevertheless, to the extent that there are segments of the urban labour market where workers have no monopoly power—one of which may be the market for casual labour—the estimate of employed surplus labour has an upward bias.

Divergence between social and private marginal product can also arise where there are income-sharing conventions in family enterprises or where distribution of custom among workers is random. If the group as a whole, family or non-family, has a degree of monopoly power in the market in which it is trading, and the average product of the group exceeds rural marginal product, then there will be an underestimate of the magnitude of employed surplus labour. If the group as a whole exercises little monopoly power and thus has an average product close to the sector marginal product and less than rural marginal product, there may be an overestimate of employed surplus labour. Furthermore, as there are no measures of rural marginal product in Tanzania, average rural product is used as the income criterion contributing to an upward bias in the measure of employed surplus labour. However, the gap between average product and marginal product is likely to be narrow in rural Tanzania, given the low capital/labour ratio and easy availability of land. There is a strong presumption that the cost of living is somewhat higher in town than in the countryside. Lack of data on cost-of-living differentials results in an underestimate of employed surplus labour. While better estimates of employed surplus labour must await further improvements in the data base, the allocative efficiency approach to the measurement of urban surplus labour provides the basis for a rigorous separation between the problem of abnormally low incomes and the more general problem of poverty in less developed countries.

5. SUMMARY

The resource costs of urban surplus labour do not appear to be very high. In order to adjust for 'hidden unemployment' and for 'hidden employment', rates of unemployment were calculated under alternative labour force participation criteria and definitions of employment. The result was a range of 8–12 per cent of the urban labour force, with 10 per cent as the best single estimate of the level of open unemployment. Based on the premise that, given the prospect of eventually finding a high-wage job, some urban residents will accept an urban income below what they could earn in the rural areas, marginal product in the rural areas is the income criterion appropriate for the measurement of urban surplus labour. Transferring this urban surplus labour—those earning less than rural marginal product—to the rural sector would increase total output. The application of a rural income criterion yields a significantly lower estimate of the proportion of the urban labour force that is surplus than does the application of a crude sectoral or minimum-wage criterion. Nevertheless, 10 per cent of the employed labour force is estimated to be surplus. However, taking the wage rigidities (which appear to be the major causal factor) as given, the output to be gained by the employment of the one-fifth of the urban labour force that is unemployed or employed surplus labour is unlikely to add more than 1 or 2 per cent to national income.

Nor are the subjective costs of urban surplus labour particularly high: for the open unemployed they are lower than they would be in industrialized countries in the absence of a formal social security system. This is so, not because the unemployed in Tanzania have a greater store of assets on which they can draw, but because the subjective costs are distributed by intra-family transfer from the unemployed to those with jobs and because the agricultural sector is available as an employer of last resort. Similarly the availability of alternative opportunities in rural areas suggests that the subjective costs of employed surplus labour are low. The exception to these conclusions would be surplus workers whose contacts in rural areas are so weak as to limit their rural employment opportunities and restrict their escape from extreme privation in urban areas. However, in Tanzania the number of such workers still seems to be very small.

VII

THE STABILITY OF URBAN MIGRANTS

MIGRATION in the colonial period was short-term and circular, the migrants' strongest ties continuing to be with their rural origins. Absence from home was frequently less than a year and rarely more than three or four years, though the total time spent in wage employment might be longer, as migrants often made several short trips during their working lives. High turnover in urban employment condemned migrant workers to unskilled labour, seemingly in perpetuity, and during the 1950s the phenomenon was viewed with increasing concern. The U.N. Visiting Mission to Tanganyika in 1954 (U.N. 1955), the East African Royal Commission of 1955 (Great Britain 1955), and the 1954 Carpenter Commission on African Wages in Kenya (Kenya Colony and Protectorate 1954) considered this the most pressing of East Africa's urban employment problems, sufficient in magnitude to raise doubts about the economic viability of a modern industrial sector. Consideration of the causes of high turnover and the subsequent stabilization of the labour force provides another perspective on African decision-making and, more importantly, a background for the analysis of wage determination in the post-independence period under conditions of urban surplus labour.

1. INSTABILITY IN THE COLONIAL PERIOD

The African pattern of circular migration differed radically from the European experience of a once-for-all shift from rural self-employment to urban wage employment and residence. The main thrust of much of the early work on African migration by economists such as Barber (1960), Berg (in Kuper 1965), Elkan (1959), and Yudelman (1964) was to demonstrate that circulating between agricultural self-employment and wage employment represented economically rational behaviour in the social and economic context then existing in many areas of tropical Africa. The change over time of a migrants' costs and returns to migration indicates why absence tended to be short: costs tended to rise disproportionately with length of absence while returns remained constant or fell.

Migration in the colonial period yielded an extremely low level of money returns. Though wages did not decline as length of absence increased, their low level ensured a negative relationship between non-monetary returns and length of absence. Wages were referred to as 'bachelor wages' because they were too low to support a family on the estates or in the towns. The only employment generally available to women was the maintaining of the family's *shamba*, in the source areas. A rural resident desiring to take advantage of distant wage-earning opportunities in order to increase family income had to split his family. The rise in psychic costs applied equally to unmarried migrants, who would not meet many of their own tribe in town. Since inter-tribal marriage was a rarity and men in the rural areas tended to marry young, prolonged absence from home meant delay in establishing a family.

For a rural head of household to migrate, the wages he could earn must be greater than the decrease in output from the family *shamba* resulting from his absence.[1] If the husband left for only the slack part of the agricultural year, the light work necessary to maintain output could be done by his wife and children. If production was entirely for family consumption, even an absence of a year or two might not have a significant impact. Absences of greater duration, however, would lead to a deterioration of those fixed capital assets for whose maintenance the husband was predominantly responsible. Cash crop production could not be maintained much beyond the period of a seasonal absence, because heavy work was often involved in this type of cultivation. Thus family opportunity costs of migration increased with the length of the migrant's absence.

Three other causes of short-term circular migration need to be mentioned. First, positive incentives for longer stay in employment were not built into the colonial wage structure. Partly because most workers were employed in occupations requiring no training, wages did not rise with experience, and there were virtually no opportunities for upward mobility. Second, employment opportunities were plentiful. Owing to the scarcity of labour in the colonial period a migrant ran little risk of future unemployment by quitting a job to go home. As a consequence of the low level of wages the labour market did not impose negative incentives on the practice of taking up

---

[1] Evidence shows that most migrants, though young, were married at the time of migration, though among first-time migrants the proportion unmarried was likely to be quite high. See Gulliver 1955.

employment for a series of short periods. Finally, many unskilled jobs, both in agriculture and in the urban areas, did not offer stable employment. Seasonal fluctuations in the demand for labour were a common feature of plantations and such industries as construction, food processing, and transport. For a permanent migrant holding an unstable job, the long-term money returns in the receiving area would have to cover the cost of an annual period of economic inactivity.

2. THE CURRENT LEVEL OF STABILITY IN URBAN WAGE EMPLOYMENT

If, by 'labour force stability', we mean how long workers remain in urban wage jobs, then the distribution of the current labour force by length of time in employment is inadequate as a measure, because we cannot know how long those currently in employment will remain employed. However, since we know that before Independence most wage employees remained in employment for short periods only, the distribution in Table 7.1 gives us some basis for assessing the change in stability in the 1960s and 1970s. Among regular employees, who comprise 61 per cent of the total urban wage labour force, stability has increased dramatically; 77 per cent have been in employment for over one year, 51 per cent have held the same job for over three years, and over one-third have been in the same job for over five years. The level of stability is high not only in relation to the Tanzanian past but also in relation to industrialized countries. However, before we make quantitative comparisons we need a measure of stability statistically comparable with those used elsewhere.

Ideally we should distinguish between employment terminations that are voluntary and those that are involuntary, owing to redundancy or inadequate performance on the job. The extent to which terminations are a result of demand side factors will influence our assessment of the determinants of the workers' decisions on length of stay. For example, the fact that over 60 per cent of all casual wage employees have been in their job for less than one year does not imply that they want to work only for short periods, but that they are daily paid workers for whose services the fluctuations in demand are particularly severe. In fact, the most striking aspect of the seniority distribution for casual workers is that over one in eight

TABLE 7.1
Seven towns: adult wage earners—seniority by status of employee

Seniority	Status of employee		
	Casual	Regular	Total
	%	%	%
1 year or less	62·3	22·5	26·8
Over 1–3 years	23·8	26·2	26·0
Over 3–5 years	6·9	16·5	15·4
Over 5–10 years	5·2	16·3	15·1
More than 10 years	1·7	18·5	16·7
Total:	100·0	100·0	100·0

Source: NUMEIST 1971.

has been in the same job for more than three years. The explanation lies in the fact that, given the pressures resulting from a pool of urban surplus labour and the government's inability to police the labour market for infractions of legislation, employers can pay lower wages and, more significantly, avoid paying supplementary benefits by listing workers as casuals.

Measuring stability by rate of turnover avoids the problem of how much longer the workers currently employed will remain on the job. The rate of turnover is the number of changes in employees, as measured by hirings or terminations, in a given stock of jobs over a set period of time. Unfortunately, we cannot calculate such a rate with precision because we do not have data on a stock of jobs continually in existence over time. We can, however, move towards establishing such a constant set of jobs by adjusting the present stock for the growth in the number of jobs in a given period. The data in Table 7.1 indicate that 51 out of every 100 current regular wage earners were in the same job three years earlier. Adjusting for employment growth over the three-year period will allow us to eliminate from the remaining 49 those who could not have been in the same job three years earlier because it did not exist. We are here concerned with gross rather than net employment growth, as a job created during the three-year period, replacing a job which lapsed during that time, would still not have been available for a continual three-year employment. The difference in net and gross change in employment is likely to be significant because of the short-term nature of some jobs in such sub-sectors as domestic service, construction, and food processing.

A conservative estimate is that, given net wage non-agricultural, non-mining annual employment growth of 5–10 per cent between 1966 and 1970, gross employment growth was in the range of 7–14 per cent a year (Tanzania, Central Statistical Bureau, Various years). The implication of this growth rate is that three years earlier between 18 and 33 of any current 100 jobs would not have been in existence; or, conversely, that between 67 and 82 jobs of any currently existing 100 jobs would have been in existence then. This adjustment to the stock of jobs raises our estimate of stability, as the fact that 51 per cent of all current wage earners were in the same job three years ago implies that between 62 per cent and 76 per cent of those in employment three years ago are still in the same jobs. For males only, the range is between 66 per cent and 81 per cent. On the basis of these calculations, we can say that for the period 1967–70 the minimum average monthly rate of turnover or separation for the entire urban wage labour force was between 0·7 and 1·0 per 100 jobs. Only the minimum is established because we do not know how many turnovers there were in the 27–40 per cent of jobs not occupied continuously over this period.

In calculating the turnover rate, our assumption has been that there was only one change of job holder for each of the jobs in that category. Nevertheless, the monthly turnover rate is extremely low. Even doubling or tripling the assumed number of job holders for each job not continually filled over the three-year period only raises the over-all turnover range from 0·7–1·0 to 1·4–2·0 or 2·1–3·0 per month. These rates, which are for the entire spectrum of urban wage employment and include turnover in such relatively unstable sub-sectors as construction, compare favourably with turnover rates in American manufacturing industry, where separations, from 1960–8 were at an average monthly rate of approximately 4 per 100 jobs (Reynolds 1970). Not only is Tanzania's urban labour force highly stable compared to the colonial period, it is also extremely stable by international standards.

There is another way of measuring stability. Instead of examining a constant stock of jobs and documenting the number of holders in a given period of time, we can examine a constant stock of employees, document the number of jobs they have held, and calculate a job change rate. Table 7.2 shows, for all those in current

TABLE 7.2
Seven towns: adult wage earners in regular
employment: rates of mobility

Average months in wage employment	Number of employees	Number of job changes	Number of job changes per 100 months of employment
6	14 319	2 220	2·6
18	22 810	10 212	2·5
48	16 927	10 822	1·3
90	21 589	20 646	1·1
156	30 969	39 960	0·8
78	106 615	283 660	1·0

Source: NUMEIST 1971

employment, the average total number of months they have spent in wage employment no matter whether in one or more jobs.[2] It also shows the total number of job changes made by this group and calculates the number of job changes per 100 months of wage employment. The job change rate for Tanzania's urban wage employed is strikingly low, 1 per 100 months of employment, which is consistent with our findings on turnover. Disaggregating by length of experience in wage employment, we find that the shorter the period of time in wage employment, the higher the job change rate. A possible explanation for this is that migrants go back home if they do not find a regular wage job after a period of moving from one casual job to another.

3. STABILIZATION OF THE WAGE LABOUR FORCE

One of the explicit aims of the legislation introducing nationwide minimum wages in 1961, at a level considerably higher than the prevailing level of wages, was the stabilization of the wage labour force. While the sensitivity of labour demand to higher wages was

---

[2] The employment history section of *NUMEIST* gathered information on up to four former jobs for each respondent. For those with more than four jobs, their earliest jobs would have gone unrecorded. However, since a very low proportion of current wage earners, less than 10%, held as many as four jobs, the degree of underestimation of the job change rate is minimal.

recognized, the Territorial Minimum Wages Board believed that the welfare and productivity benefits of stabilization would outweigh its social costs. In the words of the Board, 'in the conditions of Tanganyika higher minimum wages will lead to redundancy, but the smaller labour force will be much more settled and efficient, and families of urban wage earners will be able much more easily to live together as family units' (Tanganyika 1962). What is the relationship over the past two decades between increases in migrants' length of stay in employment and increases in wage income, whether from minimum wage legislation, government wage leadership, union activity, or the desire of private employers for a stabilized, industrially disciplined labour force?

There are a number of ways in which higher wages influence the decisions of migrant workers to remain in employment for longer periods of time. The first is that the increase in urban wages has meant the end of 'bachelor wages'. It is important to recognize, however, that payment of wages high enough to support a family in town does not necessarily mean that migrants will bring their wives and children to live with them. Splitting the family's economic activities between rural and urban areas, with the wife maintaining the family *shamba* and the husband drawing his urban wage, would maximize family income at a high as well as at a low wage, given the low level of economic opportunities for women in the urban area. For a migrant to change the pattern of family splitting, it is necessary that the loss of income from the family *shamba* be compensated by the psychic benefits of having the family living together as a unit.

This condition appears to have been met in Tanzania. The evidence presented in Chapter III shows that females have been an increasing proportion of the migrant stream (with women actually in the majority in the year and a half preceding the survey) and that only 7 per cent of all female migrants to Dar es Salaam and the six towns came to take up a job or to seek employment, while 73 per cent came as dependants. In addition we now know that, while the majority of males are unmarried at the time of leaving home, 47 per cent of those who were married were preceded or accompanied to the town by their wives; an additional 15 per cent of the wives came within six months of their husband's arrival and 12 per cent followed later on. Thus only 25 per cent of the men who were married at the time of arrival did not have their wives with them at the time of the survey and a sizeable proportion of these were recent arrivals

TABLE 7.3
*Migrant males: percentage with dependants (wives/children)
living at home*

	Dar es Salaam	Six towns	Total
No dependants	38	34	37
No dependants at home	44	40	43
Some dependants at home	10	16	11
All dependants at home	8	10	9
Total	100	100	100

Source: *NUMEIST* 1971.

(*NUMEIST* 1971). Migrants who are unmarried at the time of arrival frequently marry soon after establishing themselves in town. Sixty-four per cent of migrant males living in town are married, and over 80 per cent of these have their wives with them.

Over 80 per cent of migrant males with children have at least one child living with them in their urban home. Table 7.3 summarizes the evidence on the current location of immediate dependants of male migrants. Only 9 per cent of all migrant males and 15 per cent of those with dependants have all their dependants in the rural areas. The change in the family pattern of migration is both an index and a cause of the increase of stability of the urban labour force. With their families in town the migrants' psychic costs are less likely to increase over time, as they did in the colonial period of circular migration.

Migrants' willingness to forgo income from the family *shamba* is influenced not only by the level of urban wages but also by that of rural income. If the income a family could earn by leaving the woman to work the family *shamba* had risen in step with urban wages, men might not have been so quick to bring their families to town. Because rural–urban income differentials have been widening, income from the family *shamba* has been a decreasing proportion of total family income. If the marginal utility of income diminishes with higher income, then the additional income the *shamba* represents decreases in value compared to the benefit of having the family together, a value presumably independent of total income. Also, without the husband's intermittent presence on the *shamba*, the wife and children probably could not maintain its income over a longer period. Stagnating rural incomes and rising wages mean that the wage income forgone while the migrant returns home to do his share of work on the *shamba* rises relative to the value of output from his contribution to the *shamba*. These factors have contributed to the changing family pattern of migration and the stabilization of the migrant labour force.

Wage structures that reward employment experience are also important in encouraging migrants to stay longer in wage employment. In the colonial past, there were no job ladders or wage differentials for seniority in agricultural wage employment or in much of urban employment. Table 7.4 shows the change that has taken place and documents a strong positive relationship between income and seniority, the length of time spent in the present place of employment. The median income falls in the bottom half of sh 200–249 range for employees with less than twelve months on the job, rising to sh 350–499 range for employees of more than ten years. Mean monthly wages rise from sh 284 for the former group to sh 630 for the latter.

Income differentials by seniority provide an incentive for a longer stay in urban employment. A migrant who left employment to return home used to forgo only his wage for the period he was gone, whereas now he also forgoes the increase that would have accrued to him had

TABLE 7.4
Seven towns: adult wage earners—seniority by wage income

Wage income: (sh) per month	Seniority in years				
	1 year or less	More than 1–3 years	More than 3–5 years	More than 5–10 years	More than 10 years
	%	%	%	%	%
Up to 149	10·3	5·6	1·4	2.0	1·9
150–99	24·9	21·5	19·9	13·3	8·0
200–49	21·5	22·9	19·3	17·7	15·0
250–99	8·9	10·3	12·5	16·3	9·6
300–49	7·1	14·0	9·8	11·2	8·0
350–499	7·7	9·9	12·8	14·3	22·7
500–999	18·1	10·5	16·9	13·9	16·9
1000 and over	1·6	5·4	7·4	11·2	18·0
Average monthly wage (sh)	100·0 284	100·0 382	100·0 454	100·0 512	100·0 630

Source: NUMEIST 1971

he remained in employment. For income differentials by seniority to discourage intra-urban mobility, as well as urban–rural mobility, they must be greater than income differentials by employment experience in general. Table 7.5 compares income differentials by employment experience of those who have accumulated the total of their experience in one job (Group a) and those who have accumulated it in two or more jobs (Group b). Regressing income on employment experience for each of these two groups, we find:

$$\text{Group a: } y = 211 + 35\cdot2x \qquad r^2 = 0\cdot97$$
$$\text{Group b: } y = 221 + 22\cdot8x \qquad r^2 = 0\cdot97$$

For workers who have accumulated their employment experience on one job only, each additional year of experience adds an average sh 35·2 to their income per month. This is sh 12·4 more than a year of experience yields for those who accumulated their experience in two or more jobs. While the urban labour market does reward employment experience, it offers a greater incentive to the accumulation of experience (seniority) in one job only.[3]

Another factor contributing to the employment stability of migrants is the shift in the balance of labour supply and demand from scarcity to surplus. When there was labour scarcity, a worker who quit a job to return to his *shamba* could be sure he would find another equally well paying job if he came back. Under conditions of labour surplus, a worker who leaves employment for several months or a year or more is aware that the probability of finding wage employment in the future is less than one. Even if the increase in family income from a short stay on the *shamba* were greater than the wages forgone during his absence from work, the worker might still find it to his benefit to remain in his urban job, as future urban

[3] The returns to general employment experience for the regularly employed are likely to be overstated because uneducated, low-income earners in unstable employment are not likely to remain in town for long periods, in part just because their incomes do not improve significantly over time. Thus there is a larger proportion of workers from the lower end of the income distribution concentrated in the categories of the least experienced. In addition, there is a small group of relatively highly educated high-income earners whose administrative or technical skills are not employer specific and are in scarce supply, for whom employment experience in general is likely to yield returns nearly equivalent to the returns to seniority. They would comprise a greater proportion of the groups with high experience. Most workers have skills specific to a particular firm and gain little from intra-urban mobility. The industrial sector is so small that there may be only one or two firms employing workers in particular types of production processes. Thus the incentive to remain with one firm rather than move from firm to firm is greater than our two simple regressions would suggest.

TABLE 7.5

Seven towns: adult wage earners average wage income by total employment experience

Total wage employment experience: years	Those who obtained all their experience in the same job (sh per month)	Those who obtained their experience in more than one job (sh per month)	All wage earners (sh per month)
1 or less	228	209	224
More than 1–3	320	260	297
More than 3–5	358	366	362
More than 5–10	403	377	387
More than 10	747	541	613

Source: NUMEIST 1971.

earnings would have to be discounted by the probability of finding a job.

So far, in analysing the determinants of stability we have adopted a time series view. We can examine our hypotheses also from a cross-sectional perspective of differences in seniority among educational, occupational, and industrial sub-groups of members of the wage labour force. The difficulties of controlling for different employment opportunity growth rates and differences in turnover arising on the supply and demand sides of the labour market are particularly severe. Nevertheless, the cross-sectional view yields some additional insights.

Figure 7.1 relates seniority to educational level. The relationship between seniority and education varies by age. Young workers with post-primary education have levels of seniority no higher than workers with less education though they hold jobs with higher income and greater security, because their longer education has brought them later into wage employment. Among older workers, the more educated have higher levels of seniority, mainly because the higher level jobs to which they have access are less subject to labour demand fluctuations. This is supported by Table 7.6 in which all wage employees who have held other wage jobs are distributed by education and by whether the separation from their last job was voluntary. The proportion of involuntary separations rose from 17 per cent among post-primary school leavers to 47 per cent among those with no formal education.

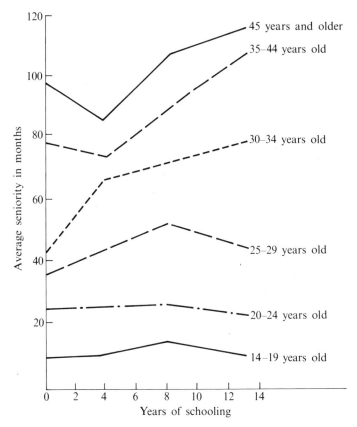

Fig. 7.1. Seven towns: adult wage earners: seniority by education for six age groups (from *NUMEIST* 1971)

Though the level of seniority for older uneducated workers is lower than for the educated, it still increases markedly with age, clearly indicating that not all low-level jobs are subject to demand side instability. The high levels of seniority of older uneducated workers may be explained by the fact that those who find stable employment hold on to their jobs because their probability of finding another is low. At the same time, those who do not find stable employment, but move from one low-level job to another without income increases for seniority or experience, may return to the rural areas at a relatively young age.

Rankings of occupations, industries, and type of employer by

TABLE 7.6

Seven towns: wage earners with employment experience: education and reason for leaving last job

	Voluntary separation	Involuntary separation	Total
	%	%	%
No formal education	53	47	100
Std 1–4	57	42	100
Std 5–8	61	39	100
Form 1 or more	83	17	100

Source: *NUMEIST* 1971.

average number of months' seniority of employees are presented in Table 7.7. At the bottom of the seniority ranking, we find three unskilled occupational categories plus sales workers, while at the top we find white-collar and skilled occupational categories. While there appears to be a correlation between the desirability of job categories, measured by income and work conditions, and length of stay in employment, we cannot reach any firm conclusions since the more desirable jobs appear to suffer less from fluctuations in labour demand, making it difficult to distinguish between the effect of demand and supply factors on differentials in seniority. Demand side instability in the industries in which lower level occupations are concentrated derives from fluctuations in product demand and from the fact that in such industries as construction and domestic service it is not possible to use inventories as an adjustment mechanism to smooth out fluctuations. The high seniority ranking of cleaners, messengers, and public servants appears to be an exception to the rule that low-level occupations suffer from greater than average demand side fluctuations. A large proportion of such workers, however, are in government which offers even low-paid, low-skilled workers a high degree of security of tenure. It is for this reason rather than higher pay or better working conditions that government employees are ranked at the top of both seniority distributions.

It is difficult to draw conclusions from the cross-sectional analysis. Nevertheless, demand side factors appear dominant as causes of differentials in seniority among occupational and educational sub-groups. The greatest influence on a migrant's decision on length of employment is the size of the rural–urban rather than the intra-urban differential and this is large for all categories. In addition, the

TABLE 7.7

Seven towns : ranking of occupations, industries, and types of employer by seniority

Occupation	Average no. of months' seniority	Industry	Average no. of months' seniority	Type of employer	Average no. of months' seniority
1. Management					
Administration	97	Railways & Harbours	96	Government	64
2. Professional	77	Comworks (Ministry of Com-	77	Parastatal	62
Technical		munications and Industry)			
3. Semi-technical	72	Government	69	Private firm	44
4. Skilled	68	Public utilities	67	Private individual	36
5. Drivers	65	Local government	63		
6. Public servants	64	Other services	53		
7. Cleaner, Messenger	59	Other transport	48		
8. Craftsmen	58	Manufacturing	47		
9. Machine operators	56	Commerce	47		
10. Clerical	48	Construction	42		
11. Unskilled	48	Domestic service	31		
12. Sales	42	Hotel, Bar, etc.	25		
13. Hotels, Bar	38				
14. Domestic	32				

Source: NUMEIST 1971.

increased stability of high-income, high-level, high-education occupations is counterbalanced by the incentive for workers in low-level, low-education occupations to stay in the same job, because finding another job is difficult and employment experience is not rewarded so well as seniority.

4. RESIDENTIAL STABILITY AND RETURN MIGRATION

A corollary of the stabilization of migrants in wage employment is their stabilization in urban residence. Tanzania's urban areas are no longer mere dormitories for peasants supplementing agricultural income by a short stint in wage employment; they are now centres of family life. Table 7.8 indicates that 52 per cent of the migrant population of the seven towns has been in continual urban residence for more than three and a half years and 33 per cent for more than six years. Stability is greater if we subtract from the total migrant population the net increase over the migrant population of three and a half years earlier, the justification being that this portion of the population arrived after the start of this period and could not have been in town for its full length. With a conservative estimate of 9 per cent net annual growth in the urban migrant population, we find that 77 per cent of migrants living in the urban areas in 1968 were still living in town in mid-1971.[4] The implication is that the urban migrant population of Tanzania has a large residentially stable core.

These newly settled urban residents have severed three of the threads that tied them to the countryside: their locus of residence has shifted from the rural to the urban areas; they no longer derive income from economic activity in their home areas; and they no longer maintain their immediate families in the rural areas.[5] Nevertheless, even for the stable core of urban migrants, ties with the countryside continue to be strong.

Table 7.9 indicates that 70 per cent of all male migrants had

[4] Estimated growth of total adult population between 1968 and mid-1971 in the seven towns is 21%. We know that migrants comprise two-thirds of all urban adults. Thus, with an assumed natural growth rate of 3%, the migrant population grew at a rate of 9% per annum.

[5] Elkan (1960) concluded that, because of a lack of a positive and continuing social, residential, and economic commitment to the urban areas, the majority of urban migrants in Uganda were not proletarians. A large majority of the present urban migrants in Tanzania's towns are proletarians in Elkan's terms. They have a continuing and positive commitment to both urban employment and urban residence. But are they proletarians in the equally important sense of having severed their rural ties irrevocably?

TABLE 7.8
Seven towns: migrant population: length of time in town

	Less than 6 months %	7 months–1 year 6 months %	1 year 7 months–3 years 6 months %	3 years 7 months–6 years 6 months %	6 years 7 months–9 years 6 months %	9 years 7 months–12 years 6 months %	12 years 7 months–15 years 6 months %	15 years 7 months and over %	Total %
Dar es Salaam	8	15	19	21	9	7	5	16	100
six towns	19	18	19	16	7	3	13	11	100
Total	12	16	19	19	8	7	4	14	100

Source: NUMEIST 1971.

RESIDENTIAL STABILITY AND

TABLE 7.9
Seven towns: migrant males: frequency of visits home by length of time in town

Frequency of visits	Length of stay in town			
	Less than 1 year 6 months	1 year 7 months– 9 years 6 months	9 years 7 months and more	Total
Once a year or more	32	70	56	56
Once every few years	4	12	24	14
Never	5	9	20	13
Not yet had a chance	59	2	—	17
Total	100	100	100	100

Source: NUMEIST 1971.

TABLE 7.10
Seven towns: migrant males: frequency of remittances by length of time in town

Frequency of remittances	Length of stay in town		
	Less than 1 year 6 months	1 year 7 months– 9 years 6 months	9 years 7 months and over
Six times a year or more	18	20	14
One to five times a year	14	26	16
Irregularly	15	28	26
Never	51	26	44
Total	100	100	100

Source: NUMEIST 1971.

returned to their home area for a visit at least once since arriving in town. More than half the migrants who had not been home claimed that it was only because they had not yet had a chance to do so, and the fact that 89 per cent of this group had been in town for one and a half years or less supports this claim. Approximately 84 per cent of the stable urban migrant core had been home and 80 per cent of those did so at least once a year. The proportion going home regularly is higher for migrants who have been in town for 1·5–9·5 years than for new arrivals or migrants who have been urban residents for more than 9·5 years. Though this suggests that contacts with the home area weaken somewhat with length of time away, 80 per cent of long-term absentees still visit the areas of their birth at least once every few years.

Table 7.10 shows that 61 per cent of all male migrants remit at least part of their urban income to their home areas in the form of cash or goods; and 72 per cent of the stable core of urban migrants make such remittances. Sixty per cent of those who make remittances do so at least once a year or more. Whether it reflects a decline in the strength of contacts with the home area over time or the fact that the rural responsibilites of older migrants may be less because of the death of parents and the independence of former young dependants, the frequency of remittances is lower for long-term absentees. Table 7.11 presents estimates of the annual average value of remittances and the proportion of urban income remitted for the 38 per cent of male migrants who regularly send money home. The 18 per cent of migrants who remit frequently transfer annually a sum in excess of the average rural per capita income, which represents 14–20 per cent of the urban earnings of the large majority. The 20 per cent of migrants who remit less frequently transfer smaller sums which are a smaller proportion of their earnings. The income transfer from urban migrants to rural dependants is substantial. There is no significant difference in the average size of the last remittance made by those migrants who remit frequently and those who remit occasionally. This, of course, implies that those who make remittances more frequently send more money home in a given year.[6]

The strength of rural ties is not the same for all groups of migrants. Those earning sh 1000 a month and over go home and make remittances less frequently than other migrants. Thirty-four per cent visit once a year or more, compared to twice that proportion for migrants earning sh 250–sh 500, while 51 per cent never make remittances, compared to half that proportion for other migrants.

[6] Thus any relations drawn below between income and other variables and frequency of remittances can also be drawn between those variables and the magnitude of total annual remittances. See *NUMEIST* 1971.

TABLE 7.11
*Migrant males: value of remittances
by frequency of remittances*

Frequency of remittances	Proportion of all migrants (%)	Proportion of migrants who remit (%)	Annual average value of remittances (sh)[a]	Estimated proportion of urban income[b] (%)
Six or more times a year	18	30	536	14–20
One to five times a year	20	33	170	3–6

[a] The value of migrant's last remittance was used as a proxy for value of the average.
[b] 75% of frequent remitters earn sh 500 or less; 82% of less frequent remitters earn sh 500 or less.
Source: NUMEIST 1971.

Since migrants in the upper income bracket are only 8 per cent of the total, their influence on the over-all pattern is minimal. As urban real incomes continue to rise, however, visits and remittances to rural areas may continue to diminish and so lead to a widening social gap and a reduction of the ameliorative effect of transfers on the increasingly unequal distribution of income between urban and rural areas. We must remember, however, that those with the highest income have probably been at work longest and away from home longest. Thirty-seven per cent of migrants earning sh 1000 or more a month have been in town for eleven years or more, compared to 25 per cent of migrants in the lower income brackets. Their lower level of remittances may be due less to a decrease in willingness to accept responsibility for people in the rural areas than to a decrease in actual responsibilities (*NUMEIST* 1971).

Migrants earning less than sh 250 also tend to go home and make remittances infrequently. This is partly explained by the connection between income and employment experience. Twenty-four per cent of low income earners had been in town for less than one and a half years at the time of the survey, compared to 13 per cent for migrants earning above sh 250. More fundamentally, given the high cost of living in town at even minimum standards, the lower the wages, the lower the surplus available either for remittances or for trips home.

How often migrants visit their home villages depends on where those villages are. In Dar es Salaam, 40 per cent of all male migrants from the surrounding Coast Region return home at least three times a year, compared to less than half as many for more distant regions (*NUMEIST* 1971). Cost of transport is a factor as is travelling time. The dominant pattern, however, is of frequent visits even to the most distant regions. Sixty-three per cent of the migrants from West Lake, Mara, and Mwanza and 43 per cent from Kigoma and Shinyanga make the 1200–1600 mile trip home and back to Dar es Salaam at least once a year.

The frequency of remittances does not vary with region of origin as the frequency of visits does; physical distance is not a problem in terms of time or money. Since the postal system is widespread, secure, and inexpensive, there is no need to fear losing funds in the mail. Most migrants use the postal system to transfer remittances. Although 72 per cent of migrants to Dar es Salaam from the Coast Region visit home once a year or more, compared to 53 per cent for all other regions, only 37 per cent of them make remittances once a year or more, while the proportion from all other regions is 39 per cent, with six of the ten more distant regions having a higher proportion than the Coast (*NUMEIST* 1971).

The strength of the contacts between urban migrants and their home areas appears inconsistent with the high levels of urban employment and residential stability we have documented. The apparent inconsistency is resolved by the fact that stabilization has not meant the end of circular migration. We have indicated that 75 per cent of the migrants in urban areas in 1968 were still living there three and a half years later. Just as controlling for employment growth allowed us to calculate a minimum turnover rate, so here we are able to calculate a minimum rate of return migration to the countryside of approximately 8 per cent.

There appear to be two streams of urban–rural migrants. The first consists of short-term migrants who decide to return home after visiting family or friends, searching for work, or a period of self-employment or unstable low wage employment. The second stream of urban–rural migrants is more important for an understanding of the maintenance and strength of urban–rural contacts. A high proportion of recent arrivals, the group that includes short-term circular migrants, have not visited their home area or made remittances. Whether this is the result of relative poverty or inadequate opportunity, it implies that most of the contacts with rural areas are maintained by the stable urban core of long-term migrants.

Nearly two-thirds of long-term migrants intend to retire to the countryside. This provides the link between urban–rural contacts and the existing pattern of circular migration. There is a clear association between the strength of urban migrants' contacts with their home villages and their intention to return there. Only 20 per cent of those migrants who make remittances intend to remain permanently in town, compared to 36 per cent of those who never make remittances. It is not clear whether this is because those who have maintained strong contacts are more likely to return home, or whether the maintenance of strong contacts is a means of ensuring acceptance at home on retirement. Probably both motives play a part. It is clear that remittances are not used to support the wage earner's wife or children.

Two-thirds of the migrants making remittances regularly and 75 per cent of those who visit home once a year or more do not have immediate dependants in the rural areas (*NUMEIST* 1971); nor do their visits and income transfers sustain *shambas* or other economic activity from which they derive direct benefit. As a result of the stabilization of the labour force and the regularization of work patterns, urban migrants can take only a few weeks' holiday a year and do not have time to cultivate a *shamba*. Over 75 per cent of the migrants' last visits home were for less than three weeks and only 24 per cent of migrants claim to have participated in any economic activity while visiting their home areas (*NUMEIST* 1971). The funds apparently are for the use of parents, members of the worker's family, or for building a retirement house.

The intention to return was expressed by relatively high income earners as well as by low income earners (*NUMEIST* 1971). Given the current structure of the Tanzanian economy, returning home to retire makes economic sense. Once the migrant retires from urban employment the real rural–urban income differential shifts in favour of the countryside. Less than 5 per cent of all migrant wage earners supplement their wages from other sources such as self-employment or renting rooms. Once a migrant has left his job, he is no longer tied to the city by his source of income. His small savings or low pension can go home with him, where the lower cost of living means that his income will extend much further. In addition, the likelihood of receiving support in old age from relatives and others might be greater in the rural areas, where traditional tribal obligations are still strong.

In conclusion, we have established that, while the labour force and migrant population have been stabilized, the pattern of circular migration has not come to an end. Rather, for most of the migrants living in urban areas the rural areas still provide an informal social security system. How much longer this system will be maintained depends on the availability of land. At present land is still plentiful in most parts of Tanzania and most migrants know there will be a plot available for their retirement. As an indication of what will happen when land becomes scarce, four times as many of the few urban migrants without access to land intend to remain in town (*NUMEIST* 1971).

5. SUMMARY

The short length of time spent by colonial migrants in employment before returning home is not to be explained by a unique African labour supply function, but by low wages which made dividing the family and moving back and forth income-maximizing behaviour. When conditions in the labour market changed, the behaviour of migrants in regard to their length of stay changed. The rise in urban wages increased the opportunity cost of leaving urban employment for trips home to tend the family *shamba*, and made it possible for a migrant to support his family in town. Stagnating rural income minimized the opportunity cost of uniting the family, while higher wages led to a labour supply in excess of demand, adding the cost of future job searches to the opportunity cost of leaving a current job. The introduction of complex wage structures also served to increase the opportunity cost of leaving a wage job.

Migrants have responded by increasing their length of stay in wage employment. The stability of the wage labour force, measured by turnover and mobility rates, is high by international standards; much of the turnover is initiated on the demand rather than the supply side of the labour market. Those who claimed that the instability of African labour precluded efficient industrialization have been shown to be wrong. However, if high turnover is a serious constraint on labour productivity, we return to the question first raised in Chapter I, why did not employers raise wages throughout the colonial period? The answer lies in the difference in the stability–

productivity relationship on estates and in industrial employment, an issue with which we will be concerned in the next chapter.

The stabilization of the labour force has accounted for much of the change in the sex composition of the migrant stream and has brought a more normal demographic pattern to Tanzania's urban areas. It has also produced a core of stable urban residents. A significant number of urban migrants still return to the rural areas, however, after only a short time in town looking for a wage job. And even the migrants who are successful in finding a job maintain strong contacts with home and intend to return there on retirement.

VIII

WAGE DETERMINATION UNDER CONDITIONS OF SURPLUS LABOUR

OUR findings suggest that for any given positive differential between urban wages paid and the supply price of labour in Tanzania, there is a level of unemployment that will result in a labour market equilibrium.[1] Conversely, if there is urban surplus labour, then the rural–urban differential must be excessively wide when viewed from an aggregate supply and demand perspective. Similarly, neoclassical models of regional income disparities clearly predict that factor mobility, of which migration is one component, should contribute to a convergence of marginal products between high and low income regions.[2] But our evidence has in fact shown that the rural–urban differential has widened more rapidly since the problem of urban surplus labour has emerged. If the differential is wide and is moving in a direction contrary to that required to eliminate urban surplus labour, then there must be mechanisms outside the realm of supply and demand impinging on the labour market, and in particular on income determination.

In this chapter we identify two alternative mechanisms that could be responsible for this situation in Tanzania and attempt to assess their importance. We take urban wages as the key element in the rural–urban differential because we have already examined the factors accounting for the stagnation of rural incomes, and, more importantly, because the burden of adjustment to excessive differentials and surplus labour should theoretically fall on the urban sector. Given a rural sector much larger than the urban, we would expect the same level of factor mobility to have a greater effect on the income of the smaller sector. Except in the unlikely circumstances of an elasticity of demand for labour much higher in rural than in urban areas, a migrant stream should have its greatest impact on the rural–urban differential by lowering urban marginal products rather than raising rural marginal products.

[1] See Chapter IV.
[2] See for example Borts 1960, Okun and Richardson 1961.

1. MARKET JUSTIFICATION FOR WAGE INCREASES

We begin by considering changes in labour supply and demand consistent with the view that wage increases were no more than would have occurred in an unconstrained labour market. Two conditions would appear to have necessitated some increase in wages to achieve balance between supply and demand, even without any other changes in the market. The first and most obvious was the labour market imbalance of the colonial era. With rural earnings constant or rising, some increase in wages might appear to have been justified in order to eliminate the scarcity. Since, however, during the 1960s the growth of wage employment was below the rate of increase of the national labour force, it is unlikely that there was any need for higher wages to ensure an adequate supply of wage labour. The second condition has to do with a shift in the occupational structure of labour demand. The decline in sisal employment and the expansion of non-agricultural employment have resulted in a rise of the non-agricultural/agricultural wage employment ratio from 0·89 to 2·45 over the period 1952–70 (see Table 2.11). This industrial shift has in part been responsible for the equally dramatic shift that has characterized the occupational structure of demand in the post-war era.

TABLE 8.1
*Distribution of employment of adult African males
by skill level and industry 1953*

Industrial division	Workers with some skill	Unskilled	Skilled/ Unskilled
Total Agriculture	24 761	158 811	0·15
Sisal	16 244	110 422	0·15
Total Non-agriculture	74 754	103 527	0·72
Mining and quarrying	4 346	12 298	0·35
Manufacturing	6 105	9 682	0·63
Construction	4 690	9 281	0·50
Public utilities	442	589	0·75
Commerce	5 510	5 589	0·98
Transport	2 221	4 660	0·48
Non-government services	6 622	4 952	1·33
Government	44 818	56 476	0·79

Source: Tanganyika, Labour Department 1954.

Table 8.1 is a crude index of the occupational structure in 1953. Every one of the eight non-agricultural categories has a higher skilled/unskilled employment *ratio* than the sisal industry or the agricultural sector as a whole, where 87 per cent of the labour force was unskilled. Only in mining and quarrying does the concentration of unskilled workers approach that found in agriculture; in non-government services, which include teachers and other professional Africans, there are more skilled than unskilled personnel. Overall the ratio of skilled to unskilled jobs is nearly five times as high in non-agricultural as in agricultural employment. The post-war growth in the importance of non-agricultural labour demand has meant an increase in the skilled component of labour demand. Moreover, as Table 8.2 indicates, the skill intensity of demand for labour in non-agricultural industries has increased. The proportion of unskilled workers in manufacturing decreased from 61 per cent in 1953 to 30 per cent in 1971. There have been similar declines in construction from 66 per cent in 1953 to 29 per cent in 1971, and in public utilities from 57 to 35 per cent. Only in commerce and the service sector has there been no appreciable change.

We would expect this change in occupational structure to contribute to the rise in average wages, under the assumption that there is a positive wage differential for workers with greater skill, an assumption confirmed by our examination of wage structures in Chapter IV (see Table 4.2).

TABLE 8.2

Seven towns: adult wage earners in industrial employment by occupation

	White[a] collar 1971	Production[b] 1971	Unskilled 1971	Total 1971	1953 Unskilled as proportion of total
Manufacturing	17	53	30	100	61
Construction	14	57	29	100	66
Commerce	38	12	50	100	50
Govt. & non-Govt. service	45	7	49	100	54
Transport	28	31	42	100	68
Public Utilities	26	40	35	100	57

[a] Including professional, technical, managerial, clerical, police, nurses and other public servants, semi-technical workers.
[b] including drivers, mechanics, foremen, skilled workers, craftsmen, machine operators.
Sources: NUMEIST 1971; Tanganyika, Labour Department 1954.

The market justification for skill differentials lies in the correlation between skill and productivity, and in the investment necessary for equipping personnel with the required skills. Here it is important to make a distinction. If training is carried out within the formal educational system, skill differentials can be seen as necessary to encourage others to invest in their own training. (Since the state meets most of the direct costs of education, it is important to remember that the student or his parents must still absorb education's opportunity costs.) Skill differentials also provide the mechanism by which scarce skills can be allocated among competing uses (Berg in Smith 1969). If, however, training is carried out within the firm at no cost to the individual worker, what is the justification for wage differentials by skill? One explanation which, as we shall see, has considerable relevance in Tanzania is that the higher wage is the means by which the firm is assured of an economic return on its investment in training. Higher wages provide an incentive for the worker to remain on the job for a longer period, and so increase the period over which the employer benefits from worker training.

We are here concerned with the market explanation of differentials, but not all occupational differentials need arise from the interaction of supply and demand. In our analysis of institutional factors that may have contributed to a rise of wages above the level justified by supply and demand, we include distortions in occupational wage structures. Also, when considering the relationship between changes in the occupational structure and the increase in average urban wages we should not dismiss the possibility that the causality runs in the other direction as well, rises in wages for reasons other than changes in the occupation mix may have contributed to changes in that mix. This could occur if the wage elasticity of demand is higher for unskilled than for skilled labour or if wages at the bottom of the distribution are rising faster than those above. Despite these qualifications, it would appear that at least some of the increase in average wages has been justified by the shift in occupational structure.

2. EXCESSIVE WAGE INCREASES: THE INSTITUTIONAL HYPOTHESIS

Elimination of labour scarcity and the increasing skill of the labour force can be seen as consistent with a market clearing explanation of the increase in wages and the widening income gap between the

agricultural self-employed and the wage employed. What can explain
a rise in wages in excess of that necessary to equilibrate demand and
supply? Two alternative, though not mutually exclusive, sets of
hypotheses can be put forward. The first posits that non-market
factors result in wages above the market clearing level, and may be
called the institutional hypothesis.

In Fig. 8.1 S and D are supply and demand schedules, w_1
represents the equilibrium wage, w_2 a wage level in excess of labour's
equilibrium supply price, with L_1–L_3 constituting the resultant
labour surplus. The allocation of the surplus between unemployment
and low wage employment was discussed in Chapter VII. Here we
are focusing on non-market forces that might account for a wage gap
such as w_1–w_2 in Tanzania. Three institutional changes which
occurred during the period of rapid wage increases have influenced
the process of wage determination and may have contributed to an
excessive wage rise.

2.1. *Trade union activity*

First there is the growth of trade union strength. Unions only began

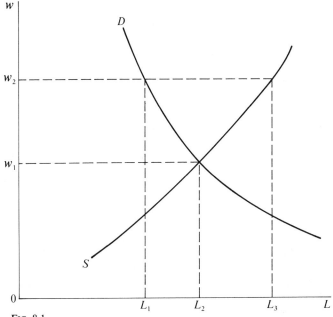

FIG. 8.1

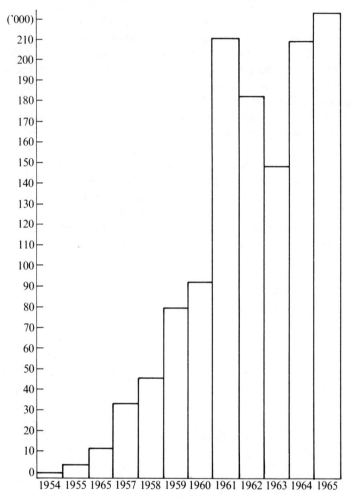

FIG. 8.2. Number of trade union members (from Tanganyika. Labour Department, 1969)

to develop in Tanzania in the 1950s. The high turnover of the migrant labour system made union formation difficult. The workers' continuing ties with widely scattered source areas hindered the development of coherent organization among them and the informal social security system provided by these ties lessened the need for such cohesion. In 1954, as Fig. 8.2 shows, there were only some 1500 union members, an insignificant proportion of a total wage labour force of over 400 000. By 1965 there were more than 220 000 union members, comprising more than 50 per cent of the labour force. While the explanations for this rapid growth are beyond the scope of the present inquiry, the emergence of educated leaders, the identification of the unions with the nationalist movement, and the stabilization of the labour force can be identified as contributing factors (Stephens 1968, Friedland 1969).

In Tanzania as elsewhere trade unions have brought pressure to bear on wages by both political action and collective bargaining. Whether such pressure could increase labour's share of the value of output in the wage sector is an open question. In an economy in which that sector generates only a small proportion of total output and an even smaller proportion of total employment, however, unions could so far improve the position of the wage employed in relation to the agricultural self-employed that the wage level would exceed the equilibrium supply price of rural self-employed labour to the wage sector.

2.2 *Minimum wages*

Legislated minimum wages could also lead to wage levels above the market clearing level. The colonial government passed enabling legislation for wage fixing in 1939 to accord with I.L.O. convention 26 (Chesworth 1972). However, it was not until 1957, following the recommendations of the 1955 East African Royal Commission and of a United Nations Visiting Mission of 1954, that the first minimum wage, applying to workers in Dar es Salaam, was actually enforced (Great Britain 1955, U.N. 1955). In 1959 the Jack Report recommended extending the ordinance to cover all workers and in 1963 a territorial minimum wage was imposed (Jack 1959, Chesworth 1967).

Minimum wages have a direct effect on the wage level to the extent that actual increases in wages are necessary to comply with the law. The minimum fixed for Dar es Salaam in 1957 was sh 82–82·50, more than twice the average wages of the 20–30 per cent of the labour force covered by the legislation. It is not possible to calculate precisely the effect of this increase on average real wages, though in the short run it was clearly upward. Raising the wages of the lowest strata would have a direct effect on the average, as would the contraction of demand for the lowest paid types of labour; while the compression of differentials and the pressure to raise wages above the minimum would have an indirect effect.

The minimum wage for urban areas, established in 1972, was sh 240. Though more people were covered,[3] the change in amount is not likely to have had any greater effect than the original law of 1957; the new minimum wage was only 33–41 per cent above the previous minimum, which was already the earnings level of most of the people affected. Certainly the new minimum was not double the average wage of those eligible for the increase. If we assume no change in employment, the direct effect of the rise on the total wage bill, and hence on average wages, was only some 5 per cent (*NUMEIST* 1971). The indirect effects cannot be calculated, though they are likely to be less significant than in 1957, because in 1972 the government had an incomes policy and administrative machinery that was relatively successful in enforcing it.

In any one instance the effect of minimum wages on the average does not appear to be highly significant. Unfortunately it is not possible to determine the effect of the changes over the period 1957–72 because we do not know what would have happened in the absence of legislation. If minimum wage increases only anticipated increases that would have occurred anyway owing to market forces or employer action, the net effect on the wage level would be zero. (This applies also to wage increases resulting from union pressure.) We cannot assume an identity between the apparent and real effects of institutional forces on the level of wages. This is particularly important in Tanzania where there is considerable evidence that it was in the employers' interest to raise wages during this period. Before we consider why this is so, there is another institutional phenomenon whose possible contribution to a rise in wages above labour's equilibrium supply price must be examined.

2.3. *Government wage policy and Africanization*

Government policy has influenced the level of wages in ways other than minimum wage legislation. Since the government is the largest single employer in the country, employing 20–30 per cent of the wage labour force, the wages paid to government workers have a significant impact on wage levels. The modest role the government has played as wage leader could also have contributed to the rise of

---

[3] In 1971 only some 40 per cent of the Dar es Salaam wage labour force earned less than the 1972 minimum.

the wages above the market rate, as higher pay for the same work by the government would put pressure on the parastatal and private sectors in the form of worker unrest and loss of productive workers to the state. The government's role as wage leader and its more general aim of raising wages were outlined by the East African Royal Commission in 1953–5 (Great Britain 1955). In the Commission's view, the migrant labour system was a social evil which led to inefficient use of labour in agriculture and in wage employment. Raising wages was expected to end the system of circular migration and increase labour productivity in both sectors.

In addition to raising wages at the bottom of the scale, government policy has contributed to the increase in average wages by raising the wages of Tanzanians at the top of the scale in the course of moving Africans into high income jobs not previously open to them. It is possible that institutional factors have led to occupational differentials in excess of those justified by supply and demand. In some countries excessive white-collar–blue-collar differentials can be explained by the rigid stratification of social classes. A man behind a desk in India is paid more than a man working a machine, not because of his scarcity or his greater contribution to national output, but simply because he belongs to a social group with traditional élite status (Berg in Smith 1969). In Tanzania there are no such rigid class distinctions. However, during the colonial period most high-level manpower posts were held by Europeans, who received incomes 20 to 30 times those of African manual workers. Although the difference was used to establish the Europeans as an élite, these high incomes were primarily determined by the alternatives available in the rich metropolitan countries rather than by opportunities in the colonial dependency.

The 1960s witnessed the rapid Africanization of the Civil Service. Table 8.3 shows the progress made since Independence in replacing non-citizens in senior and middle level posts, where the greatest concentration of colonial civil servants was to be found. In 1961 only 26 per cent of such posts were held by Tanzanians. By 1970 the proportion had increased to 85 per cent; since the number of posts had doubled over the period, this implied a sevenfold increase in the number of Tanzanians in high level positions. From our perspective the significance of Africanization is in its contribution to institutional pressures on wage and salary income.

The colonial wage and salary structures were not dismantled at

TABLE 8.3
Africanization of the Civil Service 1961–1970

Period ending	Officers serving in senior and middle grade posts on permanent terms			
	Total	Citizens	Others	% Citizens
1961	4452	1170	3282	26·1
1962	4723	1821	2902	38·5
1963	5049	2467	2580	48·9
1964	5389	3083	2306	57·2
1965	5962	3851	2011	66·2
1966	6262	4364	1898	69·7
1967	6754	4937	1817	73·1
1968	7827	6208	1619	79·3
1969	7474	6123	1351	81·9
1970	9419	8042	1377	85·6

Source: Tanzania, Bureau of Statistics 1971a.

Independence, since to do away with what many people regarded as the fruits of Independence would have been politically untenable. In addition, the physical structure, the big houses, the cars and garages, the restaurants and clubs, remained after the British left. If Tanzanians were to use these facilities, and in some cases it seemed to make economic sense to do so, they would have to be paid a salary high enough to maintain them. Government employees with higher education and training are still paid less than some expatriates working in Tanzania, who receive world market rates for high level skills. However, very few Tanzanians yet have skills that are marketable internationally. More important is the fact that the ratio of wages and salaries of higher level government officials to those further down the occupational ladder is higher in Tanzania than in most developed countries. Equally important is the fact that this wage structure has been adopted by the private and parastatal sectors as well.

Table 8.4 compares incomes of occupational groups in government and non-government employment in Tanzania and the United Kingdom. The skilled–unskilled differential is only slightly higher in the former series, but the differential between clerical workers and unskilled workers is nearly twice as great in Tanzania as in Britain. Equally significant is the fact that clerical jobs on average pay 37 per cent more than skilled manual jobs, while in Britain the situation is

TABLE 8.4
Adult wage earners in Tanzania and Great Britain:
Average wages by occupation: comparative tables

Occupational groups	United Kingdom: wage earners		Tanzania: wage earners in seven towns	
	Average wage £ per month	Index	Average wage sh per month	Index
Professionals	1375	266	863	349
Clerical	532	103	551	223
Skilled	754	146	407	165
Semi-skilled	482	93	277	112
Unskilled	516	100	247	100

Sources: *NUMEIST* 1971, Routh 1965.

reversed, with skilled workers receiving 45 per cent more than clerical workers. While British wage structures cannot be adopted as a norm, the size of the differential between white-collar and blue-collar workers in Tanzania provides evidence of continuing institutional rigidity.

While some of the increase in average wages due to the shift in the occupational structure may have been justified in market terms, some at least was due to the adoption of the outmoded colonial structure of occupational differentials. The consequent distortion had indirect as well as direct effects on the average level of wages, as the existence of a highly paid African élite put pressure on the government to narrow differentials by raising the wages of the lower stratum.

This distortion is not likely to attract surplus labour to the towns in significant numbers. Though wages paid to high level civil servants and white-collar workers are probably considerably higher than their supply price, there is no excess supply because of the limitations imposed by manpower planning on secondary and post-secondary school expansion.[4] Rural residents are aware of the strict educational requirements for high level occupations and the resultant

[4] The fact that the secondary school system expanded at a faster rate than planned was noted in Chapter VI. The resulting excess of secondary leavers began to filter down into lower level occupations. This process indicates that the scarcity of educated output was a problem of the past in Tanzania. Except in the few occupations requiring post-graduate training, there is no justification for such wide income differentials in the argument that payment of scarcity rents will assure that trained individuals will be used where their marginal products will be highest.

stratified labour market, and thus are not attracted to town by the extremely high income available in these occupations. While this by no means implies that the distortion has not had negative consequences,[5] it does mean that our primary concern in the surplus labour problem is with the wage gap facing the less well educated.

3. EXCESSIVE WAGE INCREASES: A LABOUR COST MINIMIZATION MODEL OF WAGE DETERMINATION

We now consider the hypothesis that the employers themselves were primarily responsible for the dramatic wage increases of the late 1950s and 1960s. There are circumstances in which it is economically rational for urban employers, independent of government legislation, trade union pressure, or other non-market forces, to raise wages above the level necessary to attract a sufficient number of workers. We can show that, when employers expect wage-related gains from increased productivity and decreased non-wage costs of labour to be greater than the costs of increased wages, the wage per man that minimizes total costs per efficiency unit of labour is greater than that which clears the labour market.

We can now visualize a situation in which there are no institutional distortions and yet there is a gap between the wages paid and the equilibrium supply price of labour. In this section we examine a simple formal model that makes explicit three key aspects of the wage–labour cost relationship and demonstrates the conditions necessary for the wage gap to emerge in an unfettered labour market.

3.1 *The wage–nutrition–productivity linkage*

We start by assuming a positive relationship between the supply of labour, L, and the wage rate, w,

$$L = L(w), \qquad L'(w) > 0.$$

Also there is a positive relationship between physical productivity per worker, o, and the wage rate,

$$o_1 = o_1(w) \qquad o_1'(w) > 0.$$

Here we are isolating increases in productivity associated with the improved physical well-being of the worker and assuming that at least part of any wage increase will be devoted to more nutritious

---

[5] The negative effects of this distortion on the demand for secondary school places and on the nature and content of primary education were discussed in Chapter V.

diet, better housing, better medical care, or other items of consumption having direct effect on physical well-being.[6] The total number of physical productivity units, O, supplied at any designated wage rate is given by

$$O = o_1(w \cdot L).$$

In Fig. 8.3, L–L represents the supply curve of labour and O–O the aggregate supply curve of physical productivity units. The important point to note here is that because of the positive relationship between wages and physical productivity O–O is always more elastic with respect to the wage rate than L–L.

The wage cost per physical productivity unit supplied is given by

$$c_1 = \frac{W \cdot L}{O}$$

and this cost curve is represented in Fig. 8.3 as C_1 – C_1. The level of productivity of a worker at wage w_2 is arbitrarily chosen to equal one productivity unit, and it is assumed that it is at this wage level that the supply elasticity of physical productivity units per man with respect to wages is unity. To the left of A^1 the elasticity is greater than one; to the right of A^1 it is less than one. Examining the relationship between wages and the cost per productivity unit, we find

$$\frac{dc_1}{dw} = \frac{o_1 - wo'}{o^2} = \frac{1 - w/oo'}{o_1}.$$

Whether an increase in wages results in an increase or a decrease in cost per productivity unit, whether in other words dc_1/dw is positive or negative, thus depends upon whether $w/o_1 \cdot o_1'$, the wage elasticity of supply of physical productivity units per head, is greater or less than unity. Thus it is at A^1 that the average cost curve of physical productivity units is at its minimum.

The situation in which the demand curve intersects the supply

[6] Numerous authors have emphasized that the linkage of increased income → improved nutrition and health → increased physical productivity should undermine the economist's confidence in the rigid distinction between consumption and investment. Increasing consumption in this situation can also be seen as an investment in human capital. See Myrdal 1968, Streeten 1972. Several authors have brought this relationship to bear on the issue of wage determination: see Bottomley 1971, Leibenstein 1973, and Harris 1971 whose geometric analysis of the wage-productivity relationship is extended here.

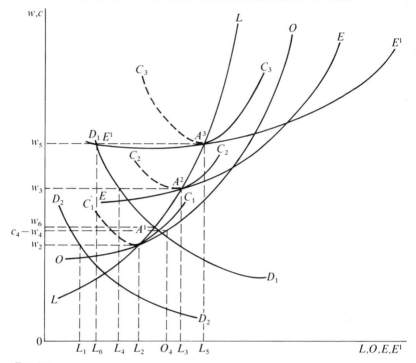

FIG. 8.3

curve to the right of A^1, where the elasticity is less than unity, is of little interest. Here, conventional labour market clearing adjustments take place through numbers hired and wage rates, though demand is defined in terms of physical productivity units of labour, and labour costs are calculated per physical productivity units. A shift in the demand curve to the right will increase the number of workers hired and the wage rate, though by a degree less than if there were no wage–productivity relationship.

It is the case where the elasticity of physical productivity units per head is greater than one that is of interest. We are assuming that, with a given capital stock, in order to maximize profits firms will seek to set wages so as to minimize labour costs. Thus to the left of A^1, if the relevant demand curve is D^2, labour costs will be minimized by setting wages at w^2 which is $w_2 - w_1$ above labour's equilibrium supply price. The result is that $L_2 - L_1$ workers would be unemployed.

The relevance of the model as it stands is limited in the Tanzanian case as it is unlikely that in the period we are examining the demand curve intersected the supply curves in the range where the elasticity of supply of productivity units per worker with respect to wages was greater than one. While there is no satisfactory definition of an adequate diet, it does not appear that Tanzanian workers were suffering from acute malnutrition in the 1950s and 1960s. Furthermore, the wage–physical productivity relationship must be qualified in any circumstances since the marginal propensity to consume (nutritious) food, or other goods that improve physical well-being, relative to all other consumer goods, may be low and since the most significant dietary constraint on adult worker productivity may derive from the permanent disabilities resulting from malnutrition in childhood, implying that an improvement in the diet of an adult worker may have little effect on his productivity (Turnham 1971).

3.2 *The links between wages, stability, and productivity*

We can extend the model and increase its relevance by considering the consequences for productivity of the relationship between wages and stability. Two effects of the wage–stability relationship increase the likelihood that it was to the Tanzanian employer's advantage to raise wages in excess of the supply price of labour. First there is the negative relationship between the level of productivity impairment per head as a consequence of high turnover, o_2, and the level of wages.

$$o_2 = o_2(w), \qquad o_2' < 0.$$

At low wages, high turnover produces a high level of efficiency impairment as workers are not on the job long enough to overcome the handicap of inexperience. With an increase in wages, the average length of stay of the worker increases and the productivity handicap of inexperience declines. In Fig. 8.4 the functions relating wages to physical productivity per worker and to efficiency impairment per worker owing to turnover are summed to yield a curve of total efficiency units supplied per worker,

$$e = o_1(w) - o_2(w) = e(w).$$

This curve is more wage elastic than the curve of physical productivity units alone. The aggregate number of efficiency units supplied at any designated wage rate is given by the function.

$$E = e(w) \cdot L$$

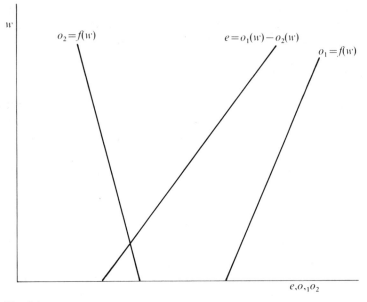

FIG. 8.4

which is drawn as curve E–E in Fig. 8.3. E–E is more elastic than O–O at any given wage rate. Thus at A^1 where the elasticity of o is unity, the elasticity of e must be greater than unity. It is for this reason that E–E crosses L–L above O–O at A^2. We have defined the level of productivity of a worker at wage w_3 to equal one and efficiency units per head can be seen to equal unity at this wage as well. The wage cost per efficiency unit supplied is given by

$$c_2 = \frac{w \cdot L}{E}$$

and this curve is drawn in Fig. 8.2 as C_2–C_2. At A^2 this curve is at its minimum value.

If the relevant demand curve for labour services is D_1–D_1, we can see that if employers consider only the wage–physical productivity relationship, O_4 productivity units of labour will be hired at a cost per unit of c_4 per unit. All the labour forthcoming at wage w_4 will be absorbed and the minimizing of labour costs does not lead to a situation in which wages paid are in excess of the supply price of labour. However, if employers also consider the stability–efficiency benefits from increased wages, the relevant cost curve will be C_2–C_2; labour cost will be minimized by paying the wage w_3; L_3 workers will be hired, each one providing one efficiency unit of labour; and L_3–L_4 workers will be unemployed. Thus if the effects of increased wages on stability and efficiency are considered, employers may find that it pays to increase wages to a level in excess of that which will attract the required number of workers.

3.3 The links between wages, stability, and cost of hiring and training

The degree of stability affects the non-wage costs of labour as well as its efficiency. Total labour costs of a firm include the cost of hiring and training workers. Included in training costs would be the increased costs of machinery maintenance that are associated with using new employees. Assuming a constant level of hiring and training costs per worker and an inverse relationship between the wage rate and the rate of turnover, there will be an inverse relationship between the wage rate and hiring and training costs per worker in a given period:

$$h = h(w) \qquad h'(w) < 0.$$

We can incorporate this additional factor into the supply curve of labour services by taking the total number of efficiency units net of hiring and training costs supplied at any given wage which is given by

$$E' = (e(w) - h(w)) \cdot L.$$

This curve, denoted as E^1–E^1 in Fig. 8.3, is more elastic than E–E and cuts L–L at A^3. The productivity of a worker net of hiring and training costs at wage w_5 is defined to equal one net efficiency unit where the elasticity of net efficiency units is equal to unity. The wage cost per net efficiency unit is given by

$$c_3 = \frac{w \cdot L}{E'}$$

amd this curve, which is at its minimum value at A^3, is drawn in Fig. 8.3 as C_3–C_3. If, in addition to the effect of wages on physical productivity and on stability-induced-efficiency, employers also take into consideration the effect of wages on hiring and training costs, then, given demand curve D_1–D_1, the wage gap will be w_5–w_6 and L_5–L_6 people will be unemployed.

4. EVIDENCE OF EMPLOYER-LED WAGE INCREASES

Has the labour cost minimization model any relevance to Tanzania during the period of rapid wage increases? Is the evidence consistent with the hypothesis that the employers themselves were a prominent factor in the wage increases? Our primary focus is on the wage–stability–productivity linkage.

4.1. The growth of wage sector labour productivity

If employers are to be considered responsible for any part of the dramatic increase in wages in Tanzania in the 1950s and 1960s, there must be evidence of a significant increase in the productivity of wage labour. The trend in labour productivity can be derived by comparing the growth of output with that of employment. The post-war period witnessed a decline in aggregate wage employment in Tanzania, accounted for by the sharp contraction in agricultural wage employment in the 1960s. At the same time, non-agricultural employment growth, at an annual rate of under 2 per cent, was less than outstanding. Table 8.5 indicates that in the sisal industry the decline of the labour force was not the result of declining output. Though sisal prices fell from their post-war high, the short-run response of growers was to maintain output. While prices were lower in 1968 than in 1961, there was actually an increase of 5000 tons in sisal production. Nor has non-agricultural output declined; on the contrary, national income data reveal that in the period 1961–8 there was an increase of over 14 per cent a year valued at constant prices. Output in manufacturing and transport and communications grew at a rate above the average; manufacturing production more than quadrupled, implying an average annual rate of increase of 23 per cent.

The gap between the rate of growth of employment and the rate of growth of output represents the increase in labour productivity. Column 7 of Table 8.5 presents estimates of the relationship between output and employment growth which may be used as an indicator of the rate of increase of productivity. The net output elasticity of labour demand, the proportionate change in employment associated with a change in output, with all other factors held constant is in its gross form and is purely descriptive. The lower the elasticity the more rapid the growth of productivity. Since sisal output was increasing even though employment was on the decline, the elasticity is strongly negative. In 1968 a labour force of 42 000 produced more

TABLE 8.5

The output elasticity of the demand for labour 1961–1968

Sector	1961		1968		Annual growth rates: 1961–8		
	(1) Labour force[b]	(2) Output (1966 prices) '000s of T£	(3) Labour force[d]	(4) Output[e] (1966 prices) '000s of T£	(5) Labour force growth rate	(6) Output growth rate	(7) Output elasticity of demand for labour (5÷6)
Agriculture:							
Sisal	128 928	198 000[a,c]	41 668	203 000	−12·199	0·357	−34·171
Non-agriculture:	196 888	81 005	242 498	205 600	3·021	14·232	0·212
Manufacturing	26 363	7 097	35 359	31 350	4·283	23·642	0·181
Public utilities	6 910	1 387	9 601	3 600	4·811	14·597	0·330
Construction	41 775	5 956	47 305	15 750	1·792	14·903	0·120
Transport and communications	21 412	8 756	31 764	30 900	5·796	19·739	0·294
Mining and quarrying	11 875	5 585	6 121	6 850	−9·033	2·960	−3·052

[a] Output in tons.
[b] Tanganyika, Labour Department 1963.
[c] Guillebaud 1966.
[d] Tanzania, Central Statistical Bureau various years.
[e] Tanganyika, Central Statistical Bureau 1964; Tanzania, various years; and Tanzania, Bureau of Statistics 1972.

than the 129 000 labour force of 1961, implying a tripling of labour productivity in only seven years. There was a similar though less marked negative elasticity in mining, while in the other non-agricultural sectors the range was from 0·330 in public utilities to 0·120 in construction.[7] This experience of rapid productivity growth and diminished rate of labour absorption in the non-agricultural sector is a characteristic of post-war economic development which Tanzania shares with a number of other developing countries in Latin America and Asia, as well as in Africa.[8]

4.2. *The wage–productivity relationship*

While the association between wage increases and productivity increases is a necessary condition for the confirmation of the labour cost minimization hypothesis, it is by no means sufficient. A high correlation between wages and output per man does not specify the direction in which the causal relationship between the two is running. Nothing in the degree of association precludes the possibility that wage increases follow increases in productivity deriving from non-wage sources. If this were so, our evidence in support of the hypothesis that employers raised wages as a means of increasing labour productivity would be diminished, but it would not significantly undermine the argument that employers were instrumental in bringing about higher wages or, what amounts to the same thing, that employers relaxed their resistance to institutional pressures for increases.

The structure of manufacturing industry in Tanzania explains why an independent rise in productivity might make employers more willing to grant wage increases. Manufacturing firms in Tanzania tend to be highly capital intensive compared to the agricultural estates. During the period of rapid wage increases they were predominantly foreign owned and sensitive to the changing

[7] No separate measures for the government or commerce sectors were included, as value added in those sectors is measured on the basis of the wage bill, making the output elasticity of demand labour a measure of the increase in wages which may or may not be related to productivity.
[8] Some estimated output elasticities of the demand for labour are: (1) Mexico, Manufacturing: 1950–60, 0·49 (Isbister 1971). (2) Colombia, Manufacturing: 1951–63, 0·44 (Zschock 1967). (3) Puerto Rico, Manufacturing: 1950–60, 0·42 (Reynolds and Gregory 1965). For a general discussion of this phenomenon, see Baer and Herve 1966, Frank 1968 and Morawetz 1974.

political balance in the country and the accusation that low wages were a sign of colonial exploitation. A high capital–labour ratio means that wage costs are a small proportion of total value added so that a given wage increase has a smaller effect on total costs in capital-intensive enterprises. In addition, many of the more capital intensive firms operated behind tariff barriers that allowed them to pass on cost increases to consumers as higher prices. The capital-intensive firms could raise wages above the supply price of labour without significant effects on profit levels.

However, increases in productivity independent of wages do not appear to have been an important factor in the wage increases that occurred. The increase in aggregate wage sector productivity was not primarily due to a faster rate of output growth in the high productivity industrial sub-sectors. Disaggregating the non-agricultural rate of productivity increase does not yield a high dispersion in rates among sub-sectors. A shift to a more capital intensive form of production and to higher levels of labour productivity may result from the response of firms to a rise in the price of labour. It can also result from the importation of labour-saving capital equipment in response to factor price movements in the producing rather than the consuming country. Though we cannot determine how much of any change in the capital intensity of production was due to changes in domestic factor prices and how much to external causes, given the recent vintage of most capital equipment in Tanzania it is unlikely that the latter could have accounted for more than a small proportion of the productivity increases that occurred.

This still leaves the question of how much of the productivity increase was due to capital deepening and how much to increasing the efficiency of labour independently of changes in technology. An increase in wages may lead employers to economize on the use of labour by adopting a more capital-intensive production technology, one consequence of which is likely to be an increase in labour productivity. Since there is no apparent reason why an employer should raise wages above the supply price of labour in order to induce a change in technology, the productivity gains relevant to the labour cost minimization hypothesis are those usually termed 'autonomous', or independent of changes in technology. These would include gains resulting from changes in management, organization and work procedures, from the improved health and nutritional level of the labour force, and—particularly important in the

Tanzanian context—from gains deriving from on-the-job training and higher levels of labour force stability.

What evidence there is, suggests that most of the productivity gain in Tanzania does not derive from changes in the configurations of capital stock, output, and labour embodied in physical plant, but from changes in the number of men used to operate the given capital stock. Evidence that the level of wages is not an important consideration in the choice of technology for firms investing in developing countries is one reason for believing that changes in labour use rather than capital equipment account for productivity increase (Aharoni 1966, Kilby 1969). In Tanzania, as in other developing countries, there is a high degree of capital intensity in the manufacturing sector despite wages that are only a fraction of those in industrialized countries. Distortions in the price of capital caused by government encouragement of foreign investment may partly account for this; scarcity of skilled supervisory personnel who often constitute a necessary complement to efficient labour-intensive techniques may also be a factor. Similarly, expensive imported inputs which require scarce foreign exchange may be more efficiently used by capital-intensive than by labour-intensive techniques. More important is a series of non-factor price considerations, including a lack of flexibility in the capital goods industries of the high-wage countries where the machinery is designed and produced. This results in equipment suited to the industrial countries rich in capital and an absence of modern labour-intensive equipment. Capital-intensive techniques are often absolutely more efficient than available alternatives over a wide range of wages, in the sense of saving on both labour and capital per unit of output. In Tanzania the choice of techniques is often further narrowed by 'tied aid' which ensures the purchasing of capital goods from the donor country. A high proportion of the firms investing in Tanzania are subsidiaries of international corporations; a policy of standardization of production techniques, rather than one of matching techniques to local factor endowments, may be profit maximizing for such enterprises. All these factors would serve to reduce the influence of wages on the choice of technology.

There are other reasons for believing that changes in labour use rather than increases in the capital intensity of technology have had the greater significance in the increase in productivity. Adjustment to factor price changes by means of capital intensity of technology is a long-term proposition because technology is embodied in capital equipment. While changes in factor prices may affect a firm's appraisal of the length of the profitable life of the equipment, they are not likely to lead to instantaneous replacement. Changes in management techniques, hours worked, and number of men per machine are likely to constitute the short-term adjustments to factor price changes. The fact that in their estimation of the elasticity of substitution in Kenyan manufacturing industry, Harris and Todaro (1969) found the unlagged relationship to be insignificant, while the lagged relationship proved significant, is evidence that in Kenya productivity gains in the late 1950s and early 1960s were predominantly of the sort involving changes in labour utilization.

Although trends in wages, output, and productivity were moving in much the same direction and with much the same degree of intensity in Kenya and Tanzania, caution should be used in transferring evidence from one East African country to another. There are, however, examples on the level of the sub-sector and the firm from all three East African countries providing conclusive proof that, in those particular instances, changing technology has not caused the increase in productivity. A study of the B.A.T. cigarette manufacturing plant in Uganda revealed that productivity was growing during the period without any investment in new equipment (Baryaruha 1967). Similarly the increase in labour productivity in the sugar-processing industry in Kenya was the result of improved labour efficiency and increased use of existing plant and equipment (Frank 1965). The Tanzanian example of increased productivity independent of change in capital equipment is in sisal, where the dramatic increase came during a period of little or no investment in capital equipment.

It is important to recognize that this minimization of wage-induced change in technology as an explanation of the dramatic increases in productivity in the Tanzanian wage sector does not contradict the growing evidence from other developing countries that firms have some choice in the capital intensity of production and are responsive to changes in relative factor prices. For example, an estimate of the elasticity of substitution in Kenyan private industry for the period 1955–66 is approximately 0·75.[9]

___

[9] See Harris and Todaro 1969. Positive and in some instances quite high, one and more, estimates of the elasticity of substitution for Puerto Rico, the Philippines, Argentina, and eight other developing countries are found in: Reynolds and Gregory

Labour productivity rose dramatically in Tanzania in the 1960s, and there seems to be a positive relationship between wage and productivity increases. The productivity increase does not appear to have derived from changes to more capital intensive technology, but from autonomous increases in labour productivity and changes in labour use. We established in Chapter VII that the stabilization of the labour force which appears to have contributed to the rise in labour productivity was caused by the increase in wages. The evidence supports our hypothesis that some of the rapid increase in wages is to be explained by the self-interest of employers. However, there appears to be a marked difference in the behaviour of employers in the agricultural estate sector and the non-agricultural urban sector.

4.3 *Wage determination and differentials in the elasticity of substitution of semi-skilled and unskilled labour*

If the employers themselves were the prime cause of the wage increases of the 1950s and early 1960s, we would expect the introduction of statutory minimum wages to have had little effect on wages paid or on level of employment. This was so for wages in the urban sector. The effect of minimum wages on estate agriculture is very different. While we estimated average wage increases of some 5 per cent in Dar es Salaam, the introduction of minimum wages in 1962 resulted in an increase in average earnings of 40 per cent in estate agriculture. At the time of the minimum wage changes in 1962–3, employment increased in manufacturing, while in agriculture there was a contraction of over 20 per cent (Tanzania, Central Statistical Bureau, various years). Apparently the agricultural estates had not significantly raised their wages or changed their use of labour before the introduction of minimum wages. The dramatic consequences of the introduction of minimum wage legislation show that the labour cost minimization hypothesis on wage determination is not relevant to agriculture. The far less dramatic wage and

---

1965, Williamson 1971, Katz 1969, Daniels 1969. Besides being aware of the weakness in the direction of causality in the relationship between wages and productivity, O'Herlihy (1972) has argued caution in interpreting elasticities estimated from aggregate data, as empirical evidence from developing countries is not in keeping with the assumptions of a constant elasticity over all outputs and time periods, of no economies of scale, and of neutral technological change, necessary for the analysis. In addition, he has noted that the result for Kenya is likely to have been an overestimate as undeflated output and wage data were employed.

employment consequences in manufacturing, however, are consistent with employer-led increases in wages.

The reasons for the different behaviour of estate and manufacturing employers lie in the technological structure of the two industries. The estates were highly labour intensive, while manufacturing was relatively capital intensive. The extent to which completely unskilled, unstable labour could be efficiently substituted for industrially disciplined, semi-skilled stable labour depended on the degree of capital intensity. The elasticity of substitution between unstable and stable labour was much higher in agriculture than in manufacturing. The 'ticket contract' and 'daily task' were aspects of a system devised by estate employers which, though wasteful of manpower and contributing to extremely low levels of productivity, could use unstable labour profitably under conditions of low wages. Since workers did not have to work in close co-ordination with machines, a loosely organized unsupervised work routine was possible. High turnover did not significantly impair the productivity of completely unskilled workers nor the productivity of complementary factors.

While it was clear that increasing the skill and discipline of the estate labour force could produce dramatic gains in labour productivity, such an undertaking, as noted in Chapter I, contained a considerable element of risk. To break the circular pattern of low wages–circular migration–high turnover–low skill–low productivity–low wages it was, of course, essential to increase wages. Since, however, the relationships between wages and stability and between stability and productivity were not precisely defined, it could not be assumed that an increase in wages would increase profits. The high-turnover, low-productivity system also yielded the employers several positive benefits. They obtained labour at rates below the cost of living of a migrant with a family, while saving on such overhead expenses as housing. As demand for labour varied seasonally, high turnover meant that it was not necessary to carry excess labour on the payroll during slack periods, and the use of migrant labourers minimized the risk of effective union organization and consequent labour troubles.

To say that manufacturing employers faced a relatively low elasticity of substitution between unstable and stable labour is to imply that they could not efficiently use unstable unskilled labour even at the very low wages prevailing in agriculture. In the early post-war period when manufacturing industry was first established in Tanzania, there was little or no difference between wages on the estates and in the factories. In 1952, 87 per cent of agricultural wage employees earned less than sh 60 monthly. In manufacturing the figure was 70 per cent, lower because there were more white-collar African workers in this sector (Tanganyika, Labour Department 1954). As we have already noted, the result of low wages was the extension of the system of circular migration to the towns.

The urban variety of circular migration, just like its rural counterpart, condemned the workers to undifferentiated unskilled labour seemingly in perpetuity. Workers who constantly circulated between agriculture and urban industry and among different jobs in the towns never acquired any specialized skills. Training received in one job served them little or not at all in the next. High turnover and lack of industrial discipline contributed to low productivity of capital equipment as well as labour. Modern machinery, which imposes regularized time and organizational patterns on the men co-operating with it, requires semi-skilled industrially disciplined workers. One of the few empirical studies of the relationship between productivity and urban employment stability carried out in Africa during this period reveals that the productivity of short-term migrants in urban manufacturing was at a level only one-third that of other employees in similar jobs who had been continuously employed for a number of years (de Briey 1955). In these circumstances an increase in wages and stability was more likely to be profitable for manufacturers than for estate owners. The difference would have been increased by the fact that high turnover would have raised training costs more for manufacturing than for the estates.

5. SUMMARY

The inadequacy of the interaction of labour supply and demand to bring about a wage labour market equilibrium is nothing new in Tanzania. Labour surplus has simply replaced labour scarcity. During the colonial period estate employers held oligopsonistic power in a situation in which it was to their advantage to use that power to hold wages below labour's equilibrium supply price. The costs, in the form of labour scarcity, that a 'cheap labour' policy entailed were minimized by the freedom of employers to generate an adequate labour supply by importing labour or using coercion, with the co-operation of the government. The productivity costs imposed by the high turnover associated with the migrant labour system (like scarcity, a consequence of low wages) were minimized. The extremely low level of capital intensity on the estates meant that managers could employ predominantly unskilled labour, requiring little or no training, so that worker productivity and training costs did not vary significantly with length of stay of employees.

The dramatic rise in wages and the transformation of labour scarcity into a problem of urban unemployment or surplus labour are largely a function of the structural shifts of the Tanzanian economy in the decade preceding and the decade following Independence. An independent government and the emergence of trade union power provided a counterweight to the power of the employers in the labour market. Union pressure on employers and government legislation for higher wages are institutional explanations for wage increases in excess of labour's equilibrium supply price.

It is not possible to determine how much of the increase in wages was due to institutional intervention and how much would have occurred without external involvement. It does appear, however, that minimum wage legislation and union pressure were chiefly responsible for the wage rises on the estates and in government, where no other mechanism could provide a plausible explanation. This is not the case in the non-agricultural wage sector, where both the minimal effects of minimum wage legislation and the existence of another explanation for the wage increase can be distinguished.

The structural shift in investment production and employment, resulting in the emergence of a substantial urban industrial sub-sector, provides the alternative wage determination mechanism. Though employers in this new sub-sector at first followed the 'cheap labour' policy of the estates, they soon found the productivity costs of such a policy prohibitive, in large part because of the relative capital intensity of the technology they employed. The estates could use the migrant labour system efficiently, the new factories could not. Our evidence, though by no means conclusive, supports the hypothesis that the employers increased wages as a means of stabilizing their labour force and justifying investment in the training of the industrially disciplined semi-skilled workers who are necessary for factory employment.

In contrast to the agricultural sector, much of the increase of wages in the urban areas preceded the implementation of minimum wages. The employers have apparently achieved their aim in raising wages: the urban labour force has been stabilized, there has been a significant increase in the skill intensity of production, and labour productivity has risen sharply. Our analysis of this productivity growth indicates that it was not due to a change in technology but to the 'autonomous' increases in labour productivity associated with increases in training and stability.

The employers and the government may have fulfilled the goals of their wage policy and thus reduced the private and social costs associated with the system of short-term circular migration. However, the structural shift in the economy and the associated change in wage policy have contributed to the growth of an urban employment problem which is increasingly causing concern. In the final chapter we consider the alternatives open to the Tanzanian government in dealing with the problem in light of the wage–productivity relationship and the apparent low level of social costs.

IX

MIGRATION AND URBAN SURPLUS LABOUR—THE POLICY OPTIONS

Low resource and subjective costs do not imply that urban surplus labour is not a social problem worthy of government remedial policy. Tanzania cannot afford to ignore any opportunity to increase national output without increasing the stock of productive resources; the reduction of surplus labour would bring an improved distribution of income to which the Tanzanian government should attach considerable importance. Unless remedial measures are adopted, the problems of surplus labour will remain or even increase. The question is whether the policies at the disposal of planners can substantially reduce surplus labour without imposing countervailing political or economic costs.

The relationship between migration and expected income is to the intersectoral misallocation model of urban surplus labour what the consumption function is to the Keynesian model. Whether in a migration function the employment probability variable is statistically significant and the elasticity of the migration rate with respect to it is quantitatively important, constitutes a 'test' of the intersectoral misallocation model of urban surplus labour. The model has been 'tested' econometrically and passed.[1] We now use it and some of the regression results, together with our knowledge of the Tanzanian labour market to assess the potential impact on urban labour market imbalance and the feasibility of remedial policies that have been tried or suggested in one or another context.

1. DEMAND-AUGMENTING POLICIES

Although the origins of the problem of urban surplus labour in Tanzania are on the supply side of the labour market, this does not mean that the remedy of augmenting demand is inappropriate. Within a certain rather restrictive set of circumstances, an increase in the demand for urban labour would be sufficient to restore the balance of labour supply and demand in a relatively short period.

---

[1] See Chapter IV.

The essence of the intersectoral misallocation model is the non-price mechanism for rationing urban jobs by which, given a constant rural–urban income differential, an increase in demand induces the increase in supply necessary to lower the probability of finding a job sufficiently to re-establish equality between rural and urban expected incomes. The interaction, however, will not interfere with attempts to eliminate surplus urban labour where the increase in demand is sufficient to provide an urban job at the prevailing wage for all rural residents who desire one.

The issue can be clarified by reference to Fig. 9.1, in which the supply curve of labour to the urban regular employment sector, S, is kinked at the equilibrium supply price of labour, because when wages are in excess of w_1 employment opportunities are rationed and rural residents contemplating migration must consider the probability of finding a job as well as the returns to employment. If the wage is at w_2 and demand is given by D, then L_1–L_3 constitutes urban surplus labour. Increasing demand by the amount of the surplus will not eliminate it. A shift in the demand curve to D_1 results in a shift in the supply curve from S–S_1, to S–S_3, with resulting surplus labour of $L_3 - L_4$. However, if the demand curve is shifted outward sufficiently, so that it intersects S–S_2 at w_2 or above, then the kink in the supply curve is not relevant to the issue of intersectoral equilibrium and there is no surplus labour.

To assess the feasibility of a demand-augmenting remedial policy we need estimates of the scope for increases in demand and of the

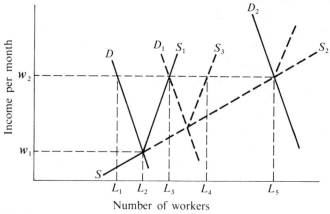

FIG. 9.1

total number of unemployed workers who would volunteer for urban jobs if they were available, L_1–L_5 in the Fig. 9.1. L_1–L_3 is the excess supply of labour actually resident in urban areas. While the measurement of the openly employed portion of L_1–L_3 is relatively straightforward, we have seen that the measurement of workers in marginal employment, employed surplus labour, presents significant problems. Nevertheless, for Tanzania we have estimated that in addition to the 10 per cent of the urban labour force that is openly unemployed, another 10 per cent is employed surplus labour.[2] In the absence of direct evidence, it is extremely difficult to measure the number of workers currently employed in the rural sector who would migrate to the urban areas if guaranteed an urban job at the prevailing wage. It would be less than the majority of rural workers whose earnings are below the urban wage, both because of the direct and psychic costs of moving involved and because withdrawal of labour from the rural sector would have some positive impact on the incomes of remaining workers, if only as a consequence of improvements in the rural–urban terms of trade. Nevertheless, the size of the rural sector relative to the urban suggests that the supply curve of urban labour is highly elastic, that the labour forthcoming would be two or more times the current total of urban wage employment, and that urban surplus labour represents only a small proportion of the total excess demand for jobs in the urban wage sector.

The achievement of significant increases in urban labour demand requires an increase in urban investment or in the labour intensity of production. Immediate and direct employment creation either by government fiat, or, as in the case of Kenya's 1964 'Tripartite Agreement', by some 'voluntary' agreement among employers, trade unions, and government, is unlikely to generate a permanent increase of employment in a system where the aim of employers is to maximize profits. The objective of the Kenya agreement was to create 40 000 jobs in a short period, which entailed 15 per cent and 10 per cent increases in the number of employees in the public and private sectors, respectively. The unions agreed to a one-year moratorium on wage increases and strikes. While in the short run a large number of jobs were created despite the financial difficulties encountered by local authorities and private employers alike, in the longer run it does not appear that any more jobs were created than

[2] See Chapter VI.

would have been without the agreement. Short-term job creation in the absence of simultaneous wage reductions could be achieved only at the expense of higher unit costs. Thus the initial effect of 'excess' labour inputs was to reduce the marginal productivity of labour to a level below the wage. Employers neutralized the short-run increase by reducing the rate of expansion of employment relative to output, or by not replacing employees who retired or otherwise left their jobs (Harris and Todaro 1968).

Government fiscal and monetary policies whose aim is to increase the demand for urban labour by stimulating effective demand for the output of goods and services are no more likely to achieve their objectives; they will more probably aggravate domestic difficulties with inflation and balance of payments deficits. Structural imbalances may cause significant slack in some industries and in certain circumstances, such as a rapid decline in export earnings, demand deficiency and intersectoral misallocation may coexist; yet urban surplus labour need not be associated with the sector-wide infinite elasticities of supply of complementary factor inputs of which Keynesian reflationary policies are designed to take advantage.[3]

An increase in the level of investment would require higher domestic savings, greater foreign inflows, or a shift in the distribution of investment in favour of the urban areas. Though the data are sketchy, aggregate savings appear to be already impressively high in Tanzania (van Arkadie in Faber and Seers 1972). The transfer of development resources from rural to urban areas could be increased, but such a course of action is likely to be counter-productive in regard to achievement of urban labour market balance. The urban bias of the government in the 1960s contributed to the stagnation of rural incomes and the emergence of urban surplus labour. To increase urban employment in this way would result in a further widening of the rural–urban differential, in effect shifting down curve $S–S_2$ in Fig. 9.1 and increasing the total number of workers desiring urban jobs. An additional squeeze on the agricultural sector would also be contrary to the policy of increased emphasis on rural development in the post-1967 development strategy. There are difficulties in Tanzania both with attracting foreign capital and, given the stated policy of decreasing Tanzania's dependence on

---

[3] The fiscal system may still be used to influence factor prices in a way that favours labour-intensive production or at least that eliminates discrimination in favour of the use of capital inputs. See Peacock and Shaw 1972.

foreign decision-makers within the economy, with the hosting of such investment. With the limited development resources available, whether domestic or foreign, the high capital/labour ratio prevailing in urban industry, which implies a high cost per job created, is another constraint on the potential effectiveness of a remedial policy that relies on employment generation.

The hypothesis that the capital intensity of production in the urban industrial sectors of developing countries is due to fixed factor proportions embodied in techniques imported from countries where labour is relatively scarce has not been substantiated. On the contrary, the evidence suggests that there is considerable scope for substitution between capital and labour both *ex ante* and *ex post* (investment). The evidence also suggests, however, that, although altering the product mix, eliminating capital intensive biases in tariff, tax, and wage structures, and providing an environment suitable for the local development of appropriate technology may have a significant impact on the growth rate of employment, such changes are unlikely to generate the quantum leap in urban wage employment necessary to achieve urban labour market balance within a relatively short period.

This brief review of the situation suggests that an employment generation policy alone cannot succeed in eliminating urban surplus labour because the scope for rapid increase in the demand for urban labour in Tanzania is insufficient. On the contrary, the estimated elasticity of 0·6 for the rate of migration with respect to the probability of finding an urban job implies that the short-run effect of a 10 per cent increase in the employment growth rate (and hence in the probability of finding a job) would be a 6 per cent increase in the migration rate. Because the base for the urban employment growth rate is much smaller than the rural base for the migration rate, the absolute increment to the urban labour force will exceed the increment to urban employment, despite a higher rate of employment growth than of migration. Feasible increases in labour demand are more likely to aggravate than alleviate the problem of urban surplus labour.

Policies focused on the supply side of the labour market must bear the burden of achieving full employment in urban areas. At the risk of over-simplification we can distinguish four types of policy instruments that can be used to regulate migration from rural areas

[4] Winston 1972. Stewart in Edwards 1974.

and hence the supply of urban labour: direct controls, urban incomes and prices policies, rural development policies, and education policies.

2. DIRECT CONTROLS ON MOBILITY

At first glance, direct controls on migration might appear to be the most effective means of reducing the flow of rural residents into the towns. South Africa has successfully used pass laws to this end by requiring a work permit as a condition of urban residence (Hutt 1971); China has reduced urban unemployment by issuing ration tickets for food and clothing that are only convertible into goods at certain locations (Reynolds 1975). But such policies raise difficult questions to which there are at present no definitive answers. How thoroughgoing must the system of controls be and how large and costly the bureaucracy to enforce such a system? To what extent does the implementation of direct controls hinder the achievement of other aspects of the efficient allocation of labour, and of social and distributional goals, thereby imposing political and economic costs in addition to the direct costs of administration?

The government of Kenya has imposed direct controls in the form of housing regulations which exclude the shanties of newly arrived migrants and the unemployed from the city centres, and it has reinforced the regulations by setting fire to such settlements. The Tanzanian government requires urban workers to have an official card certifying their employment, and it periodically 'rounds up' the unemployed and sends them back to the rural areas. Yet urban unemployment has continued to grow in both countries, suggesting that the imposition of additional controls and substantial investment would be required to make their systems work. When controls are sufficient to achieve urban labour market balance, the issue arises of how to ration urban job opportunities among rural workers. Even when a centralized system does not lead to favouritism and corruption, it may be less efficient in matching the skills of workers and the needs of employers than the decentralized rationing system (which exists even in a situation of urban labour market imbalance) in which the employers themselves select employees from all those who come to town looking for employment. Furthermore, though rationing may mean that labour that would otherwise have been idle or marginally employed in the urban area is more productively

employed in the rural areas, it does not eliminate the resource costs
of other misallocations, particularly in choice of technology, that
may arise from high and rigid urban wages. Perhaps most difficult to
assess are the political costs associated with the frustration of
workers who, despite theoretical freedom to live anywhere within
the nation's boundaries, are forbidden to move to places where other
workers with the same qualifications earn considerably more, even
though equal pay for equal work for people with the same level of
needs is a fundamental goal of societies with socialist aspirations.

3. URBAN INCOMES AND PRICES POLICIES

Narrowing the gap between rural and urban incomes is potentially
the most effective indirect means of reducing the rate of urban
migration and the magnitude of urban surplus labour. Although the
effects of decreases in urban incomes and increases in rural incomes
are essentially similar and rural and urban policies must be co-
ordinated to achieve either, we treat them separately because there
is a significant difference in the policy instruments relevant to the
different sectors.

Since our analysis implies that the rise in urban wages during the
1960s was an important factor in the emergence of urban surplus
labour, a reduction in wages would appear to be justified. In Fig. 9.1
shifting w_2 down toward w_1 reduces the excess supply of urban
labour, the difference between S_1 and D; eliminating the gap
between rural and urban incomes, $w_2 = w_1$, achieves the desired
balance between urban employment opportunities and job seekers.
The decline in real wages can be accomplished by lowering money
wages or holding them constant while prices rise. The estimated
elasticity implies that a 10 per cent decline in urban wages will
induce a 7–20 per cent decrease in the migration rate, but a
considerably greater decline would be necessary to achieve urban
labour market balance. This suggests that if the degree of money
illusion is a negative function of the rate of inflation, constant money
wages will not be any less unpopular among wage earners than an
equivalent direct cut in wages.

One objection to this policy is its consequences for the distribution
of income. Keynesian countercyclical policies are widely accepted
in industrialized countries partly because reflation benefits all
segments of the community and avoids the difficulties of specifying
what constitutes an increase in welfare. Altering relative factor

prices does raise this question. The narrowing of the income difference betwen urban wage earners and rural workers is considered beneficial, as is the rise in the income of the previously unemployed group. The functional distribution of income is the focus of concern. If, as is likely, the elasticity of substitution between capital and labour is less than unity in the urban sector, the share of wages in total income will fall, and the urban wage bill may actually be reduced if the increase in output occasioned by the decline in wages does not offset the reduction of the wage share (Ahluwalia in Chenery *et al.* 1974). Underlying the negative interpretation of this change is the presumption that the increase in the non-wage share of total income all accrues to capitalists as increased income. In fact the increase in profits may induce an increase in investment, either directly by the profiting firms (which may be in the hands of the state rather than privately owned) or by the government, which has taxed away the increment. In this case the implications of a decline in wages for the functional share translate into a choice between relatively high incomes for a relatively small group, urban wage earners, or lower incomes for that group and higher investment, thus reducing the force of the objection to a wage cut. In China wage stability combined with increases in productivity has contributed to a decline in the unit production costs of manufactured goods and a rise in profit margins and hence in the rate of capital accumulation (Reynolds 1975).

A more serious objection is the possibility that, despite excess supplies of urban labour, higher wages have been the consequence of employers' decisions rather than government policy or the pressure of unions. Though not definitive, there is considerable evidence that because of negative relationships between wages and the rate of turnover of labour in employment and between turnover and productivity, resulting in large part from higher returns to investment in on-the-job training, wage increases actually lowered the cost of labour per unit of output.[5] Thus simply to eliminate minimum wage and other institutional factors constraining downward flexibility might not in fact lead to a wage decline. Even if the current level of commitment of the labour force to wage employment precluded a return to the former system of high turnover, the smallness of the current wage bill in proportion to total costs in the manufacturing sector would make employers unlikely to risk the

[5] See Chapter VIII.

possible negative consequences of reduced incentives for productivity. This suggests that the government would have to legislate lower wages and that there is a significant likelihood that the allocative efficiency benefits associated with the elimination of urban surplus labour would be offset, at least in part, by X-efficiency costs. In a situation of declining national income the inadvisability of lowering real wages would have to be qualified. In any case it is doubtful whether this economic option is viable politically.

Either the unions have not been strong enough to resist government actions that severely reduced their power in collective bargaining, or they have come to see that fewer work stoppages and a slower rate of increase in wages is in the national and ultimately in their own interest.[6] Experience during the period 1971–3, to which we refer below, suggests, however, that unions and other organizations of the workers are still strong enough to resist a significant reduction in the real earning capacity of the wage earners. Though wage reductions may not be feasible, an incomes policy is of the highest priority for the prevention of a further widening of the differential between rural and urban incomes which would be at cross purposes with other measures aimed at reducing urban surplus labour.

Growing inequality of income distribution and a declining rate of growth of wage employment led the government, in 1967, to formulate a national policy on wages and incomes. The background report prepared for the government by the I.L.O. emphasized the importance of such a policy:

. . . The problem of incomes policy is much more urgent for the developing countries than for the advanced economies. Incomes policy involves on the one hand the allocation of resources between current consumption and the investment which is necessary to lay the foundation of future living standards. On the other hand, it involves the structure and distribution of earnings among the people, which determines the allocation of human resources and the incentives to increased production. In an advanced economy with ample resources and high living standards, the delays to growth and the waste of human or material resources which may result from errors in incomes policy are not usually critical. But in a developing economy, with much more limited resources and lower general living standards, the necessity of a sound incomes policy is crucial; it may make the difference between whether or not economic growth occurs at all, and may even involve the political stability of the country concerned. . . . (Turner 1975).

[6] In the period 1958–60 the average annual number of man-days lost through work stoppages was 761 700; in the period 1969–71 it was 1964. See I.L.O., various years.

The specific aims of the incomes policy were to restrict wage increases to a figure corresponding more closely to the actual growth of the economy and to adjust minimum wages only in a close relationship to improvements in peasant farmers' living standards. The Permanent Labour Tribunal was established to ensure the effectiveness of the wage guidelines, which limited annual increases to 5 per cent, with exceptions for genuine incentive schemes.

Whereas in the period 1961–6 wages (urban and rural estates) increased at an average rate of 13·5 per cent a year, in 1967–71 the rate diminished to an average of 3·1 per cent a year. Furthermore wages as a proportion of value added in the manufacturing sector declined from 44·8 per cent in 1968 to 37·8 per cent in 1971. The mission sent by the I.L.O. in 1974 at the request of the government to review the policy concluded that on balance '. . . the Tanzanian incomes policy, from 1966 to 1971 at least, must be reckoned one of the most successful in the world experience; and this is probably very largely due to the comparative unity the Tanzanian people have achieved. . . .' (Turner 1975.) Since the earlier period witnessed a once-for-all shift from a low income–high turnover to a high income–low turnover wage sector it is likely that the earlier rate of increase would have slowed even in the absence of an incomes policy. If one considers also the extent to which what happened after 1971 was a consequence of decisions taken during the earlier period, this conclusion seems exaggerated. For the failure to achieve one particular policy goal during this period of general success planted the seeds of the problems which, once they took root, led to the government's virtual abandonment after 1971 of the goals of the 1967 incomes policy.

As we have seen, there was no decrease in the difference between rural and urban incomes during the period 1967–71. Rural incomes continued to stagnate and the gap widened, though at a considerably lower rate than previously. This was largely due to the deterioration of the terms of trade between the agricultural and non-agricultural sectors. Total value added in agriculture at constant prices increased by 30 per cent between 1964 and 1972. While the prices of urban manufactured goods and services rose significantly, however, the price of foodstuffs did not rise. The government, which has primary responsibility for determining the prices peasant farmers receive for their produce, was able to hold the prices of foodstuffs constant, despite increases in the prices of inputs used in their production, as a means of stabilizing urban wages. Apparently the government concluded that a rapidly increasing urban cost of living would make the labour organizations less willing to abide by the terms of the 1967 incomes policy; but reducing pressure on wages in this way, which meant that most of the burden of inflation was borne by the peasant farmers, simply postponed a confrontation with the underlying issues of distribution.

Two consequences of this 'avoidance policy' of artificially low food prices were that supply was reduced and demand increased. There is evidence of an increase in the smuggling of produce into Kenya where prices that farmers received for some products were as much as 50–100 per cent higher than in Tanzania, and of an increase in the production of non-food crops, the prices of which were more closely aligned with world market prices. Not only did higher urban incomes lead to increases in the consumption of food but, in apparent contradiction of 'Engels Law', the proportion of private urban expenditure devoted to food actually increased because workers at the lower end of the distribution of income benefited the most from the combined rise in wages. In response to the growing shortage of food, producer prices were raised in 1969–70 and organized labour began to press claims for higher wages. The government reacted quite disproportionately by boosting minimum wages 40 per cent in 1972, setting off a classic wage–price spiral, as higher wages increased the demand for food and raised the price of some agricultural inputs, exacerbating the food shortage, which led to further increases in producers' prices and another 40 per cent rise in the minimum wage in 1974.[7]

The wage increases of 1972 and 1974 meant the virtual abandonment of the incomes policy and a reversion to the pre-1967 policy which insulated the incomes of wage earners but not those of rural own-account workers from adverse influences on national economic activity. Though the data are not yet available for a detailed assessment of the trends in rural and urban incomes, the net effect of the oscillation in the real income of wage earners and peasant farmers appears to have been an even more rapid widening

[7] The serious inflation and balance of payments deficits of the 1970s which followed the moderate price rises and trade surpluses of the 1960s were exacerbated by 'imported' inflation, in particular the rise in the price of oil. However, food constitutes a higher proportion of the increase in total imports than does oil and the period of rapid inflation began prior to the oil price rise of 1973. See Turner 1975.

of the rural–urban differential than in 1967–71. If this is the case, we would expect to see it reflected in an increase in rural–urban migration and a rise in urban surplus labour.

One lesson of the Tanzanian experience with incomes policy in 1967–74 is that even during a period of economic expansion the exercise of considerable political will-power is required to achieve the limited goal of holding the rate of increase in urban real wages to that of rural real incomes. A second lesson is that if incomes policy is to help reduce the surplus of urban labour it must be co-ordinated with policies on agricultural prices. In this regard the aim of incomes policy is to stabilize urban wages so that rural incomes can rise and narrow the rural–urban differential, in effect shifting curves S–S_1 in Fig. 9.1 up along curve D. Without any attempt to slow the rise in urban wages in Tanzania, the differential might have widened at an even faster rate than it did. If urban wages are stabilized by measures that effectively constrain rural incomes from rising, however, progress toward the reduction of urban surplus labour can only be achieved if changes in other factors influencing the migration rate are favourable.

4. RURAL DEVELOPMENT POLICIES

To reduce or eliminate urban surplus labour significantly in the short run, an incomes policy that stabilizes urban wages without hampering the growth of rural incomes may be necessary, but it is unlikely to be sufficient. In Tanzania rural incomes were stagnant for quite a few years before the freeze of producer prices for foodstuffs. This suggests the need for a positive policy to raise rural incomes as a complement to urban incomes policy.

From 1967 to 1971 government agricultural pricing policy reduced producer incomes below what they would have been without intervention. It is reasonable to suggest that the government might now, in the interests of urban labour market balance, raise prices above market equilibrium as a means of raising rural incomes. During the current period of shortages of domestically produced foodstuffs the world market price for these goods is in effect the equilibrium price. Given the relatively low price elasticities of domestic supply and demand, a rise in producer prices above this level is not likely to generate a problem of surplus production, because increases in domestic supply can be used to reduce reliance on imports. Even if a surplus emerged, it could be exported to earn foreign exchange, stockpiled for use in a period of drought, or distributed below market prices in particularly low income areas.

From the point of view of agricultural production and the balance of payments, as well as from that of urban labour market balance, a price support programme would yield significant benefits. The problem with this programme, however, as with the policy of directly lowering urban wages, is the feasibility of government financing of the subsidies involved. The demonstrated ability of urban wage earners to resist erosion of their real income precludes passing the price increase on to consumers. Holding consumer prices constant and raising producer prices, which would reduce the balance of payments benefits of the policy and raise the magnitude of government subsidy required, is not a means of avoiding this difficulty. If the subsidy to farmers is financed out of taxes raised from farmers, as most taxes in Tanzania ultimately are, then in terms of rural–urban differentials the policy does not yield a net gain. Since taxes that lower urban incomes are excluded from consideration and deficit financing would exacerbate inflationary problems, a price support programme appears to be financially unfeasible.

There do not appear to be any rural policies that provide a short-cut solution to the problem of urban labour market imbalance; the only way to narrow rural–urban income differentials is to raise the productivity of the rural labour force. The decision to lower urban wages in a situation of excess labour supply may raise complex questions regarding incentives and complementary changes in the urban structure of wages, and implementation is likely to require the establishment of a regulatory agency with legal authority to enforce government legislation. The decision to raise rural productivity as a means of closing the rural–urban income gap poses problems of conceptualization and, abstracting from the underlying political struggle implicit in urban incomes policy, of implementation. Lowering urban wages entails a marginal change in an economic structure that is to be left fundamentally intact, and the change can be accomplished by tinkering with a few policy variables, the effects of which are quite predictable. Raising rural productivity significantly is likely to require structural shifts in the underlying organization of the sector and co-ordination of a wide range of policy instruments where predicted effects are highly uncertain.

An assessment of Tanzania's rural development policy is clearly beyond the scope of this inquiry, but let us consider briefly several components in terms of their potential contribution to the achievement of urban labour market balance. Agricultural pricing policy was not the only government-imposed constraint on the growth of rural incomes during the 1960s and 1970s. A net flow of development capital from the rural to the urban areas was accomplished by government expenditure in urban areas in excess of urban taxes, while in rural areas taxes exceeded expenditure.

This urban bias was a consequence of the ease with which agricultural output could be taxed and of the expectation of high social rates of return to investment in urban-industrial projects and infrastructure. The low value added and profitability of the urban manufacturing sector has recently tempered enthusiasm for a strategy of rapid industrialization; domestic food deficits and rural out-migration leading to urban labour surplus have emphasized the cost of neglecting agriculture; and increased urban output from large firms with adequate accounting procedures has eased the difficulty of taxing urban incomes. The urban bias can be reduced by altering the spatial distribution of taxes or expenditure, or of both. While a reduction in rural taxation and constant government expenditure would give a direct boost to rural incomes and thus reduce urban labour market imbalance in the short run, such a policy would once again confront the government with the political obstacles in the way of lowering urban real incomes.

Altering the pattern of government expenditure so as to end the rural–urban capital flow would not mean that the rural and urban sectors would share equally in total investment, or that each sector would have to rely for development capital solely on the surplus it generates. The sectoral share of total investment would also be influenced by the distribution of foreign development capital, which was rurally oriented before Independence but has since been concentrated in urban areas. It would mean, however, that in contrast to most developing countries and most socialist countries (China being an exception in both cases (Reynolds 1975)), rural savings would be re-invested exclusively in that sector.

Nor would a policy to increase rural investment by shifting government expenditure, or by any other means, necessarily entail increased investment in agriculture at the expense of industry or social overhead capital. Romantic visions of looms in every home and iron smelters in every village have given a false impression of the nature of rural non-agricultural industry. Some goods can be fabricated efficiently in small-scale plants, and location of agricultural processing near the source of supply can yield significant savings on transport costs when weight is reduced by processing. The relationship between population density and the per capita cost of providing a given level of service may be downward sloping for some types of social overhead capital investments. For others, such as electricity, water supply, and transport, the curve is likely to be U-shaped, with minimum cost at relatively low levels of density. By bringing widely dispersed households together, the Ujamaa[8] village programme for rural development can dramatically increase the social returns to rural overhead capital investment, and compares favourably in this respect with similar urban investments.

Nevertheless, the relative abundance of cultivable land in Tanzania and the low level of capitalization of existing farms promise high returns to investment and suggest that a significant portion of any increase in development capital available in the rural areas will be directed into agriculture. During the Industrial Revolution, increases in agricultural productivity both 'freed' workers for employment in the cities and generated the food to feed them. The early dual economy models of Lewis (1954) and Fei and Ranis (1964), in which capital investment is concentrated in the 'modern sector' and withdrawal of labour provides a negative stimulus to rationalization of 'traditional agriculture' and hence to increased productivity and output, envisaged a similar role for the rural sector in currently developing countries. The suggestion that the rural investible surplus be retained within the sector as a positive stimulus to development rejects a central feature of the dual economy model, that, given the non-capitalist organization of the sector, unproductive labour with marginal product less than the free market wage will consume the surplus unless it is diverted elsewhere. Furthermore in Tanzania the withdrawal of labour will not provide much of a stimulus to agriculture. Given the high proportion of the labour force currently engaged in the rural sector and the projected rates of population growth, even at the upper limits of projections for urban modern sector employment growth, an absolute decline in the rural labour force would mean a dramatic increase in urban surplus labour. In contrast to the model and to historical experience,

[8] Ujamaa: kin, family; brotherhood, fellowship; socialism.

rural development requires simultaneous increases in productivity and labour absorption.

In Tanzania where land is still virtually a free good, the question of labour absorption translates into one of income distribution. Unfortunately the data on rural incomes are not sufficient to shed much light on the consequences for migration of changes in the intra-rural distribution of income. Conceptually, a significant increase in average rural productivity may have limited or even negative impact, if it is achieved by concentrating investments among a small proportion of farmers. Though the effect of the increase in agricultural production on prices may not cause an absolute decline in the income of the poorer farmers, an increased skewing of the rural distribution of income may nevertheless encourage migration because of the influence of the 'demonstration effect' on the rural structure of preferences. The increased ability of the richer farmers to finance higher levels of education for their children and support them through longer periods of urban job search may also increase migration.

This suggests that choice of technology is a policy issue of considerable importance, in relation both to the increasing of rural productivity and to the distribution of income in the rural sector. Factor pricing policies that encourage substitution of capital for labour are likely to impose greater resource costs in the rural than in the urban sectors. Since conceivable increases in development capital available for agriculture will not be sufficient to equip more than a small proportion of farmers with capital-intensive techniques, such policies may also contribute to increased skewness in the rural distribution of income. The identification and development of labour-intensive innovations may prove an essential ingredient of a rural development policy explicitly intended to achieve urban labour market balance.

5. EDUCATION POLICIES

The dramatic increase in educational opportunities and hence in the supply of educated workers in Tanzania since 1955 appears to have reduced significantly expected private returns to investment in education, despite the fact that the rural–urban income differential has widened considerably. School-leavers must now discount the

monetary returns to education by the probability of finding a high
wage job and, as a consequence of filtering-down and displacement,
even when they find a job, it is generally lower on the occupational
and wage scale than it would have been a few years earlier. There is
evidence that at the primary school level the excess private demand
for education has changed to an excess of school places in
consequence.

Expected net private returns to investment in education are in
excess of net social returns, both because the government subsidizes
costs and because the urban labour market overvalues educational
credentials. As a consequence of the recent changes in the urban
labour market, net social returns to investment in education are
probably lower than the social returns to other human capital
investments in which the government participates, such as health
care, the facilities for which have expanded far less rapidly; they are
probably also lower than the returns to investment in physical
capital. The apparently negligible contribution of education to rural
productivity and the high proportion of school-leavers who return to
peasant farming after an unsuccessful period of job search, suggest
that the net social returns to investment in education may be
negative. Even if these assertions, for which the supporting evidence
is all circumstantial, could be substantiated by more rigorous
empirical analysis, it may be premature to recommend reducing the
rate of investment in education (Edwards and Todaro 1973).
Underlying such a recommendation is the assumption that schooling
is a homogenous service, or that the content of education is perfectly
responsive to changes in requirements for skills as the occupational
distribution of school-leavers changes over time. It would be possible
instead to change the curriculum to prepare students better for rural
vocations, or to shift resources from conventional formal education
to farmer extension services or adult education programmes of
demonstrated effectiveness in rural areas. If students are receiving
an education unsuitable for their ultimate occupation, the policy
implication of zero or negative net social returns may be a shift in
the composition of investment from types of training yielding lower
returns to types yielding higher returns. Of course the possibility that
such shifts are unfeasible means that the option of reducing the rate
of investment in education cannot be excluded.

Our analysis suggests that changes in educational policy will have
only an indirect impact on urban labour market imbalance.

Increasing the social rate of return to investment in education by making it more appropriate for a rural vocation implies, in apparent contrast to the period 1955–70, a kind of schooling that would increase the productivity of at least one segment of the rural labour force and thus contribute to the narrowing of the rural–urban income differential for educated workers. Making education more appropriate for agriculture may reduce the rate of migration of educated rural residents regardless of the effect of such a change on the rural–urban income differential. The relationship between propensity to migrate and level of education posed the problem of separating the influence of economic from non-economic costs and returns. The econometric analysis suggests that a positive relationship between economic returns to migration and education level is part of the explanation of the educational structure of migration rates. However, the alternative hypothesis, that for a given income differential the educated are more likely to migrate than the uneducated was also accepted. While this may be because the educational system selects rural residents who are more open to change or more urban oriented, it may also be due to changes in preference induced by the urban orientation of the curriculum. If the latter factor is significant, an increase in the rural orientation of the school system may reduce the propensity of educated workers to migrate, even if the rural–urban income differential remains constant.

Reducing the flow of educated migrants from rural areas would lead to a decline in urban surplus labour in the educated segment of the urban labour force and in the proportion of educated workers in total urban surplus labour; but given the high proportion of rural residents with little or no education, it is unlikely to make a significant impact on the over-all rate of urban surplus labour. This is the issue of the influence of a change in the rural distribution of income on migration in another guise. Just as raising rural incomes by concentrating capital investment among a small group of farmers could lead to higher over-all migration rates, so improving the returns to investments in human capital when the income benefits of those investments are confined to a relatively small group of rural residents could also lead to a constant or higher aggregate rate of migration. In addition to the potential negative effects of an increase in the rural productivity of the educated on the incomes and preferences of the uneducated, a reduction in the migration of the educated will slow the process of filtering-down and displacement and result in a higher job-opening rate for the uneducated. As a consequence we would expect the rate of migration and of urban surplus labour of the uneducated to increase.

A decrease in the rate of investment in education rather than an increase in the social rate of return would avoid these distributional complications, if the resources saved were invested in the rural sector in a way that would benefit educated and uneducated alike. Since urban taxes would not have to be raised, such an increase in rural investment would have the additional advantage of avoiding the political constraint of lowering urban real incomes.

Limiting the supply of educational opportunities could be used to achieve urban labour market balance by implementing a system of low level manpower planning. There is virtually no unemployment among high level manpower in Tanzania and few workers with Form 4 or more education have filtered down into lower level occupations. Manpower planning, practised in Tanzania since the mid-1960s, takes labour demand, projected on the basis of planned rates of expansion of industry sub-groups and of surveys of employers' current skill requirements, as a given and controls supply of high level manpower by the manipulation of only one policy variable, namely the number of entrants into the various post-primary streams of the educational system.

Urban surplus labour could be eliminated by regulating Standard 1 entrance and applying a strict educational criterion for hiring in unskilled and semi-skilled jobs. The supply and demand for workers with primary education could be strictly equilibrated and since for workers without the necessary educational credentials the probability of urban wage employment would be zero, by implication the rate of urban surplus labour would also be zero. However, since the annual number of primary school-leavers entering the labour force is already more than four times the total annual increase in non-agricultural employment, such a policy would require a drastic reduction in the size of the school system; a move which would be in obvious conflict with the government's commitment to universal primary education by 1989. Even if politically acceptable, such a policy would simply substitute the rationing of school places for the rationing of urban jobs, would increase the rigidity of the process whereby workers' skills and employers' needs are matched, and would institutionalize the inability of the formal educational system to make a positive contribution to the increased productivity of rural workers.

6. CONCLUDING REMARKS

The evidence is quite strong that urban labour market imbalance in Tanzania is due to excessive rates of rural–urban migration which, in turn, are a consequence of high and downwardly inflexible urban wages. Not surprisingly, the implications for remedial policy of the intersectoral misallocation model of urban surplus labour focus on the supply side of the urban labour market. Reduced to simplicity, the advice an economist, convinced that a downturn in economic activity is Keynesian in nature, would give to a government anxious to achieve full employment is 'intervene in the market so as to increase effective demand for goods and services'. To simplify the policy implications of our analysis of urban labour market imbalance in the same way, the advice we would give to the Tanzanian government is, 'intervene in the market so as to narrow the difference in income between rural and urban areas'. To adopt such a policy would improve income distribution and allocative efficiency and thus increase national output and reduce the social problems associated with urban surplus labour. Our review of the alternatives has touched on a number of economic factors that would have to qualify the recommendation of vigorous application of those policy instruments which could achieve this goal relatively quickly. However, the most significant qualification concerns the political feasibility of following a course designed to improve the welfare of the society as a whole when a small segment of the population with disproportionate ability to influence the government would have to bear the transition costs. If there is no alternative to accepting this constraint, there are other policies that can accomplish the task, though over a much longer period.

APPENDIX A

NUMEIST—1971: SAMPLE SELECTION AND ENUMERATION PROCEDURES

IF applied economic research on labour markets in LDCs is to yield meaningful tests of theories or meaningful measures of economic categories and relationships, a necessary, but by no means sufficient, condition is that the data must be both appropriate and 'accurate'. We have indicated that the standard census and labour force survey questionnaires are inadequate for the analysis of the issues raised by recent advances in our understanding of LDC labour markets.[1] However, even where data are generated by surveys utilizing a well-designed questionnaire they are not acceptable if the statistical picture of the sample is not a precise reflection of the population from which the sample was drawn. There are opportunities at each step of the administration of a survey for statistical distortion to arise: a review of how sampling issues were resolved in the case of *NUMEIST* and how the survey was administered may be of use to researchers intending to embark on field-work. A brief assessment of the reliability of the data is included to assist the reader's judgement of our findings.

A.1. THE SELECTION OF TOWNS

Tanzania's urban hierarchy is characterized by high primacy. The capital, with a population in 1967 over four times the size of the next largest mainland town, is the predominant non-agricultural economic centre, as well as the administrative, political, and cultural focal point of the country. No study of urban migration and employment conditions could be complete without Dar es Salaam. There are fourteen other concentrations of population on the Tanzanian mainland officially classified as towns. The selection of Arusha, Mwanza, Tabora, Dodoma, and Mbeya for inclusion in the sample was determined by three criteria: (1) current population size and economic importance; (2) geographic distribution; and (3) designation of the town as an urban growth area in the Second Five Year Plan.

Tanga, Mwanza, and Arusha are the second, third, and fourth largest mainland towns, respectively, and are the principal urban centres of the north coastal, north central, and great lake geographic zones. They are also the three principal centres for the location of industrial projects outside Dar es Salaam. As many new projects have been allocated in these three areas since 1961 as in all the other smaller urban areas combined.[2] Tabora, Dodoma, and Mbeya have also been designated as growth towns, though intensive development has not yet progressed very far. The main reason for

---

[1] See Introduction, Sabot, 1977b.
[2] Tanzania, Ministry of Economic Affairs and Development Planning, 1969–70.

selecting these towns is that they serve as the principal urban, administrative, social service, and economic centres of the vast central and southern zones of Tanzania.

A.2. DETERMINATION OF SAMPLE SIZE

In this study the characteristics of the sample population have been presented as the characteristics of the urban population as a whole. This is justified because the survey covered an unbiased random sample of the urban population. The present section discusses the procedures involved in determining the size of the sample, and section A.3 discusses the method of sample selection.

Four variables determine ideal sample size: the size of the population, the variations in the characteristics being measured, the number of ways in which the data are to be stratified in the analysis, and the precision required of the data. The effect of these factors on the required sample size is readily seen. The larger the sample as a proportion of the total population, the more reliable are the results. With very large populations the size of the population is of little significance, however, as both the low and high values of the range of feasible sample sizes would constitute only very small proportions of the total, and the statistical consequences of the difference between two such proportions would be negligible. The greater the variation in a characteristic of the population that is to be measured, the larger the sample required to achieve a given level of confidence. The greater the number of ways in which the data are to be stratified for analytic purposes, the bigger the sample size must be to provide sub-populations large enough to ensure the required level of confidence. The greater the accuracy and/or confidence level required of the results, the larger the absolute size of the sample must be.

The problem is that it is frequently difficult, if not impossible, accurately to quantify these variables *prior* to the running of the survey itself. The necessary population characteristics, its total size, and the variation in characteristics of the total population and of the sub-populations may not be documented. This leads to the unfortunate implication that in order to establish the sample size, 'certain unknown properties of the population . . . must be estimated' (Cochran 1953). Likewise, the exact nature of the analysis may not be known until after the survey is completed, making it difficult to estimate the degree of stratification or the level of confidence required. It is recognized that 'for multi-purpose surveys, short of taking a sample large enough to give the desired precision for all the variables which would rarely be possible, there is no perfect solution' (Moser 1958).

The problems faced, and a suggested solution, are summarized in Moser's description (1958) of a British national market survey:

. . . For a simple random sample the size required to achieve a given precision is fairly readily determined, but this simplicity disappears with the more complex samples usual in large-scale surveys. The sample in this case was to be stratified by several factors and to be spread over four sampling stages. Little about the population, about the relative variability in different strata, and between and within clusters, was known in advance and the computation of *desired* sample size was a very approximate one. It was agreed that the sample should be of the order of 3,000–4,000: the actual number finally decided on, 3,000, was determined mainly by the number of interviewers available and how many interviews could be managed in the time at the survey's disposal.

Similar problems were involved in choosing the sample for this study. An estimate had to be made of the current population of the urban areas. More importantly, though many of the ways in which the sample was to be stratified were known in advance, little or no data were available that would allow prediction of the variations within strata, and within and between the geographic sampling clusters.[3] Hence it was all but impossible to determine the relationship between sample size and levels of confidence.

The point of departure for the determination of sample size was the consideration that the Dar es Salaam and six towns' samples were to be analysed separately, while being stratified by the primary demographic, income, employment, and mobility variables. Taking this into consideration, it was estimated that a sample of some 7200 in Dar es Salaam would yield between 3500 and 4000 usable 'adult' questionnaires, based on the assumption of 15 per cent non-response,[4] and on the fact that about 36 per cent of the urban population was below 14 years of age.[5] This was deemed a sufficiently large sample to meet the requirements of the survey. The 1967 population of the Dar es Salaam urban area,[6] and our estimates of its growth since then, placed the total estimated population at about 400 000. On the basis of this it was decided to proceed by fixing the sampling fraction at 1·8 per cent (7200 × 100/400 000). The same fraction was also used to select the samples in the other six towns, Tanga, Arusha, Mwanza, Tabora, Dodoma, and Mbeya.

Taking the sampling fraction as fixed meant that the actual sizes of the usable samples would differ from the projected size to the extent that population, non-response, or the proportion of children were wrongly estimated. In spite of the fact that non-response was actually pushed below the 10 per cent level, the Dar es Salaam survey yielded only 3307 properly completed questionnaires. Although some uncertainty remains as to the

[3] The possibility of running a pilot survey to estimate the variance of key variables was considered. However, in this case the survey of industrial wage employees which functioned as a pilot survey in other respects could not provide such information, as sampling was done at the place of work rather than in the home. See Cochran 1953, Moser 1958.
[4] In fact, non-response was kept below 10%. See section 5 below.
[5] Dar es Salaam was defined as the administrative area plus all the contiguous census enumeration areas. Whereas the city proper had a population of 272 000 in the 1967 census, the area as defined for this survey had a population of 298 000. See Chapter III.
[6] Population of the Dar es Salaam area was 298 000 in 1967. If we assume a 7–8 per cent per annum growth rate, the present number must be very close to 400 000. A 1·8 per cent sample of that makes 7200, which with 15 per cent non-response would reduce to about 6100.

precise proportion of the population below 14 years of age, and some small deviation from the intended sampling fraction of 1·8 per cent is not unlikely, our results suggest that the growth of Dar es Salaam since 1967 has been a percentile or two lower than the previously assumed 7 to 8 per cent. In 1967 the combined population of the six towns was equal to 67·9 per cent of Dar es Salaam's total population. Since the same sampling fraction was applied in all seven towns, the relative rates of growth of Dar es Salaam and the six towns can be estimated by a comparison of actual sample size. With a similarly low level of non-response for the six towns, the final sample was 2238, or 67·6 per cent of the Dar es Salaam sample. This implies that Tanzania's capital city and the six regional centres in the sample have been growing at approximately the same rate since 1967, thus ending the post-war trend of higher population growth rates for the major urban area (Tanzania, Central Statistical Bureau 1968).

A.3. SAMPLE SELECTION

Once the size of the sample had been decided, it remained to establish a procedure to select a sample that would be administratively feasible, and as unbiased as possible. The first issue to arise was whether or not to stratify the sample prior to selection. It is advisable to do so wherever possible since stratification reduces the variance of the characteristics to be measured by sampling from within more homogeneous groups. However, the large number of relevant variables, as well as the fact that sub-populations characterized by one or more of these variables were not identifiable, meant that such stratification was not feasible. The possibilities of stratifying the sample according to income levels, or according to areas differentiated in terms of their rates of growth, were considered, but rejected for want of a practical way of identifying the various sub-groups.

If the sample is not stratified, then, ideally, a random sample of 7200 individuals or 1·8 per cent of the population would be chosen from a complete list of the total population of Dar es Salaam. No such list existed, and indeed, even with such a list, the task of identifying and finding 7200 individuals dispersed over the city would have been insurmountable. Under the circumstances, it was necessary to turn to some form of spatial sampling, and this required that population clusters be identified.

With cluster sampling it is necessary to make decisions on the size and hence the number of clusters, based on the criteria of administrative convenience and the degree of intra-class correlation. Statistical problems are minimized when clusters are of equal size, though variations in size can be compensated for by sampling with probabilities proportionate to size. If size differs widely and the extent of the variations is unknown, the reliability of the sample is dramatically reduced. A first stage cluster sample is often taken even where complete sampling frames in the form of population lists are available, because of the practical advantages of concentrating interviews in a limited number of areas. What is often a matter of mere convenience is a vital consideration in LDCs where there are rarely satisfactory sampling frames providing more or less complete lists of population. Thus it is necessary that a listing of some kind has to be made specially, and here it is obviously advantageous to be able to confine the special listing to a few areas or groups (Moser 1958).

Given that some form of clustering was essential, the clusters could be based either on aerial survey maps or on the already mapped 1967 Census enumeration areas. The use of aerial surveys allows the determination of cluster size. Relatively small clusters can be used, though, of course, the smaller the clusters, the less the practical advantage derived, since the sample will be more dispersed. If relatively large clusters are used, however, a problem arises because such clusters will vary considerably in size though the extent of this variation cannot be known. The Census enumeration areas, on the other hand, represented relatively large clusters whose variation in size was known from the Census itself, and allowance could therefore be made for this variation in cluster size.

It was decided to use aerial survey maps for five of the up-country towns. Their relatively small size made sample dispersion less of a problem, and in any case the use of Census enumeration areas was ruled out, because those towns contained relatively few such areas, and their use for a first stage sample would have entailed excessive clustering. The use of aerial survey maps posed difficulties because residential patterns in these towns are closely related to socio-economic characteristics, entailing a high degree of intra-class correlation. Choosing a few areas out of a small original number could thus result in serious sample bias. For the five up-country towns, the buildings on specially enlarged aerial survey photographs were numbered, and 1·8 per cent of them were selected by means of a table of random numbers. All inhabitants in the selected houses were interviewed.

It was possible to use the Census enumeration areas for Dar es Salaam because there were 514 of them, enough for a first stage sample without excessive clustering problems. Although aerial survey techniques would have been preferable for Mwanza, the Census enumeration areas had to be used because there were no usable survey maps. The excessive clustering problem was not as severe in the case of Mwanza as it would have been in the other five towns because of Mwanza's relatively large population.

In the Dar es Salaam sample, the first stage was based on the 514 enumeration areas that made up the urban area as defined by this survey. A decision had to be reached on the number of these areas to be selected. At one extreme, the first stage could include all the enumeration areas, with a second stage selection of 1·8 per cent of the population of each area. At the other, 1·8 per cent, or nine of the enumeration areas, could be selected in a first and only stage and everyone within these areas enumerated. Both extremes were unsatisfactory: the first would negate the administrative advantages of clustering the survey population and would require the preparation of a sampling frame for the entire city; the second would introduce sampling error through excessive clustering.

With the size of the clusters and the degree of intra-class correlation given exogenously, the reliability of the first stage sample would depend on the proportion of the total number of clusters selected. Since the clusters were relatively large and intra-class correlation likely to be considerable, it was decided to begin with a large first stage sample, thus sacrificing some of the practical advantages of the process. Approximately 12 per cent, or 63, of the total number of 514 areas was therefore chosen in the first stage of the sample. Enumeration areas, weighted by population size, were drawn randomly from the total number until the selected areas included 15 per cent of the total population. This point was reached when 63 areas or 12·3 per cent of the total number of enumeration areas had been selected. Within each area, it was then decided to sample 12 per cent of the population. The selection of areas was done without replacement in accordance with the fact that when the primary sampling fraction lies between 10 and 50 per cent, variance is reduced in this way (Cochran 1953).

Weighting the enumeration areas was necessary because, although they were originally intended to be equal in population, there was in fact significant variation in their size. Since the weights used were the 1967 population figures for enumeration areas, their use in 1971 implied an assumption that all areas have grown at the same rate. This almost certainly introduced some bias into the sample, but the nature of the bias is unclear. If the fastest growing areas contain a disproportionate number of newly arrived people in the town, then there will be a bias against recent migrants. If, on the other hand, the fastest growing areas include a disproportionate number of long-term residents, who may simply be moving from one area of the city to another, then the sample will tend to over-represent new arrivals.

The last step in the sampling procedure for Dar es Salaam was to select the second stage, comprising 12 per cent of the population of each enumeration area: all the houses in each of the selected enumeration areas were counted and mapped and 12 per cent of them were chosen at random.[7] The clustering problem arising from houses with significantly different numbers of inhabitants was minimized by defining floors in high-rise flats and entrances in row houses as separate dwellings.[8] All inhabitants of the chosen houses were interviewed.

A.4. THE ADMINISTRATION OF THE SURVEY

The survey entailed two and a half months' work in the field, divided equally between Dar es Salaam and the six towns, exclusive of the time taken to map the enumeration areas, train enumerators (two weeks), pre-test and translate the questionnaire, and code the data collected.

In Dar es Salaam the 24 enumerators were divided into ten groups, each of which was responsible for interviews within a geographically clustered group of enumeration areas. For the duration of the survey the groups lived in, or near, the cluster in which they worked. This minimized transport problems, permitted the establishment of a good working relationship with

---

[7] To ensure that the second stage of the sample would be self-weighting.

[8] The exact definitions used were not as important as the need to ensure that the definition used when enumerating was the same as that used when 'mapping'. Every effort was made to see that this was the case.

the local community, and made frequent revisiting of households feasible. Four supervisors co-ordinated the work of the interviewers, who proved extremely reliable and responsible in their work. The supervisors met their respective groups from three to five times per week to check questionnaires and to help resolve specific problems that had arisen. A similar procedure was employed in the six towns, though the entire operation in each town was carried out over a period of some three to six days, and the 20 enumerators who went on the 5000-mile trip did not live in the specific areas for which they were responsible.

Both the high level of co-operation of the population and the provision for frequent revisiting (in some cases the same house was visited from eight to ten times) allowed the level of non-response to be pushed below 10 per cent. Most of this non-response was the result of households being out of town or physically unavailable. There were very few refusals to co-operate. Once interviews were completed, all responses were transferred to coding sheets using all-number codes. Each questionnaire was coded twice and then checked, to minimize error at this stage. Codes for the small number of relatively open questions were selected after an examination of a random sample of questionnaires. The data thus coded were then punched and verified. Each questionnaire occupied seven 80-column computer cards, making some 40 000 cards in all. Finally the data were transferred to computer tapes.

TABLE A.1
Dar es Salaam population: region of birth[a]

	NUMEIST %	1967 Census %
Arusha	1	1
Coast	43	40
Dodoma	1	1
Iringa	2	2
Kigoma	1	1
Kilimanjaro	4	5
Mara	1	1
Mbeya	3	3
Morogoro	13	15
Mtwara	10	10
Mwanza	1	1
Ruvuma	4	4
Shinyanga	1	1
Singida	1	1
Tabora	3	3
Tanga	6	6
West Lake	1	2
Zanzibar	3	1
Total	100	100

[a] Those born in Dar es Salaam are excluded from this Table.

A.5. THE RELIABILITY OF THE DATA

The results of the survey strongly suggest that the techniques used yielded a sample with basic demographic characteristics very similar to those of the urban population as a whole. This emerges from a few comparisons with the results of the 1967 Census. For instance, there is very close correspondence between the survey and census with respect to the age profile of males and females. The proportion of the sample population found in any 10-year age group is usually within one percentage point of the census distribution, and nowhere does the difference exceed 3 per cent. Equally encouraging is the correspondence between the census and *NUMEIST* as regards the proportion of the Dar es Salaam population born in any particular region. The figures, presented in Table A.1, require little additional comment. On balance it appears that the survey's findings can be generalized with a considerable degree of confidence.

APPENDIX B

SOURCES OF DATA AND GENERATION OF VARIABLES

THIS appendix gives the sources of the data and discusses the generation of the variables for the regression analysis and for some of the Tables in Chapters IV and V.

B.1. MIGRATION RATES

The study analyses the migration behaviour of males born in the countryside who moved to town after the age of 13. The dependent variable in the equations is defined as an average net propensity to migrate;[1] it is the ratio of the estimated number of urban residents in given age and educational groups born in a given source area to the comparable area population. Numerators were derived from *NUMEIST* while denominators were taken from the population census. The addition of four education and three age dimensions stretches the sample too thin when it is taken to its highest level of disaggregation of 17 regions of origin and 7 urban receiving areas. To increase average cell size and the significance of a value of zero in any cell, both the regions and the urban areas are aggregated into three relatively homogeneous structural groups. The three urban groups are (1) Dar es Salaam, (2) Tanga and Mwanza, (3) Arusha, Dodoma, Mbeya, and Tabora. The three regional groups are (1) Arusha, Kilimanjaro, Morogoro, Mtwara, Mwanza, and Tanga, (2) Singida, Shinyanga, Dodoma, Mara, Kigoma, and West Lake, (3) Coast, Iringa, Mbeya, Ruvuma, and Tabora. A random allocation of the total sample over all the resulting 108 cells would have less than a 1 per cent probability of leaving an empty cell.

B.2. THE RELATIONSHIP BETWEEN CURRENT AGE AND TIME OF ARRIVAL

Data on year of arrival for the current migrant age groups are used to link the dependent variable and the income and probability variables temporally. The mean date of arrival for the 20–24 current age group was mid-way through 1967. The majority of the migrants within this group arrived during the period 1967–70, and it is with average estimates of the independent economic variables for this period that the migration rates of the youngest age group are linked. Similarly, the 25–34 migrant age group, for whom the mean date of arrival was 1964, is linked to observations for the independent variables for the period 1962–6; and the age group of migrants over 34, for whom the mean date of arrival was 1957, is linked to the period 1955–61.

---

[1] Strictly defined, the dependent variable is not a migration *rate* in that it does not give the current propensity of rural residents in given population cohorts to migrate but is, instead, a demographic *ratio*.

B.3. URBAN INCOMES

To measure the income component of the returns to migration, a wage variable disaggregated by education and time period was constructed. Wage series for three occupational groups for 1957–71 were derived from aggregate average real wage series and occupational differentials for the end years. The real wage series was obtained from a published series (I.L.O., various years) for the current non-agricultural wage deflated by a price index for wage goods.

On the assumption that occupational wage ratios changed smoothly over time, the aggregate wage series is related to the occupational wages by

$$W_t = \sum_{o=1}^{3} W_{tl}\gamma_{to}\lambda_{to} \quad \text{where } t = 1955, \ldots, 1971$$

where W_{tl} are unskilled wages and γ_{to} are the occupational wage ratios, with unskilled wages as a base, obtained for intervening years from the ratios for the two end years in the series by interpolation. *NUMEIST* yielded estimates of λ_{to}, the proportion of the urban labour force in each occupational category. For each year in the series, the sum of all 1971 migrant labour force members who arrived in town prior to that year and of all 1971 non-migrant labour force members whose current age implied they were 14 or older in the given year was distributed by occupational level. Given the values for γ_{to} and W_t, the equation was solved for unskilled wages, W_{tl}, and the wages for the other occupational groups were derived.[2]

The second step in generating the wage variable involved expressing the wage by educational group as a weighted average on the wage in each occupational category such that,

$$W_{ute} = \sum_{o=1}^{3} \rho_{uteo}W_{to} \quad \begin{matrix} t = 1955 \cdots 1971 \\ e = 1 \cdots 4 \\ u = 1 \cdots 3 \end{matrix}$$

[2] It would be better to use data generated in the years in question, than to reconstruct a picture of past occupational and educational wage labour force characteristics from a contemporary sample, a procedure with two shortcomings which fortunately do not appear serious in Tanzania. The first is the implicit assumption that individual education and occupation levels remain constant over time. In Tanzania this is justified in regard to education by the scarcity of opportunities for adult labour force participants to acquire additional formal education, and in regard to occupation by the current high level of employment stability of the urban labour force and the fact that job ladders extending across our broad occupational categories are rare. The second shortcoming is the implicit assumption that rates of return migration have been uniform over all sub-groups of the employed. However, although the aggregate rate of return migration is high, the urban–rural stream of migrants is composed predominantly of migrants who were unsuccessful in their search for urban non-marginal employment. Among wage employees, return migration (other than for brief visits) is infrequent. Workers who have reached retirement age could be a second significant component of the urban–rural migrant stream, but the rapid growth of urban employment and the fact that migrants were young on arrival have meant a young average age of wage employees, contributing to low rates of retirement.

where W_{ute} is the wage in urban area u, for each educational group e, at date t. The proportion ρ_{ute}, of the labour force for each urban area in each educational and occupational category was derived from *NUMEIST* by further disaggregating λ_{to} by education.

Table B.1 presents the resulting wage data aggregated over all urban areas. Note that the disaggregation process has compressed wage differentials among educational groups as compared with the wage data in Chapter IV derived from *NUMEIST*. It was not possible to use the wage data in *NUMEIST*, which pertains only to 1971, for the statistical analysis which has a time component. The wage series in this section was constructed to provide a consistent series over the time periods used in the regression analysis.

TABLE B.1
Average urban wages (1962 sh per month)
For four education groups in three time periods
Tanzanian males

Date	No formal	Education Standard 1–4	Standard 5–8	Form 1 and above	Aggregated over education
1966–70	230	246	322	448	288
1960–66	179	194	247	336	213
1955–60	106	121	150	200	125
Aggregated over time periods: 1955–1970	81	196	253	347	221

B.4. RURAL INCOMES

The opportunity cost of urban migration is measured by rural per capita income in Tanzania's seventeen regions for each of the three time periods. Annual incomes, both monetary and subsistence, derived from agriculture, hunting, forestry, and fishing were estimated from district data. These series were deflated by a price index composed of a weighted average of separate indices for each of the components of rural income.[3] Lack of data precluded disaggregating rural incomes by education. However, occupational homogeneity, lack of institutional rigidities in income determination, and an

[3] While rural and urban income time series were deflated by production and consumption price indices respectively, no account was taken of rural–urban cost-of-living differentials. Even if the appropriate data were available, the fact that there are marked differences in patterns of consumption of goods, services, and leisure between rural villages and urban areas implies that there is likely to be a serious index number problem. The magnitude (and perhaps even the sign) of the cost-of-living differential will vary significantly, depending whether urban or rural quantity weights are used. Thus under the best of conditions there is unlikely to be one unique construct of the rural–urban income differential.

apparently weak correlation between formal education and rural productivity suggest that intra-regional rural income differentials among educational sub-groups are considerably narrower than urban differentials if they exist at all. (See the discussion in Chapter IV.) Table B.2 gives the resulting series, averaged for the periods related to the migration rates and with the seventeen regions aggregated according to the three rural areas used in the study.

TABLE B.2
Regional monthly rural income per capita (1962 sh)

Date	Region			All regions
	1	2	3	
1966–1970	42	32	36	37
1960–1966	45	25	29	35
1955–1960	45	25	29	35
1955–1970	43	28	32	35

Whether to introduce the urban and rural incomes into the migration function in discounted form raised a measurement problem. The discounted value of urban and rural income streams over the time horizon, T, are:

$$WD_u = \sum_{t=0}^{T} \frac{W_u}{(1+i)} t \quad \text{and} \quad WD_r = \sum_{t=0}^{T} \frac{W_r}{(1+i)}$$

where i is the discount rate. Since precise information on time horizons, discount rates, and changes in income over time are not available for Tanzania, the use of the discounted variable would require experimentation with different levels for these factors (Bowles 1970). This, however, is not a practical procedure when the value of i is known to be fairly low, say less than 6 per cent, and the value of T is high. In such circumstances the level of the estimated discounted value of the rural and urban income streams will be highly sensitive even to small differences in the choice of discount rate or time horizon, with the consequence that results will be dependent on an ultimately arbitrary set of decisions.

This problem can be avoided by relating the migration rate to the average value of income in source and receiving areas (Laber and Chase 1971). The assumptions that the time horizon is unlimited and that income differentials and discount rates are constant over time can justify such a procedure. In Tanzania, however, the rate of increase in urban wages owing to secular increases in the wage level and increases associated with seniority on the job are likely to exceed rural income increases over the course of an individual's working life. Therefore, since the composition of the urban labour force is skewed toward younger, less experienced age groups, the acceptance of this set of assumptions entails a degree of mis-specification of the wage variable. An alternative justification is based on an assumption that the appropriate time horizon is not unlimited but, on the contrary, is so short that changes in income differentials and discount rates are not likely to occur within it. Which of the two justifications is adopted depends on our view of the length of time over which potential migrants estimate the returns to migration.

It would be convenient analytically to assume, as Todaro does, that potential migrants have a short time horizon (Todaro 1969). However, the evidence suggests that this is not the case in Tanzania. During the colonial period, migration was circular and rural males left their families behind while they participated in the wage sector of the economy. In these circumstances the migratory journey was short term as was, presumably, the time horizon of the migrants. Today, with higher urban wages and the stabilization of the labour force, migrants who are successful in finding urban employment tend to bring their families to town and to remain in town for the remainder of their working lives (see Chapter VII). Moreover, the fact that the introduction of wage structures that increase with seniority has meant that starting wages in sought-after urban jobs are often less than average incomes in a number of regional rural areas, suggests that the time horizon of migrants is no longer short term. Thus, the use of average incomes, rather than the present value of the rural and urban streams of income, as a means of avoiding an arbitrary selection of precise levels of the discount rate and time horizon obscures the influence on migrant decisions of expected changes in income differentials over the individual's working life.

B.5. URBAN EMPLOYMENT PROBABILITIES

The probability that a migrant of educational group e arriving in town u in time period t will find a job within four months of arriving in town is:

$$P_{ute} = \frac{r_{ute}(1 - U_{ute})}{U_{ute}} \quad 0 \leqslant P < 1$$

where U is the unemployment rate and γ is the net rate of growth of employment. The two available sample surveys (*NUMEIST* 1971 and Ray 1966) yielded the education specific unemployment rates for 1971 and 1965 respectively. For 1957 estimates made by the Tanganyika Department of Labour were used. Observations for interim years were obtained by interpolating the trend for each educational sub-group. Employment growth rates for four-month periods, the estimated average time spent in job search,[4] were calculated from annual data for aggregate male employment in town.[5] To disaggregate these rates by educational sub-group, the educational distribution of total employment in each urban area in each year over the period 1955–71 was estimated by aggregating P_{ute} by averaging

---

[4] The need for a specific search period arises because growth and unemployment rates, and thus job probabilities, are time specific. Since no information is available on return migration, the length of the job search period was estimated from the length of time of unemployment and the length of time to find a job for the current urban stock of migrants. Estimating the equations with alternative job search periods of three months, six months, eight months, and one year had little impact on the results.

[5] For dates prior to 1965 the data are available only for Dar es Salaam, Tanga, and Mwanza. For the four smaller towns, estimates of total male employment were made, using the ratio of male employment to male population for Tanga and Mwanza to estimate the employed proportion of the male population for Arusha, Dodoma, Mbeya, and Tabora.

annual observations within each of the time periods by which the model was disaggregated.

If we were analysing migration to the sisal estates in the 1950s it would be illegitimate to use a measure of probability that abstracts from turnover because, with the system of short-term circular migration then prevailing, most job openings arose from turnover. The current level of stability of the urban labour force is extremely high and turnover is only a small proportion of total job openings. Nevertheless, the omission of turnover from our calculations introduces a downward bias to our estimate of employment probabilities and this bias is more serious for the less well educated who hold jobs with rates of turnover above the average.

Similarly a bias, in this case upward, results from the omission of urban employed surplus labour from the probability variable. But the statistical significance of the estimated probability coefficient will only be affected if there are significant intertemporal and demographic cross-section differentials in the proportion of marginal employment in the total of urban surplus labour. The magnitude of the temporal bias would have to be highly speculative because of the lack of time series data on the magnitude of urban marginal employment. For 1971, however, there appears to be a similar pattern in unemployment and marginal employment rates by educational sub-groups and among urban areas suggesting a minimum bias along this dimension of the model.

B.6. DISTANCE AND URBAN POPULATION

The distance variable, $DIST_{ru}$, is an average of the linear distances between each receiving town and regional centre weighted by town and regional population. Urban population, UP_u, is the average of the town populations in each aggregate urban area.

BIBLIOGRAPHY

AHARONI, Y. (1966). *The Foreign Investment Decision Process*, Boston, Harvard Business School.

ALONSO, W. &. FRIEDMANN, J. (eds.) (1964). *Regional Development and Planning*, Cambridge, Mass., Massachusetts Institute of Technology Press.

ALPERS, E. A. (1967). *The East African Slave Trade*, Historical Association of Tanzania, Paper No. 3, Nairobi, East African Publishing House.

BAER, W. & HERVE, M. E. A. (1966). 'Employment and Industrialization in Developing Economies', *Quarterly Journal of Economics*, **80**(1), February.

BALASSA, B. (1961). *The Theory of Economic Integration*, Homewood, Ill., R. D. Irwin.

BALOGH, T. (1966). *The Economics of Poverty*, London, Weidenfeld & Nicolson.

BARBER, W. J. (1960). 'Economic Rationality and Behaviour Patterns in Underdeveloped Areas: A Case Study of African Economic Behaviour in the Rhodesias', *Economic Development and Cultural Change*, **8**(3), April.

BARBOUR, K. M. &. PROTHERO, R. M. (eds.) (1961). *Essays on African Population*, London, Routledge & Kegan Paul.

BARNUM, H. & SABOT, R. (1976). *Migration, Education and Urban Surplus Labor*, Paris, O.E.C.D.

―― ―― (1977). 'Education, Employment Probabilities and Rural–Urban Migration', Oxford Bulletin of Economics and Statistics, 39 (2), November.

BARYARUHA, A. (1967). *Factors Affecting Industrial Employment: A Study of Ugandan Experience 1954–1964*, Nairobi, Oxford University Press.

BEALS, R. E., LEVY, M. B. & MOSES, L. N. (1967). 'Rationality and Migration in Ghana', *Review of Economics and Statistics,* **49**(4), November.

BEAN, L. H. (1946). *International Industrialization and Per Capita Income, Studies in Income and Wealth*, Vol. 8, New York, National Bureau of Economic Research.

BECKER, G. S. (1964). *Human Capital. A Theoretical and Empirical Analysis, with Special Reference to Education*, New York, National Bureau of Economic Research.

BERG, E. J. (1961). 'Backward-Sloping Labour Supply Functions in Dual Economies—The Africa Case', *Quarterly Journal of Economics,* **75**(3), August.

―― (1965). 'The Development of a Labour Force in Sub-Saharan Africa', *Economic Development and Cultural Change,* **13**(4), July.

BERRY, B. J. L. (1961). 'City Size Distributions and Economic Development', *Economic Development and Cultural Change,* **9**(4), July.

BERRY, R. & SOLIGO, R. (1968). 'Rural–Urban Migration, Agricultural Output and the Supply Price of Labour in a Labour Surplus Economy', *Oxford Economic Papers,* **19**, July.

BEVERIDGE, W. H. (1931). *Unemployment: A Problem of Industry*, New ed. London, Longmans, Green.

BHAGWATI, J. (1973). 'Education, Class Structure and Income Equality', *World Development*, **1**(5), May.

BIENEFELD, M. & SABOT, R. (1971). *The National Urban Mobility, Employment and Income Survey of Tanzania (NUMEIST)*, Dar es Salaam, Ministry of Economic Affairs and Development Planning, and Economic Research Bureau, University of Dar es Salaam.

BORTS, G. H. (1960). 'The Equalization of Returns and Regional Economic Growth', *American Economic Review*, **50**, June.

BOTTOMLEY, A. (1971). *Factor Pricing and Economic Growth in Underdeveloped Rural Areas*, London, Crosby Lockwood & Son.

BOWLES, S. (1970). 'Migration as Investment: Empirical Tests of the Human Investment Approach to Geographical Mobility', *Review of Economics and Statistics*, **52**(4), November.

BREESE, G. (1966). *Urbanization in Newly Developing Countries*, Englewood Cliffs, N.J., Prentice-Hall.

BRETT, E. A. (1973). *Colonialism and Underdevelopment in East Africa. The Politics of Economic Change, 1919–1939*, New York, NOK Publishers.

BYERLEE, D. (1974). 'Rural–Urban Migration in Africa', *International Migration Review*, **8**(4).

CALDWELL, J. C. (1969). *African Rural–Urban Migration: The Movement to Ghana's Towns*, Canberra, Australian National University Press.

CALLAWAY, A. (1963). 'Unemployment Among African School Leavers', *Journal of Modern African Studies*, **1**(3).

CAMERON, J. & DODD, W. A. (1970). *Society, Schools and Progress in Tanzania*, Oxford, Pergamon Press.

CHENERY, H. et al. (1974). *Redistribution with Growth: Policies to Improve Income Distribution in Developing Countries in the Context of Economic Growth*, London, Oxford University Press.

—— & SYRQUIN, M. (1975). *Patterns of Development, 1950–1970*, London, Oxford University Press.

CHESWORTH, D. (1967). 'Statutory Minimum Wage Fixing in Tanganyika', *International Labour Review*, **96**(6), December.

—— (1972). 'Statutory Wage Fixing in Tanganyika', Mimeo.

CLAESON, C. & EGERO, B. (1971). 'Population Movement in Tanzania: An Analysis of Birthplace Data in the 1967 Population Census', Research Notes No. 11, Dar es Salaam, Bureau of Resource Allocation and Land Use Planning, University of Dar es Salaam, April.

CLARK, C. (1957). *Conditions of Economic Progress*, New York, Macmillan.

COCHRAN, W. G. (1953). *Sampling Techniques*, New York, John Wiley & Sons.

CONDE, J. (1971). *The Demographic Transition as Applied to Tropical Africa*, Paris, O.E.C.D.

CORDEN, M. & FINDLAY, R. (1975). 'Urban Unemployment, Intersectoral Capital Mobility and Development Policy', *Economica*, **42**, February.

COURCHENE, T. J. (1970). 'Interprovincial Migration and Economic Adjustment', *Canadian Journal of Economics*, **3**(4), November.

COWAN, L. G., O'CONNELL, J. & SCANLON, D. G. (eds.) (1965). *Education and Nation Building in Africa*, New York, Praeger.

DANIELS, M. R. (1969). 'Differences in Efficiency Among Industries in Developing Countries', *American Economic Review*, **59**(1), March.

DAVID, P. (1973). 'Fortune, Risk and the Micro-Economics of Migration'. Mimeo, Harvard Institute of Economic Research, Cambridge, Mass., Harvard University.

DE BRIEY, P. (1955). 'The Productivity of African Labour', *International Labour Review*, **72**, August.

DENISON, E. F. (1962), 'Education, Economic Growth and Gaps in Information', *Journal of Political Economy*, **70**(5), Pt. 2, Supplement, October.

DUMONT, R. (1966). *False Start in Africa*, London, André Deutsch.

EAST AFRICAN COMMUNITY (various years). *Annual Trade Report of Tanzania, Uganda and Kenya*, Mombasa, East African Customs and Excise Department.

EAST AFRICAN STATISTICAL DEPARTMENT (1953). *Report on the Enumeration of African Employees, July 1952*, Dar es Salaam.

ECKAUS, R. (1955). 'The Factor Proportions Problem in Underdeveloped Areas', *American Economic Review*, **45**, September.

EDWARDS, E. (1974). *Employment in Developing Nations, Report on a Ford Foundation Study*, New York, Columbia University Press.

—— & TODARO, M. P. (1973). 'Educational Demand and Supply in the Context of Growing Unemployment in Less Developed Countries', *World Development*, **1**, March/April.

EICHER, C. K. &. WITT, L. (eds.) (1964). *Agriculture in Economic Development*, New York, McGraw Hill.

—— et al. (1970). *Employment Generation in African Agriculture*, East Lansing, Institute of International Agriculture, Michigan State University, July.

ELKAN, W. (1959). 'Migrant Labor in Africa: An Economist's Approach', *American Economic Review*, **49**(2), Papers and Proceedings, May.

—— (1960). *Migrants and Proletarians: Urban Labour in the Economic Development of Uganda*, London, Oxford University Press.

EVANS, P. C. C. (1962). 'Western Education and Rural Productivity in Tropical Africa', *Africa*.

FABER, M. & SEERS, D. (eds.) (1972). *The Crisis in Planning*, London, Chatto & Windus.

FEI, J. & RANIS, G. (1964). *Development of the Labor Surplus Economy: Theory and Policy*, Homewood, Ill., Richard D. Irwin.

FELLNER, W. (1946). *Monetary Policies and Full Employment*, Berkeley, University of California Press.

FIELDS, G. S. (1972). 'Private and Social Returns to Education in Labour Surplus Economics', *East African Economic Review*, **4**(1), June.

—— (1974). 'The Private Demand for Education in Relation to Labour, Market Conditions in Less Developed Countries', *Economic Journal*, **84**, December.

FISHER, I. (1966). *The Nature of Capital and Income*, New York, Macmillan.

BIBLIOGRAPHY

FRANK, C. R. (1965). *The Sugar Industry in East Africa*, East African Studies No. 20, East African Institute of Social Research, Nairobi, East African Publishing House.

—— (1968). 'Urban Unemployment and Economic Growth in Africa', *Oxford Economic Papers*, **20**(2), July.

—— (1970). 'The Problem of Urban Unemployment in Africa', The Woodrow Wilson School, Discussion Paper No. 16, Princeton, Princeton University, November.

FRIEDLAND, W. (1969). *Vuta Kamba: The Development of Trade Unions in Tanganyika*, Stanford, Calif., Hoover Institution Press.

FRIEDMAN, M. (1953). *Essays in Positive Economics*, Chicago, University of Chicago Press.

FUGGLES-COUCHMAN, N. (1964). *Agricultural Change in Tanganyika, 1945–1960*, Stanford, Calif., Stanford University Press.

GALLAWAY, L. E. (1967). 'Industry Variations in Geographic Labour Mobility Patterns', *Journal of Human Resources*, **2**(4), Fall.

GHAI, D. (1964). 'Territorial Distribution of Benefits and Costs of the East African Common Market', *East African Economic Review*, **2**(1), June.

GREAT BRITAIN (1925). *Education Policy in Tropical Africa*, Cmd. 2374, London, H.M.S.O.

—— (1955). *East Africa Royal Commission, 1953–55 Report*, London, H.M.S.O.

GREENWAY, P. J. (1944–5). 'Origins of Some East African Food Plants', *East African Agricultural Journal*, **21**.

GUGLER, J. (1968). 'The Impact of Labour Migration on Society and Economy in Sub Saharan Africa: Empirical Findings and Theoretical Considerations', *African Social Research*, December.

GUILLEBAUD, C. W. (1966). *An Economic Survey of the Sisal Industry of Tanzania*, 3rd edn., London, James Nisbet.

GULLIVER, P. H. (1955). *Labour Migration in a Rural Economy*, East African Studies No. 6, Kampala, East African Institute of Social Research.

—— (1958). *Land Tenure and Social Change among the Nyakyusa*, Kampala, East African Institute of Social Research.

HARBERGER, A. (1971). 'On Measuring the Social Opportunity Cost of Labour', *International Labour Review*, **103**(6), June.

HARRIS, J. R. (1971). 'Wage Rate Determination with Limited Supplies of Labour in Developing Countries: A Comment', *Journal of Development Studies*, **7**(2), January.

—— & TODARO, M. P. (1968). 'Urban Unemployment in East Africa. An Economic Analysis of Policy Alternatives', *East African Economic Review*, **2**, December.

—— —— (1969). 'Wages, Industrial Employment and Labour Productivity: The Kenyan Experience', *East African Economic Review*, **1**(1). June.

—— —— (1970). 'Migration, Unemployment and Development: A Two-Sector Analysis', *American Economic Review*, **60**, March.

HAZLEWOOD, A. (1966). 'The East African Common Market: Importance and Effects', *Bulletin of the Oxford University Institute of Economics and Statistics*, **28**(1), February.

HEIJNEN, J. D. (1968). *Development and Education in Mwanza District. A Case Study of Migration and Peasant Farming*, Rotterdam, Bronder-Offset.

HELLEINER, G. K. (1964). 'The Fiscal Role of the Marketing Boards in Nigerian Economic Development 1947–61', *Economic Journal*, **74**, September.

—— (1968). 'Agricultural Export Pricing Strategy in Tanzania', *East African Journal of Rural Development*, **1**, January.

—— (1972). 'Socialism and Economic Development in Tanzania', *Journal of Development Studies*, **8**(2), January.

HERRICK, B. H. (1965). *Urban Migration and Economic Development in Chile*, Cambridge, Mass., Massachusetts Institute of Technology Press.

HUTT, W. M. (1971). *The Economics of the Colour Bar*, London, Merrit and Hatcher.

HUTTON, C. (1971). 'The Good Life: Attitudes of Peasants and School Leavers Towards Agriculture', Mimeo, Conference on Urban Unemployment in Africa, Institute of Development Studies, University of Sussex, September.

ILIFFE, J. (1969). *Tanganyika Under German Rule, 1905–1912*, Cambridge, Cambridge University Press.

—— (1971). *Agricultural Change in Modern Tanganyika*, Historical Association of Tanzania, Paper No. 10, Dar es Salaam, East African Publishing House.

INTERNATIONAL BANK FOR RECONSTRUCTION AND DEVELOPMENT (1961). *The Economic Development of Tanganyika*, Baltimore, Johns Hopkins Press.

INTERNATIONAL LABOUR ORGANISATION (1959a). *The International Standardisation of Labour Statistics*, I.L.O. Studies, New Series, No. 53, Geneva, I.L.O.

—— (1959b). *Why Labour Leaves the Land*, Geneva, I.L.O.

—— (1966). *Measurement of Underemployment—Concepts and Methods*, 11th International Conference of Labour Statisticians, Report IV, Geneva, I.L.O.

—— (1970). *Towards Full Employment: A Programme for Colombia*, Geneva, I.L.O.

—— (1971). *Matching Employment Opportunities and Expectations: A Programme of Action for Ceylon*, Geneva, I.L.O.

—— (1972a). *Employment, Incomes and Equality: A Strategy for Increasing Productive Employment in Kenya*, Geneva, I.L.O.

—— (1972b). *Fiscal Measures for Employment Promotion in Developing Countries*, Geneva, I.L.O.

—— (various years). *Year Book of Labour Statistics*, Geneva, I.L.O.

ISBISTER, J. (1971). 'Urban Employment and Wages in a Developing Economy: The Case of Mexico', *Economic Development and Cultural Change*, **20**(1), October.

JACK, D. T. (1959). 'Report on Methods of Determining Wages in Tanganyika', Dar es Salaam, Government Printer.

JEFFERSON, T. (1939). 'The Law of the Primate City', *Geographical Review*.

JENSEN, S. (1968). 'Regional Economic Atlas: Mainland Tanzania', Dar es Salaam, Bureau of Resource Allocation and Land Use Planning, University of Dar es Salaam.

—— & MKAMA, J. (comps.) (1968). *District Data, Tanzania 1967*, Dar es Salaam, Ministry of Economic Affairs and Development Planning.

JOHNSON, G. (1971). 'The Structure of Rural–Urban Migration Models', *East African Economic Review*, 3(1), June.

KAMARCK, A. (1971). *The Economics of African Development*, Revised edn., New York, Praeger.

KATZ, J. M. (1969). *Production Functions, Foreign Investment and Growth: A Study Based on the Argentine Manufacturing Sector 1946–61*, Amsterdam, North Holland Publishing Co.

KELLEY, A., WILLIAMSON, J. & CHEETHAM, R. (1972). *Dualistic Economic Development*, Chicago, University of Chicago Press.

KENYA COLONY AND PROTECTORATE (1954). *Committee on African Wages, Report*, Nairobi, Government Printer.

KEYNES, J. M. (1961). *The General Theory of Employment, Interest and Money*, London, Macmillan.

KILBY, P. (1969). *Industrialization in an Open Economy: Nigeria, 1945–66*, Cambridge, Cambridge University Press.

KIMAMBO, I. N. & TEMU, A. J. (eds.) (1969). *A History of Tanzania*, Nairobi, East African Publishing House.

KNIGHT, J. B. (1966). *The Costing and Financing of Educational Development in Tanzania*, African Research Monographs No. 4, Paris, UNESCO/International Institute for Educational Planning.

—— (1968). 'Earnings, Employment, Education and Income Distribution in Uganda', *Bulletin of the Oxford University Institute of Economics and Statistics*, 30(4), November.

—— (1971a). 'Measuring Rural–Urban Differentials', Mimeo, Conference on Urban Unemployment in Africa, Institute of Development Studies, University of Sussex, September.

—— (1971b). 'Wages and Employment in Developed and Underdeveloped Economies', *Oxford Economic Papers*, 23(1), March.

KUPER, H. (1965). *Urbanization and Migration in West Africa*, Berkeley, Calif., University of California Press.

KUZNETS, S. (1966). *Modern Economic Growth*, New Haven, Yale University Press.

LABER, G. & CHASE, R. (1971). 'Interprovincial Migration in Canada as a Human Capital Decision', *Journal of Political Economy*, 79(4–6).

LAL, D. (1973). 'Disutility of Effort, Migration and the Shadow Wage Rate', *Oxford Economic Papers*, 25(1), March.

LEIBENSTEIN, H. (1973). 'The Urban Unemployment Absorption Problem: An X-Efficiency Analysis', Paper No. 295, Cambridge, Mass., Harvard Institute of Economic Research, May.

LESLIE, J. A. K. (1963). *A Survey of Dar es Salaam*, London, Oxford University Press.

LEVY, M. & WADYCKI, W. (1974). 'Education and the Decision to Migrate: An Econometric Analysis of Migration in Venezuela', *Econometrica*, March.

LEWIS, W. A. (1954). 'Development with Unlimited Supplies of Labour', *Manchester School of Economics and Social Studies*, **20**, May.

—— (1966). *Development Planning: The Essentials of Economic Policy*, New York, Harper & Row.

LINDSAY, C. (1971). 'Measuring Human Capital Returns', *Journal of Political Economy*, November.

LIPTON, M. (1968). 'The Theory of the Optimizing Peasant', *Journal of Development Studies*, **4**(3), April.

LISTOWEL, J. (1968). *The Making of Tanganyika*, London, Chatto & Windus.

LITTLE, I., SCITOVSKY, T. & SCOTT, M. (1970). *Industry and Trade in some Developing Countries*, London, Oxford University Press.

MACDONALD, L. D. & J. S. (1968). 'Motives and Objectives of Migration: Selective Migration and Preferences towards Rural and Urban Life', *Social and Economic Studies*, **17**(4), December.

MASON, P. (1958). *The Birth of a Dilemma*, London, Oxford University Press.

MBILINYI, M. (1970). 'Traditional Attitudes Towards Women: A Major Constraint on Rural Development', East Africa Social Science Conference, Dar es Salaam.

MBILINYI, S. (ed.) (1976). *Agricultural Research for Rural Development*, Nairobi, East African Literature Bureau.

MINCER, J. (1970). 'The Distribution of Labour Incomes: A Survey with Special Reference to the Human Capital Approach', *Journal of Economic Literature*, **8**, March.

MIRACLE, M. & FETTER, B. (1970). 'Backward-Sloping Labour Supply Functions and African Economic Behaviour', *Economic Development and Cultural Change*, **18**, January.

MITCHEL, C. (1971). 'Continuities and Developments in the Sociological Study of African Involvement in the Cash Economy', Mimeo, Conference on Urban Unemployment in Africa, Institute of Development Studies, University of Sussex, September.

MORAWETZ, D. (1974). 'Employment Implications of Industrialization in Developing Countries', *Economic Journal*, September.

MORIS, J. R. (1971). 'The Youth Employment Problem in the Rural Areas', Mimeo, Department of Political Science, University of Dar es Salaam.

MOSER, C. A. (1958). *Survey Methods in Social Investigation*, London, Heinemann.

MYRDAL, G. (1957). *Economic Theory and Underdeveloped Regions*, London, Methuen.

—— (1968). *Asian Drama: An Inquiry into the Poverty of Nations*, 3 vols., Harmondsworth, Penguin.

NELSON, P. (1959). 'Migration, Real Income and Information', *Journal of Regional Science*, **1**(2), Spring.

NUMEIST, see, p. 264, Bienefeld and Sabot (1971).

NYERERE, J. K. (1965). *Education for Self-Reliance*, Dar es Salaam, Government Printer.

—— (1971). *Ujyama, Essays on Socialism*, London, Oxford University Press.

O.E.C.D. DEVELOPMENT CENTRE (1971). *The Challenge of Unemployment to Development and the Role of Training and Research Institutes in Development*, Paris, O.E.C.D.

O.E.C.D., THE STUDY GROUP IN THE ECONOMICS OF EDUCATION (1965). Report by the Study Group: *Residual Factor and Economic Growth*, Paris, O.E.C.D.

O'HERLIHY, C. St. J. (1972). 'Capital/Labour Substitution and the Developing Countries: A Problem of Measurement', *Bulletin of the Oxford University Institute of Economics and Statistics*, **34**(3), August.

OKUN, B. & RICHARDSON, R. (1961). 'Regional Income Inequality and Internal Population Migration', *Economic Development and Cultural Change*, **9**, January.

OLIVER, R. & MATHEW, G. (1963). *History of East Africa*, Vol. I, Oxford, Clarendon Press.

ORDE-BROWNE, G. (1946). *Labour Conditions in East Africa*, London, Colonial Office, H.M.S.O.

PEACOCK, A. & SHAW, F. (1972). *Fiscal Policy and the Employment Problem in Developing Countries*, Employment Series No. 5, Paris, Development Centre, O.E.C.D., February.

PEIL, M. (1971). 'Education as an Influence on Aspirations and Expectations', Mimeo, Conference on Urban Unemployment in Africa, Institute of Development Studies, University of Sussex, September.

PHELPS, E. *et al.* (1970). *Micro Economic Foundations of Employment and Inflation Theory*, New York, W. W. Norton.

PHELPS-STOKES FUND (1924). *Education in Africa*, London, Phelps-Stokes Fund.

PIGOU, A. C. (1933). *The Theory of Unemployment*, London, Macmillan.

POWESLAND, P. (1957). *Economic Policy and Labour*, East African Studies No. 10, Kampala, East African Institute of Social Research.

RAY, R. S. (1966). *Labour Force Survey of Tanzania 1965*, Ministry of Economic Affairs and Development Planning, Dar es Salaam, Government Printer.

RESNICK, I. N. (1968). *Tanzania: Revolution by Education*, Arusha, Longmans of Tanzania.

REYNOLDS, L. (1969). 'Relative Earnings and Manpower Allocation in Developing Economies', Economics Growth Center, Paper No. 134, New Haven, Yale University.

—— (1970). *Labor Economics and Labor Relations*, Englewood Cliffs, N.J., Prentice Hall.

—— (1975). 'China as a Less Developed Economy', *American Economic Review*, **66**, June.

—— & GREGORY, P. (1965). *Wages, Productivity and Industrialization in Puerto Rico*, Homewood, Ill., Richard D. Irwin.

ROBERTS, A. (ed.) (1968). *Tanzania Before 1900*, Nairobi, East African Publishing House.

ROBINSON, R. (1971). *Developing the Third World*, Cambridge, Cambridge University Press.

ROSS, W. (1915). *The Works of Aristotle*, Vol. IX, Oxford, Oxford University Press.

ROUTH, G. (1965). *Occupation and Pay in Great Britain, 1906–60*, Cambridge, Cambridge University Press.

RURAL DEVELOPMENT RESEARCH COMMITTEE (1976). *Rural Socialism in Tanzania*, Dar es Salaam, Tanzania Publishing House.

RWEYEMAMU, J. F. (1971). 'The Historical and Institutional Setting of Tanzanian Industry', Economic Research Bureau, Paper 71.6, Dar es Salaam, University of Dar es Salaam.

SABOT, R. H. (1972). 'Barriers to Development in Africa', *African Affairs*, **71**(284), July.

—— (1977a). 'The Meaning and Measurement of Urban Surplus Labour', *Oxford Economic Papers* (November).

—— (1977b). *The Social Costs of Urban Surplus Labour*, Paris, O.E.C.D.

SAHOTA, G. S. (1968). 'An Economic Analysis of Internal Migration in Brazil', *Journal of Political Economy*, **76**(2), March/April.

SCHULTZ, T. P. (1971). 'Rural–Urban Migration in Colombia', *Review of Economics and Statistics*, **53**(2), May.

SCHULTZ, T. W. (1961). 'Investment in Human Capital', *American Economic Review*, **51**(1), March.

—— (1962). 'Reflections on Investment in Man', *Journal of Political Economy*, **70**, October.

SEN, A. K. (1975). *Employment, Technology, and Development*, Oxford, Clarendon Press.

SHEFFIELD, J. R. (ed.) (1967). *Education, Employment and Rural Development* (Proceedings of a Conference held at Kericho, Kenya, in September 1966), Nairobi, East African Publishing House.

SIMON, H. (1966). 'Theories of Decision-Making in Economics and Behavioural Science', in *Surveys of Economic Theory Resource Allocation*. Prepared for the American Economic Association and the Royal Economic Society, Vol. 3, Surveys 9–13, London, Macmillan.

SJAASTAD, L. A. (1962). 'The Costs and Returns of Human Migration', *Journal of Political Economy*, **70**(5), Pt. 2, October.

SMITH, A. D. (ed.) (1969). *Wage Policy Issues in Economic Development*, New York, St. Martin's Press.

STAHL, K. (1951). *The Metropolitan Organization of British Colonial Trade*, London, Routledge & Kegan Paul.

STEPHENS, H. W. (1968). *The Political Transformation of Tanganyika 1920–67*, New York, Frederick A. Praeger.

STIGLITZ, J. (1974). 'Alternative Theories of Wage Determination and Unemployment in LDCs: The Labour Turnover Model', *Quarterly Journal of Economics*, **88**, May.

STREETEN, P. (1972). *The Frontiers of Development Studies*, London, Macmillan.

SUTTON, J. E. G. (1970). 'Dar es Salaam: A Sketch of a Hundred Years', *Tanzania Notes and Records No. 71*, Tanzania Society, Dar es Salaam.

TANG, A. (1958). *Economic Development in the Southern Piedmont, 1860–1950: Its Impact on Agriculture*, Chapel Hill, University of North Carolina Press.

TANGANYIKA (1962). *Report on the Territorial Minimum Wage Board*, Dar es Salaam, Government Printer.

TANGANYIKA. CENTRAL STATISTICAL BUREAU (1963). *African Census Report, 1957*, Dar es Salaam, Government Printer.

—— —— (1964). *The National Accounts of Tanganyika, 1960/1962*, Dar es Salaam, Government Printer.

TANGANYIKA. EDUCATION DEPARTMENT (1960). *Annual Report*, Dar es Salaam, Government Printer.

TANGANYIKA. LABOUR DEPARTMENT (1927–69). *Annual Reports, 1927–1965*, Dar es Salaam, Government Printer.

TANGANYIKA. PROVINCIAL COMMISSIONER, WESTERN PROVINCE (1963). 'Memorandum on the Supply and Welfare of Native Labour', Tabora.

TANZANIA (1972). *Annual Plan for 1971/72*, Dar es Salaam, Government Printer.

—— (various years). *Background to the Budget, An Economic Survey*, Dar es Salaam, Government Printer.

TANZANIA. BUREAU OF STATISTICS (1969–71). *1967 Population Census*, Dar es Salaam, Government Printer.

—— —— (1971a). *Annual Manpower Report to the President, 1970*, Dar es Salaam, Government Printer.

—— —— (1971b). *National Accounts of Tanzania 1966 to 1968: Sources and Methods*, Dar es Salaam, Government Printer.

—— —— (1971–2). *1969 Household Budget Survey*, Dar es Salaam, Government Printer.

—— —— (1972). *National Accounts of Tanzania 1964 to 1970*, Dar es Salaam, Government Printer.

TANZANIA. CENTRAL STATISTICAL BUREAU (1968). *Recorded Population Changes 1948–1967*, Dar es Salaam, Government Printer.

—— —— (various years). *Survey of Employment and Earnings, Annual*, Dar es Salaam, Government Printer.

TANZANIA. MINISTRY OF ECONOMIC AFFAIRS AND DEVELOPMENT PLANNING (1964). *Tanganyika Five Year Plan for Economic and Social Development, 1st July 1964–30th June 1969, I: General Analysis, and II: The Programs*, Dar es Salaam, Government Printer.

—— —— (1969–70), *Tanzania Second Five Year Plan for Economic and Social Development, 1st July 1969–30th June 1974*, Dar es Salaam, Government Printer.

TAYLOR, M. C. (1970). *Taxation for African Economic Development*, London, Hutchinson Educational.

THOMAS, I. D. (1967). 'Population Density in Tanzania 1967', Dar es Salaam Bureau of Resource Allocation and Land Use Planning, University of Dar es Salaam.

TODARO, M. P. (1969). 'A Model of Labor Migration and Urban Unemployment in Less Developed Countries', *American Economic Review*, **59**, March.

TODARO, M. P. (1971). 'Income Expectations, Rural–Urban Migration and Employment in Africa', *International Labour Review,* **104,** July–December.

TURNER, H. A. (1966). *Wage Trends, Wage Policies and Collective Bargaining: The Problems for Underdeveloped Countries,* Department of Applied Economics, Occasional Paper No. 6, Cambridge, Cambridge University Press.

—— (1975). 'The Past, Present and Future of Incomes Policy in Tanzania', Mimeo, Geneva, I.L.O.

TURNHAM, D. (1971). *The Employment Problem in Less Developed Countries,* Paris, O.E.C.D.

UNITED NATIONS (1957). *World Situation: 1957,* New York, United Nations.

UNITED NATIONS. DEPARTMENT OF SOCIAL AFFAIRS. (1949). *The Population of Tanganyika,* New York, United Nations.

UNITED NATIONS. TRUSTEESHIP COUNCIL. (1955). *United Nations Visiting Mission to Trust Territories in East Africa, 1954. Report on Tanganyika,* New York, United Nations.

UNIVERSITY OF NATAL. *The African Factory Worker,* Cape Town, Oxford University Press.

WATSON, W. (1958). *Tribal Cohesion in a Money Economy. A Study of the Mambwe People of Northern Rhodesia,* Manchester, Manchester University Press.

WELLISZ, S. (1968). 'Dual Economies, Disguised Unemployment and the Unlimited Supply of Labour', *Economica,* **35.**

WILLIAMSON, J. G. (1965). 'Regional Inequality and the Process of National Development: A Description of the Patterns', *Economic Development and Cultural Change,* **13**(4), Pt. 2, July.

—— (1971). 'Capital Accumulation, Labour Saving, and Labour Absorption Once More', *Quarterly Journal of Economics,* **85**(1), February.

WINSTON, G. C. (1972). 'On the Inevitability of Factor Substitution', Research Memorandum No. 46, Williamstown, Mass., Center for Development Economics, Williams College, April.

WOLFF, R. D. (1969). 'Economic Aspects of British Colonialism in Kenya, 1895–1930', unpublished Ph.D. thesis, Yale University, New Haven.

YUDELMAN, M. (1964). *Africans on the Land,* Cambridge, Mass., Harvard University Press.

ZSCHOCK, D. K. (1967). *Manpower Perspective of Colombia,* Princeton, N.J., Industrial Relations Section, Princeton University Press.

INDEX